SIMPLE MAN'S DREAMS

STORIES OF THE HUNT

VICTOR SCARINZI

SIMPLE MAN'S DREAMS
STORIES OF THE HUNT

iUniverse books may be ordered through booksellers or by contacting:

iUniverse
1663 Liberty Drive
Bloomington, IN 47403
www.iuniverse.com
1-800-Authors (1-800-288-4677)

Because of the dynamic nature of the Internet, any web addresses or links contained in this book may have changed since publication and may no longer be valid. The views expressed in this work are solely those of the author and do not necessarily reflect the views of the publisher, and the publisher hereby disclaims any responsibility for them.

ISBN: 978-1-5320-4401-4 (sc)
ISBN: 978-1-5320-4403-8 (hc)
ISBN: 978-1-5320-4402-1 (e)

Library of Congress Control Number: 2018905443

Print information available on the last page.

iUniverse rev. date: 05/14/2018

Introduction
You Could Say I Truly Live to Hunt!

Hello, everyone. I am Victor C. H. Scarinzi, Italian redneck. Now, I'm no expert, but I've been hunting on my own since I was about nine years old, just like many folks in these stories. I love exchanging stories about hunting, fishing, trapping—anything to do with the outdoors and Mother Nature. Also, as well as helping other hunters in any way I can, you could say I truly live to hunt. I believe God gave nature and all that's in it for us to enjoy. Where else but in the woods, lakes, mountains, swamps, and deserts can you find a peaceful place to go think while sorting out your problems and dreams and planning your future? That's where I learned to appreciate all things in my life and where I am most assured there must truly be a God.

And so I invite you to come along with me to hunt the African plains, fish down the Amazon, face the Alaskan elements, and travel to many more places my hunts have taken me to. Follow along with me tracking moose, hogs, turkeys, bears, caribou, and other challenging animals I have been blessed to have the opportunity to take. Share in the companionship with my friends in our journey to achieve some of our lifetime goals and enjoy nature's beauty. The outdoors and the critters present there are truly a blessing to all to ponder.

Meanwhile, do yourself and your children a favor, and get outdoors together. Most of all, try to protect the outdoors and all that's in it. Destroying nature destroys us all. We are but a strand in the web of life, and to hurt the strand is to hurt ourselves.

First Bear and Big Mule Deer

This story kinda came about after I was lucky enough to get out of school to go hunt in Colorado with my friends Ray McComic; his dad, M. A., an ex-warden; Reed, Tommy, and Teddy Dowden; and many more. This was part of my first childhood dream—to live in the mountains, not just hunt in them. Out of high school, I worked oil fields on work boats, jack-up rigs, and platform rigs. It fell in around 1987. So, kinda let down and not too much in debt for a young man, I decided to move to the mountains. I just packed up my Toyota 4×4 with camp gear and left to figure it out when I got there. In midspring, I met some folks—Harry Landers (Wild Horse Harry) and M. J. Hackler—who were starting guide trips on horseback for a new resort being built near Vallecito Lake. It was located just out of Bayfield, Colorado, and was run by Wits-End Guest Ranch and Resort. I started out working there, pretty much for spending money and food, taking folks on trail rides and camping trips. It wasn't long before those trails weren't working for me, so I made new ones to prettier places than the forest service trails. I didn't realize that wasn't gonna go over very well, and I kinda got into trouble. Funny thing is—five years or so later, I found out that my trails were now new trails. I always have to choose a different path. I made a friend named Dan McClure from Tiffany, Colorado. He was a wrangler at the ranch and a true cowboy. We had many adventures together chasing girls, getting into bar fights and gunfights, and getting kicked in the back and chest by mules and horses—especially Rufus, who was a big mule who put us on our butts a few times.

After spring and summer, we ended up in South San Juan Wilderness with Harry and had camps scattered throughout the mountains, darn near the top of Wolf Creek Pass. It is beautiful country and became my home. Home had been a tepee, and now it was an outfitter's tent. Every foot of game trails and mountains became just part of another adventure. I never grew tired of extending my walks over the next mountain. The rougher and steeper terrain just meant not many had been there before me. Now I was going to be a guide for deer, elk, and bear, as well as help Dan with some packing and all shoeing of the horses. I am also a farrier and can make horseshoes from scratch. Guiding is a tough job that lasts from five in the morning till midnight in most cases.

Eventually I was foaming at the mouth, to have my time, between hunters, to cut loose on my own. Everyone slowed me down. There was one spot where we jumped a lot of big bucks, and I had often set my sights on hunting it many times. I called it Clam Shell. It looked just like a clamshell on the steep side and forced game to move around it. With all my encounters, I had learned which way the animals fled. So I stalked them from thick grove to thick grove, ripping each open spot with my eyes and I was quick to throw my gun up at the slightest movement. I was soon exhausted, so I slipped over the edge of Clam Shell and down a well-used trail for a peanut butter sandwich. I was sitting there with my gun in my lap when I heard a lot of rocks being moved over the top, and I looked up to see a fully grown cow elk standing there, fifteen yards right behind me, but she didn't see me.

True story! Without even aiming, I slowly raised my gun as she looked back. I just pointed and shot. She tumbled and missed me by a foot on her way down the mountain. When I got to her, she was broken to pieces, having tumbled down hitting rocks for about two thousand feet.

After skinning her and humping the meat back up the mountain alone, I decided to tie some of the meat to trees with plans to pack it out later. I continued to hunt on and around Clam Shell because I knew I would eventually be able to outsmart the deer I had been jumping. Sure enough, I found them—two big bucks moving up and out of some thick aspen deadfall with their backs against the rock, heading down. I knew the area as well as they did now, so I just ran at an angle to where I knew I would be able to see a good bit, hoping they would head through it like always, trying to get over Clam Shell. Every hunter is always way too slow. By the time they get to where the deer are, they are gone. I got there just in time to see them slowing to a walk. I threw my 6 mm up, finding them in the scope. After running at such a high altitude, I couldn't have steadied the gun if I had wanted to. They split in different directions and I unloaded my gun at one and believed I'd hit him. I looked for him for about thirty minutes, then realized that if I did hit him and he toppled over, down the canyon, I would be lucky to find him.

Upset and worn out, I decided to go back to the presumed impact site and regroup. I walked around and then sat down with my head hung low with grief. Then, as if in a dream, I looked up and about two hundred yards away, there came the other huge buck. I stood to fire offhand and started working that bolt action as fast as I could pull the trigger. I saw him fall just as he topped the steepest part within five miles on the mountain. Now out of shells, I eased over and saw him lying there about two hundred yards down. He was darn near straight down, head up, and very much alive but I knew he had been hit because I saw blood.

I sneaked down the mountain and got within ten yards when he saw me and tried to stand and run. His back legs were not working. I ran and grabbed his huge antlers, and it was on! The terrain was very steep, and we tumbled through rock, deadfall, and vegetation. It was a miracle I came out alive. At that time I might have weighed

120 pounds. This deer was pushing two hundred pounds. I wasn't about to let him get away. In the end, I was beaten up. It was totally exhausting for me and gruesome for him, but my big knife ended the hunt. He was four-points from being Boone and Crockett. I sat there crying with him and realized, looking into heaven, that this beautiful animal, a truly majestic rocky mountain mule deer, had given its life so I could enjoy mine and be fed at the same time. That's when I started laying my hands on game that I kill and thanking God for the animals and their souls by giving glory to the animal and what it gives me. Mounting an animal is just a continuance of the time of the hunt and glory to its life given. It is an appreciation of its beauty and so forth—not bragging. It is the realization of the power, beauty, and hardship that the wild animal went through, to grow so smart and majestic.

Hunters have a love for animals most others that don't hunt can't understand, because they never studied them to see what truly makes them so special. They also don't see the money hunters pump into the systems that help them so much. Trophy hunting is not about heads on the wall. The challenge goes way back in us all, and we don't just shoot or hunt for any animal we see or shoot them because they are there.

Through the challenge, we fall in love with land, streams, mountains, deserts, etc. Because the animals live there, we would die to protect them and their habitat. It's the hunter's money that protects them.

So back to hunting. I had been on the mountain a long time before everyone else this season, living in meadows and on top of the mountain, living and eating off the land. And in doing so, I and bears had crossed paths a few times. But there was one that, I swear, followed me. He tore up my camps and everything in them. I nicknamed him Big Black.

We had a group of hunters come in from New York. Right off I told them about bears and asked if I could bring my gun just in case I saw one when I wasn't with them, during early mornings or late evenings. They said okay. I had a lot of fun with these guys, sneaking up on them as I came back to get them. They kept saying I couldn't do it, but I did it every time. I woke up one morning, and it was very cold. I started a fire in the cook tent and headed out to the meadow to call in Whiskey, one of the horses. When he came, the rest would follow. Well, it figured, this morning he was stubborn, so I had to walk down, halter him, and lead him back to the hitching post. I noticed that one of the horse's shoes was coming unfastened, so I had to fix that. It was rough with frozen hands.

After I saddled nine horses and fed them, I went to wake the hunters for chow time. They were slow getting started this morning. The wind had picked up a bit, which made it even worse. Finally we were on horses and heading up the mountain. No words were being said. The only sound was that of the hooves hitting rock. Slowly I dropped the men off in spots I felt good about, for the first three hours of the morning. Now, this last guy, Clause, asked me what I was going to do. I said I was gonna scout a hole off the edge of a canyon and also look for Big Black. He said that he wanted to go, being as he was so cold. I said sure, but it's tough and thick country. I had tennis shoes in my saddlebags because once I got off the horse, I usually swapped them. Heavy boots, too many clothes, and heavy packs will slow you up real bad. It's risky, though, if you get in a bind in the cold.

We spooked a small group of elk tearing down the mountain through the deadfall, and we soon reached the nasty edge hole at the edge of the canyon. Just guessing, I'd say it is a thousand acres or so. I found a heavy used trail going into it. Right off we found bear scat and tracks—elk and deer as well. Now my senses were heightened from instinct that a hunter gets. I was in slow, paranoid motion. Scanning every spot I could, I soon saw where a bear had broken off a bunch of tree tops. Maybe one hundred yards down was a rock where a piece of the mountain had fallen off, and there he was—Big Black! About thirty seconds after giving Clause the shot, I pulled the trigger. He growled, balled up, biting at himself where my bullet had gone in, and tumbled through a thicket along a steep ridge. On getting to him, I was sure he was Big Black. It seemed he had been pulling tree tops over a hole—preparing to hibernate, we figured. And odder than that, he had scat all over the tops, as if using it to hold them together. Odd, I thought.

Then the fun began. We skinned him out for a full rug. Then we had to take all the meat out. It took the rest of the day and into the cold night to get it all down to the main camp. Then there was a drive to Pagoso Springs to have a warden tag it. We got it done, and the wardens said they thought, from the paw and skull measurements, that the bear was about the third or fourth largest bear ever taken out of Weminuche and South San Juan Wilderness. I still got a fine of fifty dollars for not having every piece of meat! The fine was due to one of the horses I chose to pack the meat on. Apparently he had never smelled a bear. I guess he broke away after one whiff of that bear. He lit off the mountain without us, meat and all.

After ten and one half months of hiking, camping, fly-fishing, cowboying, living off the land, and more, along with the heavy snows that come in late November, I decided my first dream was complete and it was time to get to work. I had considered moving there hard. Some of those times resting atop those high peaks and seeing across mountain ranges as far as I could see, I thought about how I would like to see my life go—that it was up to me, things that would ruin it, etc. I knew during these times that this was my way to gather thoughts from my heart and decipher the right way to turn at the crossroads. I still do this today. I also realized that God will show me the way as long as I try.

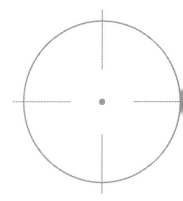

Trapping

Hello folks, I wanted to share a little bit about something that I believe can make you more of a woodsman and hunter than most anything: trapping.

In these times, most folks don't trap out of necessity. However, in many cases, it's still a good part of many folks' lifestyles. I think the reason we have a predator problem is because not as many trap like they used to. The price trappers get for selling hides is just not worth the work today. Some of that is probably because of fur farming—especially mink farming, which produces more than three hundred million pelts annually! That's a lot of income lost to a good ole boy. Fur farms are present in twenty-three states, and 85 percent of pelts used in the world's fur trade come from these small farms.

In the late seventies, I was a proud young man to be out earning a bit of my own money. I loved the lifestyle of being out of bed before daylight on a school day, running my trap lines. It's a great way to teach kids a lot about the outdoors and the critters that live in it, while spending time together. Many nights I lost sleep waiting on daylight. I couldn't wait to bring my pelts into town, meet the fur buyer, and see other trappers' catches. Most of the time I was the youngest one there. Most of what I learned I taught myself, with some help from an old friend, Mr. Taylor. There was no Google back then!

To be a trapper, you have to become familiar with which animals make which tracks, how they move, how they hunt food, where they live, and more. You have to have a very good sense of direction and also be able to remember where you set eighty-plus traps. Even twenty traps take a lot of work. They must be checked every twenty-four hours at least; every twelve is even better.

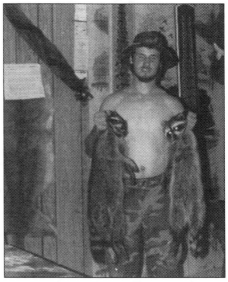

One little story I'd like to share happened when I set a line to take my little brother David Parker along. He was handicapped by spinal meningitis as a baby, which left him with one arm paralyzed and one leg partially paralyzed. But through life, he has done more than many folks with all their abilities. He is my biggest inspiration.

Anyhow, we had a little creek that ran not too far behind our house in Anacoco, Louisiana. So, I had decided to set a small trap line there so I could bring David without too much walking. It was a fairly cool morning, and we lit out to the woods. David tagged along pretty well. He was determined to go with his big brother. A few times he stumbled, and even fell down from a vine that tangled around his feet. (Because of his disability, he couldn't pick his leg up very far.) Not once did this appear to bother him. Now, the first trap we came to was tripped, and had a toe off an ole coon in it. But the next trap was a bit of a surprise; it held a big tomcat, and he was not happy. I managed to get the poor thing loose without being hurt. But David got plenty of laughs at me doing it with the cat under a small coat I threw over it. I used a lot of sardines back then to bait. They were cheap and had a strong smell. I used apples, cat food, candies—anything a poor boy could get.

Well, we ended up getting a few coons and two opossums, as best I can remember. When we got back to the house, there to greet us, with a bit of worry, was the best mom ever and the best hunting partner I ever had, Carolyn Parker. She had us a big breakfast cooked and told us to come in and eat before we skinned our catch. So we did, and about thirty minutes later, we went out to start skinning, but the opossum David had carried was gone. There were no dogs that could have toted if off. It had left the scene. It must have played opossum! Mom was a little irritated that I had given him one to carry that I hadn't made sure was dead. So, I guess you could say he was the one that got away.

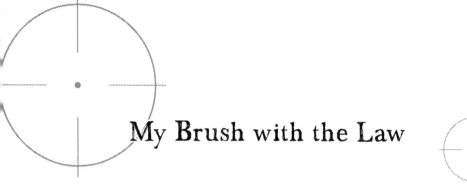

My Brush with the Law

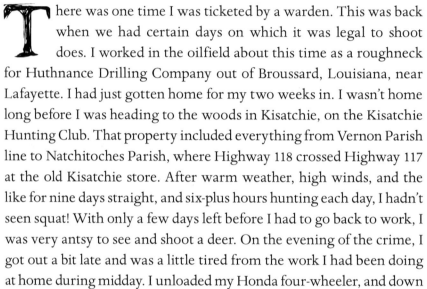

There was one time I was ticketed by a warden. This was back when we had certain days on which it was legal to shoot does. I worked in the oilfield about this time as a roughneck for Huthnance Drilling Company out of Broussard, Louisiana, near Lafayette. I had just gotten home for my two weeks in. I wasn't home long before I was heading to the woods in Kisatchie, on the Kisatchie Hunting Club. That property included everything from Vernon Parish line to Natchitoches Parish, where Highway 118 crossed Highway 117 at the old Kisatchie store. After warm weather, high winds, and the like for nine days straight, and six-plus hours hunting each day, I hadn't seen squat! With only a few days left before I had to go back to work, I was very antsy to see and shoot a deer. On the evening of the crime, I got out a bit late and was a little tired from the work I had been doing at home during midday. I unloaded my Honda four-wheeler, and down the trail I went. I had unloaded my climber and strapped it across my back, and the old .30-30 was in my hand.

I climbed to about twenty-five feet high in a good pine tree. It was really too warm for hunting, but I just had to try! I was in a good thicket with some shooting lanes: three along the front, one hard to the right, and one more hard to the left. I remembered seeing most all of the usual game, and apparently I went to sleep. When I woke up, in front of me was a small-racked buck slipping by between shooting lanes, stepping in the middle as far as I could tell. Now it was late, so the only way I could see anything was by looking through my 2×5 Leupold scope. But I was sure I had seen antlers. More time passed, and I finally saw a deer, right where I lost sight. I saw a deer's legs moving and then a partial view of the body, so I turned the scope up, dialed in on hair I could see through the brush, and popped a shot.

After waiting a while, I climbed down and went to my four-wheeler to get a bigger light.

I eased toward where I had seen the deer standing. Now it was dark enough for a light. I followed the blood trail slowly through the woods. I soon looked about seventy-five yards ahead, and right there was a doe lying there, staring at me in my light beam. At this time I was thinking I had just come upon a bedded deer. But seeing the blood trail going straight that way at about twenty yards, I knew it was the deer I shot. Not good, as doe day was not till the next morning. Well, I don't let a deer lie, much less a wounded one, so I pulled the gun up, now a good forty minutes after dark, and shot. Walking up to her, I felt a bit sick, realizing I must have shot a deer I mistook for a buck. Two deer must have been there, but it was definitely a mistake. This would be the first doe I had taken in about eight years.

I dragged the deer out, put her on the four-wheeler, and up the road I went. I had the lights on and wasn't trying to hide her. But at the time, I really didn't know what I was going to do. Pulling into where I was parked, I saw another truck. One of the other club members had heard the second shot and come to see if someone needed help. Then he saw the twelve-hour-early deer. He asked me what I was going to do about it. I said, "Well, I'm not going to leave it, and I sure don't run from my mistakes." So I planned to let our club president and friend, Charles, know about it and see what he thought. So this guy, who I figured didn't trust me, said, "Well, let's go." It did kind of make me mad at him a bit, but not pissed off, so I said, "Let's go."

I pulled into Charles's yard, and he was a bit surprised at the situation. He quickly told me he wished I hadn't done it. He was a ranger for the Kisatchie National Forest. He pretty much said that he would have to report it. I said, "No problem," and really, at that moment, I didn't figure much would come of it, considering I was turning myself in because of a mistake. It wasn't like I had been spotlighting, had tried running from them, or had it half skinned in a shed. Wrong!

Warden showed up, and it wasn't long before I saw it was going a bit the other way, with the ticket and so forth. But when he said he was going to have to take my gun, he then became nothing more than a man that wasn't my friend anymore! Really, really bad thoughts ran through my mind. This gun meant the world to me. Charles must have seen it in my eyes then and sensed what I was feeling and thinking. We are alike in a lot of ways. He said, "Don't do it." I had to do something to relieve the anger and pain after trying to do the right thing and show people the right way, so I told him the only way to get this gun was like this, and I busted it across an oak tree toward him. I then told him to, "either arrest me or get out of my face; I'm going home!" All these years later, I'm not mad at him anymore. Several months later, I showed up in court in Natchitoches Parish for my sentence.

In the courtroom, they asked, "How do you plead?"

I had to say, "I plead neither guilty nor not guilty. But if you ask me if I shot a deer illegally, I say yea. But if I did it on purpose, I say no, and y'all know it. So it's going to be up to you to show folks waiting to see the outcome of this decision."

The judge was a bit frustrated, and he said, "Well, the warden said you're guilty, and in his report he said you became angry, so you're guilty." He started reading what my fines and judgment would be for a while. He saw that I was getting upset, and I feared I was about to mess up again. He said he was going to waive it all except a $250 fine and $250 replacement fee. He then asked if I thought that was fair, and I said, "Sir," regretting it, "no, because I don't feel I should have had my gun taken." He then granted me my gun. I saw that by reading the maximum sentence that could have been given, he was helping me; and months later, I wrote him a letter saying so. This goes to show the world that sometimes running and lying to the law is not always the best way to try to get out of a situation. I've never been one to hide or lie about my mistakes too often.

White-Tailed Deer—
A Few of Many Hunts

O ne good memory I have is of a deer I took near Peason Ridge Training Area on Fort Polk Military Training Base while in high school in the Kurthwood community of Vernon Parish, Louisiana. Like many young men in my area, I lived for going camping when I could, and at the time, I loved to have friends and make new friends who were already doing it. I had a little camp built on public land. It was probably one of the first of its kind for those times, built out of reclaimed wood and corrugated metal from old chicken houses, with a dirt floor. I did manage to rustle up an old King wood stove for heat and a little cooking. I spent more time with wild horses for company than people most of the time, along with a few old hunting dogs. There was always some kind of hunting and trapping going on in those days, and it seemed there was all the time in the world.

This particular morning in November, I was on school break with Mike Gahagan and went to hunt. Mike was my neighbor's, Mr. Billy's, son. Mike was much younger than I, about twelve years old, and more like a family member than a friend. I was still a young hunter and very particular as to how I hunted, approached a stand, and so forth. We had eased down the road and onto a fire lane the government had pushed along the edge of the wildlife management area. It was closed at the time, and we were out without a light. We eased through the woods quietly. It was just cold enough for us to wish that the ole heater in the Jeep worked better. It was a good hour before daylight, if not more, and I placed Mike out near an ole slough in a thicket along a rub line.

Hunting was all old school in those days. There were no plots or feeders, and I'm thankful I learned to hunt this way. There were also few deer in the area, so we had to depend on rubs and scrape lines. I went to a stand on an oak ridge full of red oaks, sand jack trees, and post oaks that had a good many acorns at the time. In those days, you had to find crossings, food—something to better your chances. Sitting in my stand, the woods were quiet except for the falling acorns and the occasional hooting owls. The sky grew brighter as the sun came up. Now and then a light breeze rustled the leaves up, enough to blow some out of the trees. Now, I swear I did something back then that I had never seen or heard of at the time. It was said that if you fooled around like this you would push the deer away. On many occasions, I could barely see game pass through the thicket of woods along the branch in front of me. There was no clear shot; it was so thick there that sometimes I could only hear game walk by. So a week or so prior to the hunt, I got an ax and cut three lanes in front of my stand. Since then, in about a two-hundred-yard span, there were a half dozen or more scrapes made under the limbs by bucks searching out does in heat.

Sitting there, I was plenty excited. About that time, some doves flew over, and a few turkeys flew off their roost a ways down. Daylight broke through the trees with rays of morning sunlight, and I could just barely see a deer move through their branches. It was not much longer before the squirrels began to crack and gather acorns in the canopy of the trees. To top that off, some hogs down the creek were squealing—fighting over food, I assumed. It was just a morning full of life in every aspect.

About thirty minutes after daylight, way off in the distance, I heard a deer blow. I was thinking it might have come across our trail and seen Mike. Then, ten minutes or so later, a doe blew across the hill like a bat out of hell, running past me. She was moving way too fast for me to take a shot. More time went by, and I was at the edge of the seat on my little two-by-four deer stand, about ten feet high, nestled up in a tree full of limbs. Then, like magic, and like a ghost, a doe was just standing there fifty yards away, very alert, looking back with her tail straight out. She showed all the signs that another deer, or something, was behind her or following her. No sooner than I decided not to shoot, she trotted off and a small six-point came running in chasing her. The buck stopped with his head in the air—trying to pick up her scent or see her, I figured.

All the time, I was pulling my Marlin .30-30 up and getting him into my scope. I was about to squeeze off a shot when he spun around and bolted as if I had shot him from the opposite direction. In a flash, out of the corner of my eye to the left of my stand, right in the middle of my shooting lane, there he stood—the biggest buck I had ever seen in our part of the country at that time. I pulled around and shot, and the buck jumped up, kicking his back legs high into the air. He leaped into the brush ten yards out. I could see limbs and small trees moving right where he went down. Just out of fear he might get away, I shot four more times into the movement. For the first time in my life, it was all about killing and not eating. Ten minutes later, I climbed out of my stand and stalked up to where I saw him last, gun shouldered, and looked over into the brush. There he was. I was shocked, blurry-eyed, and still slam-jam full of adrenaline at what was lying there. Super thankful, I fell to my knees and thanked great God Almighty that I had just taken a true Louisiana monarch. It is something I now do always after an animal gives its life so I can enjoy mine and fill my stomach. Not only was this deer huge, but he was also nontypical with a ten-and-a-half-inch drop tine. I attempted to drag the deer and realized it wasn't going to happen alone, so I managed to get him into some thicker cover and covered him even more. I wasn't going to take a chance someone could happen upon him. I walked back to get my little buddy and the Jeep.

Mike loaded up his Harrington and Richardson twenty-gauge shotgun, and we went for my deer. Now, I might have been 135 pounds soaking wet at the time, and Mike, well, he was a beanpole at the time. Not so today. We got to the deer and attempted to drag him for one hundred yards, if that. We were doing the best we could, but it wasn't good enough to move that dead weight. So we found a small tree, bent it over and broke off the top, pocket-knifed the bottom enough to break it, and put it between the deer's legs so we could lift him off the ground and onto our shoulders. It took a few tries, and we were looking at about a quarter mile to get the deer to the Jeep.

A memorable part of this story is how little Mike manned up and had the guts to put out the effort to tote this deer, with the weight slamming him from side to side on those little legs. I was proud to see my little friend had heart. Getting the deer out of the woods and showing it off almost let it spoil. It even made the newspaper. The deer lacked three points from being Boone and Crockett, and that was unheard of in our neck of Louisiana at the time. From that hunt on, antlers were as important as the meat to me.

Hunting Trip to Africa

September 30, 2003

Well, anticipation definitely increased about one week prior to departure—especially after I finally prepared with shots, passport, work being taken care of, etc. Also, not seeing many deer while bow hunting this week at home made me ready to go. The season started September 13 in most of Louisiana.

Of course, actually leaving home slowed my desperation to hunt in Africa for a very short spell. One must consider that death can occur on such a trip. But I must say that if you have a chance to do what you have wanted to do all your life, then you should do it without hesitation. Living in fear is just as good as being dead. With a little planning, devotion, discipline, and good ole "want to," anyone can do as he or she wishes. In my case, the goal is hunting in Africa. It took me a while to go since I first dreamed about it at about twelve years old in Texarkana, Arkansas. It was then that I saw my first African animal being mounted—a Kudu. I daydreamed about what it must be like to hunt such an animal. At twelve I was already into hunting, trapping, etc. I thought then that only a few people in the world could afford the trip, and I never saw myself in that category. I tell you, it takes no more than it does to buy a pool, a used automobile, furniture, or something else you just have to have. Well, buying a trip to Africa is just the same as all of that. You just have to work for it. Like any other dream that people have in their lives, it can be achieved if it's really wanted.

One thing I noticed on my flight to Georgia is that modernization had chopped up the landscape. And to think that it's all done for our supposed better way of living. I asked myself, "Has it, really?" I wonder what God must think when he looks down here.

What I'm saying is, don't get caught up in getting more, but be happy and take your time to live a dream. Some things on Earth in our lifetime will come to pass and no longer be there to enjoy. The forests and animals most definitely feel the pressure. But it's not hunters who are killing them; it's all the people who are wanting more and more every day. Hunters want more of nature, more of animals, and more different species of animals to be taken care of, and they want it more than anyone else. Destroying nature is destroying yourself and the future for all those you love. So help when you can.

Custom Travel Agency set up my overnight stay in Atlanta, Georgia, at Double Tree Hotel, and it was good. I had an awesome meal that night at Blue Bay Fish Market & Grill: lobster, shrimp, stuffed mushrooms, scallops with rice, a baked potato, and seafood gumbo. Atlanta seemed to be a very clean and well-groomed city.

At the airport, I met two guys from my job at the embassy in Moscow, Luther and Scott, after almost four years. Small world! And I made friends with a man who sat by me; he was a banker from South Africa who lived in Atlanta. He said that, yes, there are hunting seasons in Africa. I also met a guy by the name of Ward from Dakota Arms.

We flew on a Boeing 747-400, which was a double-decker, with me on the top deck. I'll tell you that the sixteen-hour nonstop flight was tough though not unbearable. The South African Airlines plane was great. The food was great, as was the service.

The plane carried me a total of 9,034 miles, starting from Alexandria, Louisiana. Johannesburg Airport was nice and friendly. Clearing customs was no problem at all; a lot of that had to do with Bob and Peter briefing me on what to do before the trip. Bob is the booking agent, and Peter is the owner of the hunting camp.

October 3, 2003

It was my first hunting day. The ride to the ranch where we were hunting was about three and a half hours from Johannesburg by truck, with a good portion being a gravel road. Riding and driving on the wrong side of the road was different too. A lot of the mountain range looked like it does just as you get into the Rocky Mountains.

Upon arrival, the facilities were more than I expected, and they had very much of an African feel to them. Immediately the food was available, and it was very, very good too. Only two other hunters were there—one for a safari and the other for leopard hunting. My room was as nice and big as one you would pay $200 a night for in any resort. In the evenings, I could watch beautiful sunsets out of my window.

October 4, 2003

Day three ended up with three animals, all of which made record books. The first one was taken in early morning, and it was a duiker buck. Then we came in around eleven thirty in the morning to eat, and again it the food was good. We cleaned up and took a nap.

Around three o'clock we went back, seeing game everywhere. We spotted and stalked this time, looking for the right prey. We got on warthogs, impalas, wildebeest, rhinos, giraffes, etc. Later we found a lone gemsbok bull, and after intense stalking and waiting for a good shot, I took it. And he took off. Waiting left me weak in the knees like I haven't been in a long time. Instantly we went after him with no blood trail, Peter tracking him, to my amazement, by tracks and trails. With a lot of luck, we got on him, only for him to jump up and run again, but with a quick run of about fifteen yards, I got in a good enough position to shoot him in the ass to slow him down, and only then did I get a third and final shot, dropping him. My 200 Weatherby was trying to do its job. His horns were thirty-three inches long and seven and a half inches around at base, and he carried a huge body.

Later we stalked within thirty yards of two huge rhinos. And when they got spooked, all we saw after they gathered their momentum was what looked like two boulders crushing trees and bushes in their path, followed by a cloud of dust. I had no desire to shoot such a majestic animal; simply sneaking up on them was just as challenging.

We had about thirty-two thousand acres in this one location alone to hunt without imposing on another property. Other game we saw were monkeys; prairie grouse; geese; ostriches; prairie dogs;, snake eagles; an African goose, which was beautiful; and an African pigeon, which makes the sound often used on African shows.

Right at dark that day, I took a blue wildebeest with a quick hunt and kill, leaving him down at maybe forty yards. I shot him facing me straight on at around three hundred yards. This probably was the longest shot I ever made on an animal. His score was eighty-three, give or take a half inch. This animal is so much prettier than what they look like on TV. I'll tell you, though, that loading such large animals is a job. We got its head and two front feet pulled up on a tailgate, tied a snatch block to a pad eye on the back cab of the truck, tied one end of rope to the head and the other end to a tree, and moved the truck forward, pulling the animal on up.

We ended up seeing warthogs. I learned that females have two wattles on their heads and boars have four and bigger bodies. There was much more to this day, but I was ready for dreamland after I got full of eland casserole, which is considered the best African game animal for human consumption, and kudu jerky with pumpkin balls. Added to that was a good tussle with a dog …

October 5, 2003

Day four started at five thirty with breakfast. I asked for three pieces of toast with peanut butter, honey, and syrup. I also had some good ole caffeinated coffee to do my body good. Then we left with one man, one guide, and one driver for the truck to start combing the landscape with binoculars.

Peter uses a three-cylinder turbo diesel four-door Nissan to hunt out of. You don't always hunt out of the truck, but you do have to ride a lot, since thirty-two thousand acres can hold and hide animals well. We took some stalk hunts for one hour or so in strategic areas with water holes and greenery on bushes for food. It can be tough to get on a lot of these animals when you have 40 forty sets of eyes and 20 twenty sets of noses working against two eyes. You very rarely hear the animals either.

Peter says that hunting in Africa is best in the evenings. In the mornings, animals prefer not to move much and lie down from competition with each other and predators around water holes, such as leopards, black hyenas, civets, and jackals. We saw a few baboon tracks, but that's it so far. One thing about African soil I've seen: it's red like a river bottom, but it must be rich in some way for game to survive here as it does.

At this point I most definitely felt that this was another world in another country, not at all like the American South. The vast emptiness with nothing but game leaves me feeling as if all work from the year past is drifting away, letting my mind, body, and soul heal to humble me down to be happier. Hunting gives me a way to forget most of the goings-on in my life. I think it helps me realize what we need to do within ourselves to be better for ourselves and those we care for. I, myself, always felt that hunting was the first instinct God gave us, and those civilized men who don't find it in something else, such as sports or fishing, still yearn for it. For a man not to pursue a passion is not to feel like a man, I think.

The morning hunt was slow, with few animals moving. We came in for lunch. I went to visit a village near the camp and then came back for a swim. We went out at three o'clock and saw a few animals now and then, so we began stopping and walking through brush several hundred yards to water holes, glassing them over. After about three water holes, we spotted a waterbuck barely before it spotted us. We got closer, and I got into a sitting position for a shot after about fifteen minutes. He was staying under a large camel thorn tree. With the scope on him, waiting for him to move, I grew tired and lay down. This time he moved only to lie down, leaving me virtually no shot at all. We debated on me trying to make a neck shot but decided against it. We decided to get closer, so we crawled on our bellies and managed to get closer and hid behind a thorn bush. He spotted us but did not spook. He knew something was there, so the staredown was on.

Finally, after about fifteen minutes, he stood up and turned his head to look back, so I took three steps to the right of the bush right out in the open with my gun up. Another staredown was on until my arm was about to break, all along with ten bugs biting me. Then he started to break and run, and I made my shot. He was gone, but so was I—behind him in full sprint, trying to get another shot. But there was no need; he went down. I had made a perfect shot, leaving me four one-shot kills, with a few mercy shots after finding them. This was a hell of a hunt! He was a Safari Club scorer and made Boone and Crockett.

Today I wasn't even wearing my watch. Who cared what time it was! I was not living by a timepiece.

Waterbuck

The difficult part was the dry heat that was burning my eyes and lips, and drying my nose out, along with the increased quantity of flies bothering me. Peter said it was a good sign of rain to come. I learned that the big trees in Africa we see on TV are camel thorn trees, and the small ones are usually shepherd trees. We also managed to record video of a rhino with a baby. We found out that a rhino can have a baby only once every five years.

That was a heck of a day. We ended it with a fire-grilled steak with all the trimmings. Peter got his laughs by putting Louisiana hot sauce in my tea.

October 6, 2003

Africa, Africa—the institution solution for me. Every step in my nine-dollar tennis shoes was a good one.

The morning hunt was slow, though we again saw some young animals. We spotted about fifteen or so baboons taking off on a road, heading toward another road. We sped around to head them off, but they were crossing just as we got there. I managed to get a round off at about three hundred yards with a clean miss. If I'd hit him, he'd have flipped a few times.

We came in for a great lunch and to rest. The animals were all bedded down, and even a human can walk only so much area before he needs rest.

That evening, we were still mainly concentrating on a kudu bull. We spotted a big one and tried to stalk him, but he saw us and high-tailed. Then I stalked a gemsbok with my movie camera to about thirty-five yards. But the highlight of the day was chasing down a warthog till he stopped to face me. Being hell bent, we went for each other, with me taking him with my Gerber knife. The best part was that Peter caught it on video just in time. Peter said it was the first time he had ever heard of this happening in Africa.

Later we stalked to within five steps of a rhino facing us before actually seeing us. Talk about an adrenaline rush! I'll tell you, though, to kill one is to do nothing. These animals have tenfold to offer alive. Get five steps away and look into those huge eyes, and you will feel something more than seeing it dead after a two-hundred-yard shot.

Soon after that, Peter thought he would try his luck at running on a warthog. And he did, hitting him with his shooting sticks. He was a big one too. A really big warthog weighs 150 to 160 pounds, and they usually cut their victims with their bottom teeth, using the top ones to tear at the point of impact. Unfortunately, we didn't have a camera this time.

We ended the day with supper: blue wildebeest, sweet carrots, spinach, rolls, bean casserole, spicy rice, and gravy. The wildebeest was the best yet, leaving eland meat in second place in my taste test. Of course, the grand finale was Peter using me as a guinea pig with a fart machine he had, making the African employees think I had really bad gas. We almost busted a gut.

October 7, 2003

We decided on going an extra hour early this morning and trying for a zebra today. They are nothing like a horse. They are just as wild as the rest. They just can't hide as well, and they always do as the leader of the pack does. They are only as smart as he is. Peter estimated there are over two hundred of them in just his hunting area alone. That morning we had no luck finding zebras, though we came across some nice southern impalas, two females, with wildebeests mixed around them. We got up to about 150 yards and had to sit for about fifteen minutes to get a shot. I left the impala dead in his tracks, thanks to the bipod on my gun giving me a really steady hand.

I took the shot, confident I could hit him. And we ran into about eighteen giraffes in a couple of different groups. I'll tell you, no hunter should hunt them. They are like zoo animals even in the wild. You couldn't miss them, so why in the world shoot them?

It seemed that luck was trying to pass me by, but we were staying up with it. Around lunch we found a lone eland bull, the largest antelope in the world. After stalking, chasing, and hiding, we finally got a shot, leaving him about ten steps from his death. He was about 1,800 pounds; this was a damn huge animal! He scored 82 on the books out of 222 animals. Loading him was an experience. Afterward, I was ready for lunch.

After lunch we went to Peter's neighbor's place, which had about 6,500 acres to continue to hunt kudu where it was thick. Kudu like it where it is thick. We were in a bush for about two hours and found a couple of young kudu bulls and several females. Then we came across a huge one but quickly saw that something was wrong. The excellent bull had fallen victim to the drought and lack of food, and he had given up. He could not get up and lay for too long to have a chance. He could barely move his eyes. The owner of the ranch suggested that we finish him. I must add that it was a sad moment for me. But I must also tell you that there are thousands of animals that don't die for this reason like they used to in the past. First of all, the Africans realized that these animals possess great economic value due to the hunting industry. For this reason, they now supplement their feed and build water holes to help sustain them during the droughts. Without this many animals would die, and twice as many would suffer for months. They also build high fences now to control poaching and ensure the game is hunted right and is allowed to grow to full maturity. If hunters from all over the world did not come to hunt here, the locals could not afford to spend money on food and water. The more needed and valuable something is to the society, the longer it will last. So if you want to help Africa's animals and its people, go hunting there.

Back to the hunt. I'd been noticing that if there was a good bull somewhere, there was usually another one nearby. This time my instinct told me that there was another one around. Sure enough, about 400 yards away, we found a kudu bull hiding from the sun under a tree. We stalked to about 125 yards, but no clean shot could be found. After some time, he spotted us and broke to run behind some trees. Seeing that the area behind him was quite open, I ran up and knelt down and steadied as best I could on him while he was in a lope. When he slowed to cross a three-strand barb wire fence I did end up taking him. He roughly scored about two points over the record book. He had 3.25 turns with thick bases.

Greater Kudu

After all that happened that day, I was sure that the luck must end. Well, it didn't. As we were driving out, I spotted a lone warthog running off from a water hole. His tusks were very much apparent. I assured Peter he was the big one and asked him what he thought. Peter said, "Go for it," and I was gone. I figured he must have run three hundred–plus yards by this point, so I did too, before slowing down to stalk and hunt him. I was only guessing where he might go. In about twenty minutes, I spotted one standing still, and about the time I saw it was him again, he lit out like a bat out of hell. With my scope down, I threw the gun up to take a shot.

He didn't stumble or anything, so I assumed I had missed, but as always, I still was looking. By now fifteen minutes had gone by. I heard Peter yelling. I thought he was yelling to find me, but it turned out a cobra was in the process of trying to bite him. Soon we all met—him, the driver, the tracker, and me. We all were circling around, looking for signs, when I found a piece of warthog skin about four inches by six inches. From there we found tiny spots of blood, then splatters. The tracker and driver stayed on the blood trail while I and Peter stayed on their side, looking for an animal, in case he jumped to run off or charge. Tracking went on for about fifteen more minutes before we heard the tracker hollering. He had spotted him and was running after him. Then we all ran, jumping thorn bushes. The warthog ran down into an aardvark hole. Peter stood on the top with a 9 mm pistol, and I knelt down twenty yards in front in case he bolted. The warthog stuck his head out only to take four 9 mm bullets to his head before giving it up. I was worn out, breathless, and thorned nearly to death, but it was a hell of a hunt, and he turned out to have long, thick tusks to make a hell of a trophy.

I have to brag. You can bet that only a well-determined hunter and excellent guide would have finished this hunt. Peter and I always worked as a team against the animal and became one during the stalking, as well as reading the animals. His determination and my desire is what blessed me with such a fine hunt and animals that all scored. I must have seen six hundred warthogs lesser than mine. But it was not over yet.

October 8 2003

On day seven, we were in Limpopo Province, South Africa, near Botswana. Man! After this hunt, my legs feel like someone's been punching on them. This is all due to running, trying to catch animals in the open. Walking here is like walking in your kid's sandbox most of the time.

Today we went after zebra. We spent two and one half hours driving, trying just to spot some, but we never did. However, we did come across a spot on the road that looked as if three or four of them had crossed there. The wind wasn't quite right for them to go their way, so we went up a little, and in about twenty minutes we found their tracks. We walked hard and fast for another two hours nonstop, trying to get on them, before we ran into two eland bulls. We squatted and waited for them to move on to keep them from taking a chance to run, which would spook the zebras. Soon we heard zebras talking back and forth, trying to locate each other. So we slowed, only to be pegged by two eland bulls. It didn't spook them too badly; besides, it was very thick. We lost some blood from this stalk from fishhook-type thorns.

After following the tracks a while longer, we spotted them again. The first shot opportunity was no good; there were too many zebras ahead of the one we wanted, which we had a hard time keeping up with because they all look alike. Soon they paused and mingled around, with him in my scope, along with some limbs. I thought I had a hole to the vitals. I squeezed the round off on the second shot opportunity, and we knew it was a hit. He quickly went out of sight in the thick brush. In about ten minutes, we picked up a blood trail and followed it for about five minutes more. We saw him about the same time he saw us. He ran—and so did I, behind him. He ran till he assumed he had lost me. Only when he stopped and looked back did the second shot hit him right where I wanted it to—the neck. He fell in his tracks.

I must say I've picked up some tracking tips from Africa, but this kill wouldn't have happened without Peter. These animals can prove to be a challenge, but one is plenty for me in my lifetime.

We came in ready to eat, and eat we did—gemsbok and kudu mixed with a mild spicy brown gravy and rice.

That night, we decided to hunt solely for steenboks and maybe blesboks. You have a better chance to get an animal you want by concentrating solely on that animal. Each has a few areas and habits.

We started the evening hunt at about three o'clock. We went to the place where Peter's great grandfather shot a hippo years ago. Now it is a cattle farm. There has been no water there for years, though you can tell that there used to be a small river that was not very deep. We were finding some steenboks now and then, but no males. We did stalk on a few monkeys but weren't too serious about that. Then, right at dark, we spotted a steenbok and started after him, but with not much hope. The area was vast and very open, so we ran from tree to bush, stopped and squatted, and sat and waited till we thought I was in a decent range. This animal was thirty-one inches long and twenty-two inches tall. I leaned my gun's barrel against a small tree when he ran about fifty yards. I was making noise all the time, hoping he would stop. He did. I looked through the scope, and he looked so small. The reason I couldn't see him well was that I had forgotten to turn my scope from 2× to 10×. But I squeezed off a shot, dropping him in his tracks at about three hundred yards. I was surprised, as that was definitely the longest shot I have ever made—especially at such a small target. He was three-sixteenths of an inch short of making the record books, though he will be a beautiful full-body mount.

October 9 2003

On the morning of day eight, we left before daylight upon my request. I wanted to hear Africa waking up, as well as to capture some of the night sounds without the noise of the wind. I also wanted to take time to put the sounds of birds to the birds making them. We picked up an old couch and hid it under a large thorn tree about ten yards from the water hole. We didn't see any animals till about nine thirty, and between then and noon, there was always something going or coming the whole time. However, I did not see the blesboks that I was interested in. I saw a nice one on the way out, but he was moving really fast so I didn't want to take a chance at wounding him.

We came in for a fine lunch and after that sat out at front visiting with Artamon. Artamon is probably the only two-year-old castrated pet warthog in the world. He is free to come and go in the bush by Peter's house as he wishes. He has a mud hole where he takes mud baths and eats dog food every day around midday for twenty to thirty minutes, and then he leaves. However, he will stay long enough to eat a pear or an apple from you or let you have a picture with him. He was the only survivor out of nine piglets Peter found at a very young age. I'll tell you, he is a sight.

We left late for that evening hunt. I heard wildebeest and eland, as well as a few kudu. I think the moon was affecting them a little. I was content with the hunt already. Peter said he had never had anyone take the grand slam in four days. Also, all the animals had scored. We definitely were after them.

October 10 2003

At morning on day nine, we found a large herd of blesboks. They found us as well and hightailed. We tracked them for about thirty minutes before we found them. Just as we started to move in, two wildebeests got in our path. We got on our bellies and moved past them, only to get scented by them, which triggered the blesboks to run. We did all the above again, except it was some cow kudu that gave us away this time. The herd seemed to be heading to a watering hole we knew of, so we walked fast to get to the truck and ran to the watering hole. Big mistake. We were too late. There were 160-plus animals there. We sat anyway but saw only a warthog. On the way, I took a couple of potshots at baboons running at about 450 yards. The evening hunt was slow. We had only three warthogs, two cow kudu, and a snake eagle show up.

One must wonder, as I did before coming here, about insects. Well, mosquitos are not very bad, and there are no reported cases of malaria here now. I've had problems with spiders that can run as fast as a human walks. But there's nothing to worry about 90 percent of the time, since they are harmless. They just freak you out now and then. To me the flies were the most annoying, but that was usually for only about two hours during the heat of the day. Insect repellant definitely helps. Here, at Cruiser Safaris, this is all there is to worry about. You eat, hunt, and sleep, and it's all good!

October 11 2003

Day ten started out with me getting up to find all my clothes freshly washed and ironed, believe it or not. If you come to Africa to hunt, be aware that it's very dusty here; bring good cleaning gear for your guns, cameras, binoculars, etc. After breakfast, I got ready to sit on a couch in a blind for about four and a half hours. I was still hoping to see the big blesbok. I just felt he was here. Well, I sat there for about four and a half hours at the water hole, seeing a lot of game, but I didn't take anything. I'll tell you, though, just having to worry about some deer jumping out in front of you is one thing; we had a rhino running in front of our truck last night about fifteen feet from it, with us doing thirty-five miles per hour.

In the afternoon, we came in, ate lunch, and went right back to sit in the blind at a smaller water hole. It was slow at first, but then game started moving. There was one large herd of wildebeests, jackals, one good warthog, and a huge gemsbok. We saw other game as well. At dark we dragged a gut pile to attract jackals and hyenas down the road to a different location. We sat waiting for the moon to rise enough to see at night. Unfortunately the jackals came yapping within twenty yards of us before it did, so I couldn't see them. We hoped they were hyenas because that's what we were after. Between the moon rising and jackals, it was a good night hunt. I was told it is not normal to hunt at night, except for leopard hunts. We sat there till ten at night. There were a few warthogs that came by, as well as some dark spots; we just didn't know what the spots were.

October 12 2003

On day eleven, we started the morning hunt at seven o'clock and stayed in the blind till noon. We saw only nine impalas. We couldn't believe it. We thought maybe it was too windy that day, leaving it warm but not hot. The animals probably drank while we were having lunch and napping for thirty minutes.

That evening, we were on a mission for blesboks. We drove within a quarter mile of each water hole we could find, killed the truck, and stalked our way into them. We did this about seven times. Each time, we saw game but no male blesboks. At one water hole, as we were standing and waiting for the driver to bring the truck around after radioing him, a big black jackal ran to within twenty-five yards of us to drink, and then he panicked when he realized we were there.

We stalked the last water hole till we saw blesboks. And guess what? It was the same water hole we had been sitting at in the beginning. All we saw was about a dozen females. I became a little aggravated, so I walked out to let them see us, and they ran. We got back in the truck and drove for five minutes and stopped to get a picture of the sun going down. While doing that, out of the corner of my eye, I saw blesboks moving away from us at a trot. It was late, but we went after them. The sun drops like a rock here, and it is very beautiful because moisture mixes with dust to give it a brilliant hue. Well, we found blesboks—and the one I was looking for. We wound up stalking them three times as they moved without seeing us. Each time, we had trouble finding the male in the open or not blocked by females or thorn trees. Just as Hanz, the professional hunter (PH), wanted to quit, I said, "One more time." Now it was almost dark. Once again I had my gun lying across the shooting sticks, trying to find him. And I did, under a tree. Just as he turned, I aimed sharp for his asshole and put it within one quarter inch of there, folding him up, breaking his back. The problem was that I wasn't sure if it was the male blesbok that I had been after, but I knew it was a male. When I got there, I found that my persistence had paid off again, because it was him. I'll tell you, to find one animal on thirty-two thousand acres three days after seeing him the first time made this hunt a darn good one. He turned out to score 42 points on the SCI books. He needed only 39 to make it. That night, I ate till I couldn't lie down and be comfortable to sleep.

On the last day of the hunt, day twelve, we started at six o'clock, looking for another warthog. I was pumped since a man had shot one with tusks fifteen and a half inches on each side, making it the second-largest warthog killed in Peter's camp. They had found him just yards from where I shot my first warthog, which had tusks eleven and a half inches long. I'm still proud of him, though. The meat buyer said he buys around four hundred of them before he sees one that big, and that's only a few times a year. So I was glad just to see a fifteen-and-a-half-incher. The man from France who had shot it said it was his eighty-ninth African animal in his lifetime. The fifteen-and-a-half-incher was his fourteenth warthog.

Mother luck was on our side this morning. It was cool enough for a long-sleeve shirt again and very cloudy. They said hogs would not move in weather like this. Sure enough, there weren't any, so we drove very slowly, looking into thickets with binoculars. We found a few small ones—mostly females, though. In the process of stalking, we did manage to get within twenty feet of a warthog that stopped to stand his ground. The PH took a photo of us facing off. After two minutes or so, I backed off, giving him his room to go about his business.

We continued to walk from thick areas to more thick areas, being watchful of openings in between. We only caught a glimpse of one trotting away from us. At the same time, we were feeling beat. We discussed what to do. Last night they got a few raindrops for the first time in nine months. Though only a few drops, it was enough to make tracking much easier. So we decided to track after him just to see. After about thirty-five minutes, we caught up with him—but a little too close at about ten yards. He ran like hell, but it was easy to see he was a shooter. He ran, and so did I—to the point that I was seeing stars. When he stopped for one instant about five hundred yards into the chase, all I could see was his ass, so again I sent a three-hundred-grain bullet into it for an enema.

That was all she wrote. I can't officially get the score until the skulls are boiled out, but his tusk was thirteen and a half inches, making him one in about two thousand. Hunting these prehistoric-looking hogs is a blast when you get out of the truck and meet them head-on in their own environment.

That evening, we went out about four o'clock. On the way, we picked up some African kids walking home from school. They walked about two and a half miles each way for school. Hanz said they go for twelve years like in the states but are not required to; if their parents want them to quit, they can do so at any age.

Then I asked about AIDS within the African community. I learned a lot. It seems that the biggest problem is that people do not believe in condoms and think that they do not protect from the virus. In fact, they think using condoms will only make it worse. Talk about poor education from the government. I heard that witch doctors tell men that there is one way to get rid of AIDS: having sex with a virgin girl. By doing so, the men kill many girls, as young as infants to nine years old.

For the evening hunt, we took Peter's electronic game call out and set up, trying to call in jackals and tiger wolves. It took only about an hour and a half till we had some yapping nearby. A few minutes later, a jackal came out and I took a shot. I didn't really need him and still had a good final hunt.

On day thirteen, I left at nine in the morning to go to Johannesburg to drop animals off at the taxidermy shop and buy a few gifts at a curio shop, then I left for the airport to come home.

The flight home was easier than the one to Africa because I took a sleeping pill that knocked me out for about five hours. Then I watched three movies and napped again. All this made the time go by quickly. At that point, the only thing I was thinking about was seeing my wife, Vera, who so patiently helped me write this story. Having a wife that understands that hunting is my passion and doesn't give me any problems about doing it sure makes it easier on me and makes this man thankful.

I want to thank Star Pawn and Gun Archery, owner James Mckee, for helping me get the gear I needed for my safari and putting my pictures and the story on their website. Special thanks to Peter Lamprecht for an unforgettable good time with a good man who became a good friend, who asked me once, "What makes a good man?" Now, Peter, I would say a man like you is what makes a good man, since I grew to know you while hunting.

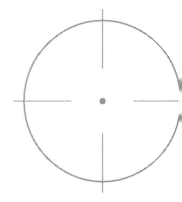

Bow Hunting

Howdy there! I'm getting happier than a possum in a persimmon tree knowing that archery season will soon be upon us. I hope that if you aren't already a bow hunter, you soon will be. I started in 1976 with a Bear bow and then a Whitetail Hunter. It took me seven years on my own to learn how to take a deer with a bow, and there haven't been many years since that I haven't.

First I have to say that the cheapest bow on the market today is better than the best bow we had ten years ago. You certainly don't have to buy the best bow on the market to take a deer. You should, however, try to stay clear of used bows unless you can take it to an archery shop and make sure the draw length is correct for you and that it's in good hunting condition.

After purchasing a bow, you have to practice, practice, and practice. Then, once your confidence is built up, you must practice some more. I recommend you practice shooting your bow while sitting down, kneeling, and from above (off your roof, for example). You can walk through the woods practicing shooting at targets and learning to judge distance. I also practice in the clothes I intend to wear hunting. One thing that'll help is a 3-D target. You can place it at different angles and distances to practice shooting. You should learn to use a range finder and take a couple of practice shots from your hunting stand in the morning before you climb down.

One of the most important things you should remember as a bow hunter is to stay within your shooting limits for you and your bow. You need to wait for the animal to come within your range and not try to stretch it. Always shoot low at a deer that is within close range. Remember: the range from the bottom of a tree to the deer will be different from that between a deer and your stand. You should range some spots while in your stand and wait for the deer to come to one of the spots you picked out. If you don't own a range finder, step off some distances by walking them out.

You have to think a little differently when bow hunting rather than gun hunting. You need to get closer to the deer and be more concealed with a good backdrop. You need to hunt right at deer crossings and funnels. Figure out where the deer are feeding, and get right in there. Look for acorns around hardwood bottoms. Pin oak acorns are usually the first ones to drop. I find them by listening for squirrels and scouting with my binoculars. If I'm in a pine plantation with no real hardwood around, I'll look for French mulberries or other berries.

One thing a lot of people hate about bow hunting is dealing with mosquitoes. The best prevention I've found is to spray just a little mosquito repellent on before walking to my stand. When I've been in my stand for five or ten minutes and I've cooled down, I apply mosquito repellent everywhere I need it. Most people perspire when walking to their stand, and this causes their spray to wear off too soon, leaving them vulnerable to mosquitoes. Don't worry too much about the deer smelling your mosquito spray; I have never had much problem with that. But it is a problem when you can't be still because you're being attacked by a hundred darned mosquitoes. What I do to help with my scent is purchase a commercial scent like fox urine. I stuff cotton in old medicine pill bottles and saturate it with the fox urine. Then I tape a loop of cord around each bottle and hang them all around me in trees and bushes.

When bow hunting, you need to take a moment before releasing your arrow and make sure everything is right. Concentrate on your target, and squeeze the release slowly, trying not to grip the handle too hard. Let your bow ride in your palm. A lot of people shoot targets well but forget all their technique when shooting at an animal. The first time I really saw this was with a group of hunters from New York that I was guiding for an elk hunt in South San Juan, Colorado. These hunters could knock your eye out at up to sixty-five yards during practice, but when I would call an elk in for them to shoot, they'd miss every time. The elk were fifty times bigger than the practice targets and as close as twenty yards, but they couldn't hit them to save their lives.

I could tell you so much more about archery hunting, but part of the fun is learning as you go. Just remember that animals deserve you taking the time to shoot as effectively as you can and not just wounding them. If you do stick an arrow in a deer, be sure to wait an hour and a half or longer before you try to follow a blood trail and look for it. It takes a little longer for them to go down than with gun hunting.

Well, get your stick and string and set yourself up in the wild for some archery hunting. I hope God blesses you with what I think is the finest nourishment for human consumption—venison.

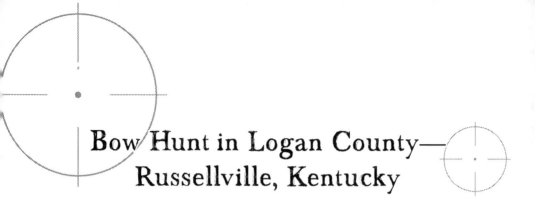

Bow Hunt in Logan County— Russellville, Kentucky

September 2006

Day 1

With deep desire to hunt somewhere new, me and my girlfriend of over a year, Debbie Thompson, left on September 15 at five thirty in the morning for the 738-mile trip to Kentucky. We were packed to hunt deer as seriously as possible. The drive took about twelve and a half hours, including stopping on Interstate 20 in Jackson, Mississippi, to eat at IHOP. The caramel-coated French toast was pretty good. The best part of the drive was along the Natchez Trace Parkway. We saw deer and turkeys all along the highway.

We were staying with Brian and Shelly Wilkins. Shelly is Debbie's cousin from Rosepine. Her parents, The Thompsons that own Your Home Town Shopper there. Bonnie Thompson helped me a lot with this book. Shelly met Brian when he was stationed at Fort Polk. He works as an electrician at Logan Aluminum, which makes four cans out of every six-pack.

Day 2

This was our first day to hunt! This afternoon we started scouting properties. We found a few good funnels where we set our climbing stands. The area was very hilly with deep ravines, thick oaks, scattered rocks, and cedar trees. Part of the area had been thinned. In a thicker area, we saw some good buck sign next to a transition of terrain types, such as rubs on trees as big as my leg, last-year scrapes and old rubs, large deer tracks, and deer droppings.

We got into our stands about five in the evening. Near six o'clock I had two does and one yearling pass about twenty yards under me. Debbie had three pass right under her, and then later two more. No bucks.

Day 3

This morning was cool enough for a small coat. We both saw deer sign but no bucks. The biggest problem was that we got infested with seed ticks. I thought that was it for Debbie. With a couple cans of OFF! and very hot water, I got Debbie back out that evening, but the weather turned hot with no breeze. We didn't lay eyes on a deer. We did see about six turkeys and a ton of cat squirrels.

Day 4

We started the morning out hunting in the rain until about eight o'clock. We waited until after nine to come down when it started to flood. Neither I nor Debbie saw any deer. I did see a cat squirrel with a white tail. I've only ever seen one other, and I have him mounted.

That afternoon, we went over to look at some of Mr. Day's property. Scouting through a cornfield, I walked up on a pack of coyotes. They scattered all around me. It was raining off and on when I walked up on two groups of turkeys. I didn't have my bow with me because I was intent on covering a lot of ground. I could've definitely taken two gobblers. I saw several deer beds and caught a few glimpses of deer running out of the edges of the cornfields. Finally the rain got heavier, so we called off our evening hunt.

Day 5

We started the day with cool weather. While walking to our stands near where we parked, we got flagged. We could see the deer from the glare of a nearby house. Neither of us saw anything during the hunt. We were let down just knowing the cool spell hadn't gotten them hopping.

After lunch we went up to Lewisburg to Jerry's farm. We scouted the area, which was an oak draw about three hundred yards wide in most places with a small branch running through it, and it sat between corn and soybean fields. We saw a lot of sign most everywhere. We jumped a smaller buck. I drew on him but didn't take the shot. We marked about four places for stands the next morning. We saw a good bit of turkey sign, so we hoped to be able to hunt deer and turkey at the same time.

That evening, we went back to our stands at the Nash place. The wind blew hard right up until dark. Debbie had a spotted fawn come under her briefly. I didn't see anything. I think Debbie did get into some turkey mites, so she took a bath with some Pine-Sol.

Day 6

We started the morning out early, trying to get in undetected at Jerry's farm. Debbie wasn't that lucky. I had three does show up early but no bucks. I spent the rest of the morning watching a hawk trying to catch squirrels. Debbie didn't see anything. I helped her move her stand, and when we were walking out of the woods, we saw a yearling by our truck. I had good and bad luck for the evening hunt. I was lucky enough to get to see a buck and get off the shot. I wasn't sure if it was a four or six point. Well my bad luck was that I found my arrow with only a few hairs on the broad head. Darn!

Day 7

I had a good evening with perfect conditions. At six thirty, deep in the woods, I saw a head first, then horns, and then all of a deer moving through the area, heading away from me. I stood up and hit my grunt call, making a contact call. The buck stopped, looked all around, and then turned right to me, walking about thirty yards. He then veered off away from me and was almost out of sight but finally turned and came off my right side in a half circle. He got to about twenty yards, but I still had no shot. I could tell he sensed that I was there, and he started walking straight away. At thirty-four steps, I grunted with my mouth, leaving him quartering away. I aimed behind the ribs, dropping him in his tracks. He was a very healthy four-point with a big body.

Day 8

The morning hunt was as perfect as it can get. At 7:13 a.m. I had a buck—probably 102 pounds, a six-point—feed his way up to about forty yards out and then suddenly bolt for about ten steps. He settled down and came back in to about twenty-five steps from my stand. I stood up and drew my bow, but of course, he stopped too soon. I held my bow awhile, locking my head to help. Finally he moved out. I took the shot with a hit. He bolted off, so I settled in my stand for a wait. Not long after that, a yearling came through. At about eight fifteen, a deer blew hard at my back. I thought I'd poo-pood my britches. It sounded like a mature buck. About nine o'clock, I took a practice shot where the buck had been standing to reassure myself. Then I climbed down and went to the kill spot. I couldn't find blood or the arrow. Zigzagging in the direction he had run, I found just a spot of blood. I followed the trail through the thickets, across a creek, through a bamboo flat, up a large hill, and to a big, open bottom. There it was, as clean as could be—just a spot of blood. I spent two hours trying to find him in all directions. I guess I have to call this one food for nature. This is always hard to swallow for me.

The highlight of this day's story is the four-point I shot on the evening of day seven. That four-point was the same one I had shot at on day six. I know this because he had a hole through his neck—all the way through—with a little red at the exit hole. It had to be him. I was shocked. I guess I just didn't hit the right stuff to kill him that first time. I assume that's why there were a few hairs on the broadhead and no blood on the arrow. Believe it or not, it's true!

Day 9

We left early this morning and got to the woods only to be met by a storm with a lot of lightning. I don't play in nature during electrical storms after having almost been hit on two occasions. (Once it came close enough to send pine bark flying in my face.) Debbie tried but was back in about fifteen minutes. She was starting to get that feeling we all get after not having gotten a shot in days. I told her it would be worse to not see anything than to not get a shot.

That evening, I didn't see a thing other than a screech owl that landed by my stand. We were still under severe storm warnings, and it was drizzling rain. Right at dark, Debbie had two different doe couples come in. She got her first shot ever at a deer but forgot to shoot low at the belly, which is what you need to do when the deer is close to you and you're on a climbing stand. She was excited and more fired up after that though.

Day 10

We had severe storms all night and into the morning. I also got sick, so we decided to sleep in. After getting up, we went to get deer meat shredded for sandwiches at Ed's Barbecue near Clarksville, Tennessee. Debbie went shopping with her cousin and missed the evening hunt. I waded my way through the swamp my stand was in. It looked like someone had mowed the place and piled up all the sticks left behind from the flooding. I didn't see a thing.

Day 11

There was still a lot of water in the trees. It had quit raining, but there were still dark skies. After daylight, there wasn't anything moving; it seemed as if the animals just wanted to rest after battling the windy storm. I certainly was feeling that way. About eight in the morning it cleared a little, and the woods lit up when eight turkeys came up on me. They fell about ten yards short of a good shot. You can shoot either sex during fall season with a bow in Kentucky. Still no deer showed up. Debbie saw two. On our way out of the woods, we saw a turkey near the truck. I almost decided to put a hunting stand in the back of the truck.

That evening, I didn't see much, but my eyes were playing tricks on me. There were about four does on the road when I was driving out to pick up Debbie. She had two does come by, but they didn't present her a shot.

Day 12

Morning was very windy up till around eight o'clock. And then it got still. I waited until nine fifteen and then came down. I was determined to see a deer before I came in, so I decided to stalk a bit. Well, twenty minutes into stalking the edges of the cornfields, I came on a place where I felt there should be a deer. I stopped and looked for a while before taking a step, and then a deer suddenly took off and then stopped, broadside. I tried the shot at sixty-five yards, but it was no good. I continued stalking and scouting. I came out in a soybean field near where Debbie was hunting, thinking I saw some turkeys way off. Two does appeared, walking right at me. I was in the wide open, so I knelt down. I drew my bow but never got a clean shot. Debbie saw only a few chipmunks.

For the afternoon, we went to Lake Malone down Highway 107. We did some sightseeing, talked to landowners, and ate lunch.

That evening was perfect, and it was cooling down. I had a doe come from behind me and stop by a deep branch near where I was sitting. I drew and felt that I could certainly make a kill, but I would've had to shoot through some limbs. Thinking the deer would hop across the branch, giving me a wide-open shot, I waited. It jumped across and didn't slow down until about forty yards out. I was trying to take a doe too now, since the landowner wanted one.

When I got back to the truck, I radioed Debbie. She was still at her stand and had made a shot. She radioed saying she'd found the arrow with only a small string of meat on it. I knew that wasn't very good.

I got my coon light and met her to start looking. I found a little blood and could tell where it had crossed the road. The doe had gone into an overgrown field. There was very little blood for a long way. I think the shot went through a leg. We didn't find her, but was sure she would be all right. She'd run about five hundred yards already.

Day 13

Neither I nor Debbie saw a deer—to our surprise, since it was a cool morning. I moved my stand and got set up for the evening. About six in the evening, I looked to the left and two does appeared. One spooked when my game camera snapped. I drew on one, and she stopped half behind a tree. I waited until I had to let down on my draw. By then another doe had come within range, and I made a shot with a hit. After dark, I radioed Debbie and found out she'd also made a hit. I went to help Debbie but couldn't find her arrow or blood. She said she'd heard it run through the cornfield. She and I, Jeremy, and a friend of Jeremy's from Georgia tried to find the doe, but once again, we had no luck.

Debbie and I went back to track my deer. We lost the blood trail, so I had Debbie hold at the last blood spot, and I started covering the area in circles with my coon light. About twenty minutes later, I found the deer curled up against a big log.

Day 14

This morning Debbie stayed in to spend the last day with Shelly until this evening's hunt. I went out but saw only a big doe walking out for the day. I came back and cut up deer meat and then went to Hunter's Den to pick up a dozen arrows to have ready for when I got back home.

That evening, we ended the trip without seeing anything, but we left with more experience and some new friends. We'd had a great time. For the trip home, we drove the entire Natchez Trace Parkway.

One of Many Scuba Diving
Trips Spear-Fishing for Catfish

About 1987 I started on an obsession that took a while to scratch out and slow down. I'm talking about swimming among logs and easing through grass at twelve to thirty feet deep, hunting catfish. I did this in the Toro River, Toledo Bend, Degray Lake, and some rivers in Arkansas.

The events of this small story happened on Toledo Bend, just out of Pirate's Cove. I hadn't been doing it long and was certified by Steve Cole from Hornbeck, Louisiana. I got my air and gear from Dick and

Sandy at Dick's Dive Shop there on the lake. I had planned to use two tanks this day. So out I went early, into the water and down to the thermocline edge at a log jam that came right up to grass that was about twelve feet high. There was fairly heavy cloud cover this day, so I had to move slowly along and stop now and then to let a cloud pass in order to see better. I came up to a large tree that looked as if it had broken at about five feet, and the tree was still attached to the stump. There was another tree across it. It was still dark when I eased up to it, kinda leaning on the log, using my clicker trying to attract some white perch. We were allowed to take a few with a permit in those days.

Not much later, the sun moved over, and on another log across from me was a huge catfish at about eye level. I exhaled deeply and saw his huge tail curled at the bottom of the log. I set the switch on my spear gun to high power and eased up, and about the same time we saw each other, he just kind of rolled off the log. He was swimming along as I popped him good. In a flash I was jerked, and I grabbed the log, and then it was skipping along with me. I could feel him jerking and swimming from side to side. My spear gun was harnessed to my wrist. The debris was so stirred up from our movement that I couldn't see two feet in any direction.

Then, quickly, there was no more pressure around my wrist. After rapidly rising up above the dirty water, I pulled my spear gun string toward me from the front to see my shaft. The steel shaft was broken, and I saw the monster just kind of swimming down into the grass with my other piece of the spear in his back area. I swam and tore through the grass, trying to catch him, but I didn't have a chance. I was sick to my stomach. I had just let a monster catfish get away! It was bigger than me—most likely the biggest cat ever speared on the lake, and maybe in the state. It turned out that what I needed was a shaft like those used in the ocean. It needed to be stronger steel, maybe with a swivel on the tip. But at that time I didn't know they existed. If I would have had that, I would have gotten him for sure. Fish all look bigger underwater, but that wasn't the case here.

I finished the rest of that tank and spent the rest of that day looking for him. I asked fishermen along the way to keep an eye out for a floating fish. I came back days later and scanned along the bank, but he never emerged. I'm guessing he just got tangled in grass and became turtle bait. There were many that died, though, and fell victim to my freezer and fish fryer as the years passed. I never saw a catfish this huge again. Once I saw a gar I estimated to be about eight to ten feet long. That's my story of the one that got away!

Hog and Predator Hunt

Day 1

I was lucky enough to make a late hunt with my brother from another mother Scott Bagi, from Ohio, and Joseph, from Alaska. Also tagging along were Mark and Casey from home.

I met Scott and Joseph at the Houston Airport, and we lit out to Eagle Pass, Texas, for the six-plus-hour drive. Mark had already made it there. We finally arrived about eleven at night, and at midnight we were hunting. With no sleep since five in the morning, it became challenging as we stayed out till well into the morning. Finally, about four thirty in the morning, our light hit a group of hogs and the bullets began flying. We ended up with two hogs down and a lot of ears hurting from the muzzle brake on Casey's gun.

Day 2

We bedded down after a good breakfast and headed out for an evening still hunt. A fox was bagged during the evening hunt. Again we bedded down for a nap, and about midnight, Casey and I went out. Night was cool, and holding the light was rough on my hands. We were hunting in a pecan orchard right on the Rio Grande River. Often we encountered the border patrol. We didn't quite understand what they were doing, though, because any Mexican who had come here illegally would see them from ten miles off, lie down till they passed, and keep walking.

Around three in the morning, we found a group of about five hogs in our light beam. As soon as they were in the light, they were leaving it, though outrunning my Nissan Pro-4 wasn't that easy, and soon they each felt a bullet that left them on the ground. I started with my AR-15 and new Laser Genetics night scope, but it wasn't working right. The next night, Joseph and I went out alone at about ten at night, and we were seeing a lot of game but no hogs. Soon Joseph got a good shot at a nice gray fox with my .17 HMR. A short time later, we got into the pigs. Joseph tried with open sights, though that can be complicated at night. I managed to light another one up, leaving it dead.

Day 3

After sleeping till about ten in the morning, we headed out toward Midland, Texas, and Pecos. First we shipped meat for Joseph to Alaska and picked up more groceries, and then we lit out for a six-hour drive to Pecos, Texas, or Loving County to meet Alan for some javelina and coyote hunting. We arrived about three in the afternoon, and by five, Joseph and I each had a javelina down. After caping mine and skinning Joseph's for a full-body mount, Scott and I were inside cooking. Then Joseph yelled, ran into the house to grab his gun, and began following a coyote that was dragging the carcass off. He actually got him, too. We spent some of the night checking the carcass with a red light that we had tied to a fence out back. The wind started howling, and the temps got down to thirteen degrees. Our butts were cold.

Day 4

We slept in as best as we could, and then Alan and I went out and sounded the predator calls. Soon, from one thousand–plus yards, here came a coyote, running to about seventy-five yards and stopped behind a bush. He spotted us and ran away, but I clipped him anyway with my AR-15. It was twenty-seven degrees. About noon, we all went out, and after several setups, we had no luck. We ended the evening with some halibut and creamed corn. It was six degrees this night.

Day 5

We woke up early, and Scott and I rode down to Alan's for breakfast. We came back to pick up Joseph and headed out. After about three setups, we got two coyotes in; we clipped one and slung lead at the other. Later we went to the river and weaved around the thickets, looking for pigs, but we had no luck. About one in the afternoon, we headed in, packed, and pulled out, headed to Tilden, Texas. Our time with Alan in Pecos was interesting. He is a person I can now call a friend. My time there with Alan was time well spent. He is the kind of man you can talk to and, in five minutes, respect him as a man's man and know he is the kind of friend we all would like to meet.

Day 6

We finally met Trent Johnson, "trailer mover," and Darrell about midnight. We unloaded, and about five o'clock we woke up and headed to the stands. This country is thick with mesquite and cactus, some being six feet high. Daylight broke with me in a box stand overlooking a small water tank—or pond, as most call them. Inside it were about fifty ducks of different kinds. Also a lot of doves and quail were there, feeding on some corn. The wildlife was nonstop.

I heard a gun crack. Joseph smacked a big boar. He said it had been lying on its back and that he headed down the stand only to see that the hog had left the area. I think another shot would have been good. Scott saw one too, and that was it for the morning.

After we all came in, we visited, napped, and went to get a truckload of corn to fill the feeders. That evening, we left out feeders as we got on the stands. While trying to get in my box, an owl, almost white, came out of it. Later, right at dark, he wanted back in and was ten feet outside the window, looking at me. It was a nice sight for about half an hour.

Two shots were fired. One was Scott losing a boar, and one was Jodie (Joseph) downing a nice sow. We all went back to look for Scott's boar but had no luck. We couldn't even find a drop of blood. That night ended with good fellowship with other campers. We had one-inch-thick steaks, halibut, silver salmon, and all the trimmings. We set in for a good night's sleep, got up, ate breakfast in town, and said our goodbyes, all while planning our next trip.

Oh yeah, I don't want to leave out a good laugh. Throw a live jackrabbit in the cab of a truck with a few buddies and see what happens. If you'd rather not, just ask Trent and Darrel. I can tell you it was funny.

All in all, I had another great hunt thanks to some friends I call my brothers. Till the next hunt, get out and enjoy, and thank God for getting to do it. And remember: each animal you take gives its life so you can have one, so give thanks for each one.

Preparing to Hunt

A re you starting to think about hunting season yet? If you're anything like me, you're restless for sure. I picked up a few extra acres of deer lease for the 2007/08 season, and same as everywhere I hunt, I've had plenty of work to do.

The first thing I do when I get on a deer lease is find the boundaries. It's important to find out who and what's around the lease and whether the boundaries are hunted. Next I ride and walk all roads and fire lanes to try to locate where the deer are crossing at different times of the year. Then I walk creeks and scout potential funnels, feeding areas, and old tree rubs. Basically, I just get out early and get to know my lease so I can find the best place to put my stand.

I located a spot on my new lease that I feel might be lucky for me. It's at the end of an old logging road next to an oak ridge with several types and ages of trees. Nearby is a clear-cut with a pine plantation on the other side. I determined that all the deer I would need were right there. I then looked for a few spots that might make good hunting stand locations. On one end I put my newly built 6 × 6 × 8–foot box stand on wheels (just for the ease of moving it). I camouflaged it well with paint and limbs. I'll probably use it when the weather's bad. Also, about three hundred yards away, I put my climber out and chained it to a tree. A climber is my choice of stand, because at least half the deer I've taken have been from about thirty feet up in that type of stand.

My next job was to start preparing food plots. I found a natural opening next to the clear-cut that consisted of about a fourth of an acre. Here I brush-hogged and then sprayed with Roundup. A week later, I disked it up and sprayed with Roundup again. (I believe this gives you more for your money.) This area I planted with Imperial Whitetail Power Plant. About sixty yards away, some weeks later, I planted iron clay and purple hull peas, being sure to leave room for a fall food plot. I never plant over spring and summer plots. Done right, there will still be plants in it for most of archery season. In the third week of September, or when the moon is on the increase and the chance of rain is apparent, I go ahead and plant iron clay peas again, mixed with Imperial Whitetail Clover and Buck Forage Oats. I try to plant seed types that are quick and will come back the next year.

About fifteen yards off the main trail of my hunting spot, I dug a hole about four feet by four feet wide and eighteen inches deep with a levee-type mound around it. Throughout the year I'll put several things in it. In March I put a few bags of stock salt in it, in May a sulfur block, in June a mineral lick, and in August I put all three plus some time-release Deer Cocaine.

At the very edge of my food plot, and kind of in the trees, I set up my feeder. In my experience, I would never put a feeder right out in the open or in the middle of a deer crossing. This is especially true for a lease where there have been few or no feeders previously. I never feed more than one second every morning and every evening. A lot of hunters tend to overfeed. I think the most important thing of all is to try to have all this done by July 15 and then get out of there until hunting season opens.

Now, you don't have to do any of this to kill a deer, but it sure makes it fun and increases your chances. A man has got to have something to spend his money on. The main thing about deer hunting is to scout your location and learn to identify what the deer are doing in that area. Be cautious about your scent, and go as often as you can.

First Trip Hunting in Missouri

Hello folks, howdy out there. I have been having to work a little harder this year. I had to pay Uncle Sam so he could give it to those who don't work. But now, September 14, I am leaving for an 862-mile trip to northern Missouri to bow hunt and embark on a quest, one more time, to possibly take a 140-plus-inch buck with a bow. I think that if I'm ever gonna do that, I have to go where they live. It will probably help also if I go during the rut. For now I go early, just because I see more deer hunting in other states than at home.

I lit out with the intentions of driving five hundred miles and stopping, and that I did, pulling my new little eco RV, which Robert, who owns the local RV sales and service business, hooked me up with. I started fast, putting my feelers out in stores, cafés, etc., trying to find somewhere to start my hunt. I decided on a small farm town with the courthouse in the center of the town and old buildings built around it. There was a corner café, which seemed like the best place to eat. The folks were all friendly and had a certain easiness about them. I managed to hear about some public land just outside of town in a real estate office. It was getting late, so I found a Dollar General store and started stocking up on groceries. I noticed a man in a truck next to me and asked him for directions, and within minutes he insisted on just taking me to show me how to get there—but not before letting me stock my truck with food and water and allowing me to plug into power at his shop. This was such a blessing from a good man whom I now call a good friend for life. It helps to have a friend when in a situation like mine—hunting all alone when no one knows where you are. Yes, Mr. John is one of those rare people we meet. His sons spent three and four tours in Iraq and Afghanistan.

My First Evening: September 15

I unpacked and hit the hay early. I planned to stalk on the ground on the first morning out, not knowing where to set up. About an hour into hunting, I spooked some deer. I just sat down right there on a log, and in about fifteen minutes a doe and yearling emerged out of the thicket right in front of me and came within fifteen yards and moseyed on by. I was just sucking up all the new sounds, sights, and smells.

This area is big farm country for sure and holds a lot of deer. It wasn't long before I felt something crawling on my arm. Yep, there they were, seed ticks. They are common in thick grass and brush around farm country. I was left feeling as if they were all over me. It wouldn't be the first time.

Slipping through the wood, I soon spooked a flock of turkeys off their roost. Late for that, I thought. I pushed my way through a canopy of large oaks, with thick cover underneath them that came up to my waist most of the time. It was also littered with a lot of dead limbs and deadfall. Watching for rattlesnakes and copperheads would be just about useless here. I finally found what I wanted in a stand of pin oaks loaded with acorns and deer sign. I spooked some nearby deer that were very close. I came in, napped, and then headed back and set my climber up and plopped down. All I saw were squirrels, and I listened to coyotes yapping their song in the background. It started cooling down.

Day 3

It is just cold enough to wear a light coat. No wind; clear skies. It was barely light when a deer walked on the road out near me. About another minute later, another deer was down the hill feeding. Soon a yearling with a few spots fed within twenty yards and then bedded down darn near under my stand for an hour or so, and then it moseyed on along. There were no bucks to be seen. That evening, I moved to a much thicker area where two draws crossed in an X shape, pretty heavily trailed, but I didn't see a deer.

Day 4

After peanut butter toast and a hard wake-up, I lit out to the stand. When I came within fifty yards of where I knew my stand was, I started looking for my glow-in-the-dark sticker on the stand, and soon I saw two glowing things. The second one was a deer within feet of my stand. I wasn't sure what to think about that. It was as though he was on my climber. He never spooked too badly, so I eased into my stand, and about thirty minutes after daylight, it decided to blow at me. I spent the rest of the morning hunt with no sightings. I came in, washed a few clothes in town at the laundry, and packed up to head for Mercer, Missouri.

After driving sixty or so miles, I saw a difference in the terrain type. I stopped in Princeton to wait for the rest of the group while eating at the Crossroads Bar and Grill. That was some fine eating right there. I soon realized there was a carnival downtown, so I went to listen to some music and check out the sights while waiting two hours for the group. Jeffery with the Missouri Outfitters soon passed, and I fell in right behind them for about a twenty-mile ride to the property we were gonna bow hunt, to set stands for the next morning. We didn't make it until noon the next day, because of a massive storm with a lot of hail and lightning. The evening hunt was scary, as if it wanted to rain, but it didn't. I slipped through a bean field and into my climber, cutting limbs on my way up. I then ranged spots all around me for yardage. I hunkered down for a four-hour wait till that magical hour before dark.

Soon a spike appeared from out of nowhere, as they can do. He moved by. Up here deer have to have four points or more on one side. There are big deer here. Only twenty miles away was where the world record was taken. We were four miles from the Iowa line, and it takes four years to get a tag to hunt there. I spent the rest of the evening being cold for the first time this season.

The cushion on my climber was damp, so I was damp, and then the wind picked up a lot. I saw a lot of squirrels, but that was it. On the way out of the bean field, I saw one deer after dark. Out of six hunters, about thirty-two deer were seen, with three does taken.

Day 5

For the morning hunt, I went to climb on the landowner's lookout. It was set between two bean fields. The sky was kind of overcast, and a light wind was blowing. No deer were seen. The wind picked up pretty fast, and it just got plumb hot. I decided to look for some acorns. Deer don't eat soybeans too much when the beans are in the middle of dying.

Moving through the woods as quietly as possible, I soon jumped a deer. I think it only heard me and didn't see me. It was a stud buck, but I had no chance at a shot. Not long after that, a yearling and doe came running toward me and stopped about twenty yards away. I managed to sling an arrow, and I believe it hit something. I wasn't really wanting a doe yet, although if I took one this way, it would have been all right. During the evening hunt, I wasn't expecting much. The moon was full, and it was hot. Sure enough, I saw nothing, but I had seven turkeys roost by me. It would have been nice to get a shot at one, since you can shoot two during the fall with a bow.

This was the first time I planned an out-of-state hunt during the full moon. I let that slip by me somehow. We did have a fine meal. I stayed with Dan Martin; I had my RV at his house. He is the owner of Hilltop Archery Shop in Mercer. He is one of those guys you seldom run across and we need so many more of.

Day 6

Morning was cool with a little breeze now and then. The moon was bright, so I left for the stand a little later than usual. I would be near where I saw the big buck. About an hour or so into the day, I spotted a deer to my left. Then, moments later, her yearling darn near got into my lap. She slipped by, and thirty minutes later I saw another doe, but no bucks. Later I came down and pulled my climber and moved about four hundred yards to a tree I found with acorns and deer sign under it. I decided to ride into Mercer, Missouri, for lunch. Mercer has a population of 320 people. I came back to scout the back half of the property, but the creek was still up from the flooding rain. While scouting I found another hot spot.

I stopped by the Hilltop Archery Shop to hang out with Dan's dad and bug his customers, as well as to shoot my bow a little. I got six new arrows and three broadheads. I favor Stingers. Dan's dad gave me a book, and about the time I decided to leave, the bottom fell out of the sky again. So I went back to camp to hang out, relaxing and reading.

Day 7

I woke up and cooked a few eggs and toast, hoping to just shoot a deer now. My heart was telling me it was time; my blood was racing, my head was pounding, I was breathing hard, and my eyes were going funny. The trophy doe would now be in my sights if she showed.

I didn't get headed out to the stand till about ten in the morning because of the heavy rain still falling. I thought, Okay, maybe this is a good thing, since the moon is full. Three hours passed while I was entertained by a red fox squirrel gathering acorns, hiding them around trees, and eating one now and then to keep his energy up. I came down to gather about half a Walmart bag of acorns from four different trees for me and Phil, the owner of the land I was hunting on. He was working hard to reforest it for wildlife.

After lunch in Mercer, I set a lock-on stand for an evening hunt. The rain had cleared out, but the wind had picked up. Nevertheless, a single doe popped out—but too far away for a shot. Actually, she seemed spooked. Moments later, a coon came out, and then, fifteen minutes later, another. Oddly, it seems that they actually spooked the little deer. Later it sounded as if a single turkey roosted behind me.

Day 8

What the heck, eggs sounded good again to start another morning. I felt maybe the day would be one for a good buck, though that would only be icing on the cake. I just love deer hunting, like many. It's a privilege to hunt, in my eyes, and I really love the meat.

Around eight in the morning, I had a doe pop out and make her way to the tree with acorns that I was sitting over in my climbing stand. The acorns were falling down a hill the tree was hanging over. The deer got up in the thickest spot it could find to feed. Finally I saw an opening, drew my bow, and released an arrow. She bellowed, wheeled around, and bolted through the brush. I waited about forty-five minutes and then climbed down, only to see meat on my arrow. I looked anyway and tracked her a couple hundred yards before finally feeling assured that she would make it. I think some vegetation got in my way. Sometimes the place where your sight is in relation to where the arrow sits on the rest is a few inches different. This is rare, but sometimes it poses a problem.

I came in to try to take a nap, though the wind was blowing so hard against my camper I couldn't sleep. The sky was blackening fast, and I was sure I would miss another day. I left anyway, with a drizzle falling now and then. About one hour into the hunt, from out of nowhere, a doe came right under my stand. I took her seven steps from the tree my lock-on was in.

On another note, I've seen that here, if caught littering, it's a $1,000 fine and one year in jail. If you hit a highway worker, you lose your license for life and pay a $25,000 fine. Louisiana needs to tighten up like that. Also, the farms place used tires painted purple on fence posts to mark private property.

Day 9

It was just a picture-perfect morning, cool but not cold. I was in the stand forty-five minutes before daylight because the moon was still up, helping see the deer early. Travis came in late, causing the deer to blow at me. They scented me in two different directions. Soon I heard a turkey yelping, and then I heard another in a different direction. The rain started coming, and I hadn't brought my rain suit, so I headed down the tree with my climber. As I was about halfway down, two deer broke over the hill.

The evening hunt around midday was still up in the air because of rain. At four in the afternoon, it was still up in the air. Finally, about five thirty, I made it out to the stand to see a yearling, a doe, and a couple of big coons.

Day 10

I went out for the morning hunt with no luck. I decided on leaving today and headed 640 miles to Louisville, Kentucky. No big bucks were taken from Missouri, but I left with a few good friends, having had a good time chasing the dream on new soil. Well, I hope the good Lord sees you with some hunting this season or just some getaway time in the woods. Catch you next time.

Atchafalaya River Hunt

Hello, folks! Looks like Old Man Winter is slipping away! For me and most of you, that means more work and less play as a hunter. Oops! I forgot about turkey season, spring food plots, fishing, diving, camping, boating, etc.

Well, I did a little more hunting down south on the Atchafalaya River at T. J. Oucoin's camp, right on the river. Behind it is a three-hundred-plus-acre lake called Cow Lake. Dannis Martin, Gary Green, Davey Jones, and I hit a bank about seven in the morning with the intent to hunt deer, set out trot lines, and duck hunt. I figured that if we did half of it, it would be a good trip. Usually I stick to one or the other at a time, but if they were game, so was I.

I struck out to scout and hunt on state land along a river behind camp, while everyone else left to put out four trot lines and jug floats.

I managed to locate a few likely spots, working my way through the swamp. A lot of the area was thick with deadfall from trees blown over by storms in the past. The swamp in the basin can leave you being surprised and bewildered in a different way than some other places in the wild. If you have never been here, get a boat and find your way into it. It is changing as we know it.

As dark fell upon me, I soon realized I had walked way too far and had become much more exhausted than I wanted to before the walk back to camp. My GPS reminded me that camp was over two miles away. Late or not, I curled up for a twenty-minute catnap to rejuvenate my energy. We had left my house at three in the morning to come down. Shortly after dark, I made it back to the camp. But I had seen no deer. The first thing I saw and smelled on arriving back was a large pot of Cajun gumbo. T. J. got it done, and none of us minded feeling miserable from eating too much of it. Camping and cooking—there isn't anything like doing those things while making new friends and being with old ones, all together.

After a lot of logs getting sawed from our snoring, we lit out the next morning, all hunting. No deer were killed until about noon. Then we had one-inch-thick steaks on the grill! Shortly after eating, we ganged up in two boats and headed to the lake to check the trot lines and shoot some ducks. T. J. and I cut across the island to Cow Lake, and the rest were supposed to go up around the canal. They had to use PVC sewer pipes to roll the boat across the bank for about one hundred yards to the mouth of the lake. Quickly they realized there was too much kelp washed in for them to make it to the lake. Meanwhile, T. J. and I shot our limit of marsh hens and pouldeau. T. J. introduced this to me for the first time and taught me to aim at the bird's tail, belly, and head, and then *bang!* That helped after I missed the first couple of ducks, which left me a little embarrassed. Then I lucked out and took a nice green-winged teal drake. I fully intended on mounting that one. This was like killing a monster buck for me. I haven't done a lot of duck hunting, but I like it so far and am thankful I was asked by T. J. to do something new. New things that I've never done are what I can't wait to find. To me, this is living! Having friends to do these things and share these things with is the blessing.

Soon we got a phone call from Davey. We had to pick up the trot lines and check them. We caught a good mess of channel cat ranging from three to five pounds.

On the evening hunt the "ole deer slayer" managed to take a small deer, and Dannis notched a few trees with his gun trying. All in all, we managed to leave the place with what we came for, all the time making memories for a lifetime, and hopefully friends as well.

That evening, we loaded the boats to the hilt for the trip downriver to Butte-Larose Marina. It seemed we had a lot more than we had come with. I almost flipped my boat changing hands on the steering stick with the throttle wide open, like a dumbass for sure. And of course it all was seen by Davey, who I knew would rag on me. So what if the current tried to consume me? (Oh! Friends, ha!) Well, that was okay, 'cause Davey went back to get T. J. and the four-wheeler and almost lost the four-wheeler in the river.

If you've never been camping with friends or have forgotten what it's like, get back out there. And if you've never been down south to do it, try it. It is truly its own world; it is separate from northern Louisiana for sure. View all you can of God's picture of Mother Earth he has allowed you to live in for a short time. If half your life has passed, then you must surely know how short it is!

Well, live on, my friends—and happy camping!

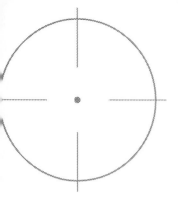

Bass Fishing

My friends, Lord knows there are many men and ladies alike that love to pitch a lure into water after a Lunker bass. A lot of folks don't understand why either. Well, for me—and I think like a lot of others—I can't wait to send a lure into any hole of water for the thrill of feeling something hit my bait and jerk my line. It's just plain fun to flip a hook with a worm on it near a treetop, put a big glob of liver on a hook for catfish, or use live shrimp for saltwater species.

I think a lot of what we fishermen enjoy is being on the water at daylight on misty mornings, seeing the sun come across the water just as doves or wood ducks fly by. Then a big thump hits your topwater bait, which skips across still water along the edge of a big stump or log, and then you feel a bass pick up your artificial worm and start to move off with it before you set the hook in its mouth.

Maybe a lot of what I love about fishing is just exploring new lakes or waterways along with an old friend or while getting to know a new one. Cutting across the water in a nice boat right at daylight and heading to a favorite fishing hole is a great way just to get that feeling that you are thankful to be alive. It's hard to beat the look on a kid's face, also, when he or she pulls in a nice white perch or something. Every serious fisherman can't wait to try to get a bigger fish than his last, whether it takes two days or two years. Of course, icing on the cake is creole seasoning, Zatarain's Fish-Fri, and some hot oil.

There are all kinds of ways to fish, making all kinds of ways to relax and reflect on life while doing it. The fish and the waters they live in are together truly one of the best blessings in God's creation. Take the time, my friends, to see this and protect it. Get out there and give it a shot. Feel the high and lows of ones caught and ones that got away.

Dog Days of Summer and Snakes

Looks like the dog days of summer have come into town. I haven't been in the woods a lot, but, when I did go, I had no problem seeing plenty of snakes and annoying banana spiders, with their big yellow webs that will knock your hat off at five miles per hour while riding down a fire lane.

I thought I would tell y'all a few things I know about snakebites. First, you're probably not going to die, though you might *wish* you were dead. I know of a twelve-year-old boy, my friend Mark Labates, who was bitten with both fangs, delivering a full load of venom into his forearm. That means a lot as to how bad your experience will be. It cost him $68,000; a big, nasty scar; two plastic surgeries, and a nickname: Pure Poison. It's one of his greatest stories now that it's over.

Get a book and learn about the poisonous snakes you have in your area and how to identify them. Just remember: red and yellow kill a fellow. This comes in handy if you just found or were bitten by a coral snake. Don't fret too much. They have to get you in a soft spot like between your fingers, on your ear lobe, etc., usually when you are curled up in a sleeping bag or dozing by your favorite oak.

In case of a bite, here are a few things you should not do: Don't give any kind of medicine to the victim. If you can't find the snake that bit the victim soon, go to the doctor. Don't use ice at all. Don't lance or cut into the bite. Never use a tourniquet; venom needs to spread. Don't give the victim food or water. If a child is bitten, don't let him or her know it is poisonous, and assure him or her it will be okay. Otherwise, their hysteria might just get you killed on the drive to the ER. Here are a few things you should do: Stay very calm and move slowly. Get to the doctor as soon as possible. Remove clothing or anything from around the bite. Take pictures before and after, in case you live. *Just kidding!*

There are a few who have died from snakebites in Louisiana.

Usually snakebite victims who die are elderly or were already very sick.

A few things will help keep you out of the way of a moccasin. When I was learning how they smell, I picked up a smashed water moccasin. It gave off an odd smell. You can often smell the moccasin before you see it. I've shown this to many people. Also, step *on* a log to cross, never over. Step over a brush pile instead of into it, when you can, and avoid likely areas as much as you can.

Don't let this stop you from enjoying the outdoors. Snakes are everywhere. They could be under your carport, on your front porch, or under your house, and they can even come through the door if it is left open too long. It happens. Lights in yea house attracts insects which attracts frogs that in return attract snakes in many cases.

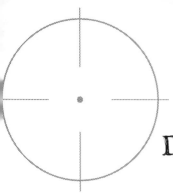

David's First Buck

David Parker

avid Parker—what can I say; he is the greatest inspiration in my life. He had spinal meningitis at nine months old, and it changed our lives forever. My little brother endured pain over and over again and yet he overcame. Brain trauma left him a little different in a special way, and it left his right arm completely paralyzed and one leg darn near paralyzed as well. But with hours of my mom's, Carolyn Parker's, love, devotion, and physical therapy—but mostly his heart to succeed—he walked again, with a limp. He wore braces for years. We loved to camp and hunt, and David was right in the middle.

So when he finally felt his time had come to hunt on his own, well, as with letting him drive, it was hard. But God always looked out for

David from the get-go, so I soon came to terms with leaving it that way. It was a cool, calm November morning in Kisatchie forest. I woke to Mom rattling the coffeepot and my stepdad, Cullen Parker, putting wood in the coals that were left from the night's fire. David and I piled out of the tent. He was excited. We had showed him a place on a draw lined with white oaks, blackjacks, and post oaks that were loaded with acorns. There was a wild horse trail leading to it. It was hard for him to walk because his little leg, as we called it, would barely clear the top surface. There were some fresh scrapes and rubs along the ridge. It was about the hottest spot that I knew. We all went our separate ways to stands in Peason WMA. Super Dave, with a monster grin, drove into the morning's darkness by himself, headed about two miles down 117.

At about nine thirty, we started coming back into camp. At ten o'clock, Mom filled with worry, couldn't stand it, and said, "Let's go check on David. He was supposed to be back at 9:00 a.m." It was about two hundred yards to Highway 117 from where I camped. About the time we got there, he pulled up; so we backed up, and he pulled in. He got out and we saw that he had blood all over him. Mom nearly fainted, and my heart stopped. But then we saw that he was grinning from ear to ear. He had shot a nice six-point with a Remington twelve-gauge loaded with three-inch buckshot shells. He had gutted it with a dull knife through a hole about eighteen inches long, dragged the deer up three hundred yards of hills, and then loaded that 150-pound deer into the back of a Chevy short-wheelbase truck all alone. Now, that is not easily done. Also, accurately shooting one-handed is not easy either. But David always surprises me. If you could spend a day doing things with David and not feel foolish about your own little hardships, it would be a miracle. For a so-called lesser man, he is more of a man than hundreds I've run across. I love him so much.

Wildlife Management Areas

I've already been thinking about WMAs for the next hunting season. They can be very rewarding. Each WMA has its own adventure to offer for hunting and exploring. I usually decide on one and then get as many maps for that area as I can find. Next I contact the game warden or a biologist for the WMA I've chosen, or I at least talk to someone who has hunted there. I basically try to learn everything I can about it before I start hunting.

I tend to enjoy WMAs later in the season, when my deer leases start to become the "same ole thing." Weekdays are best if hunting is open, because there are usually fewer people in the woods then. After a morning hunt, I'll spend my afternoon looking for other locations to hunt, but there are usually other things you can do to break up the boredom between hunts. Many WMAs offer boating, duck hunting, and even fishing.

There are a few things you need to remember when hunting WMAs. First of all, you need to make sure you know the laws and regulations. These may vary depending on the area you choose to hunt. I highly advise you to wear all of your hunter orange and keep your light on when you're coming in and out of the woods.

My last WMA hunt was at Three Rivers in north Louisiana. We went midweek and found a moderate amount of hunters, but it wasn't overly packed. The roads were decent, but the campground was lacking. I could tell that it could become wet and muddy quickly if a good rain came. As soon as we got there, I looked the roads over for deer sign but found very little. Since it was January, there wasn't much cover left for the deer to hang out in. I knew I needed to go long and deep into those woods.

On my first hunt, I hadn't decided on a stand site, so I wound up sitting on the ground. I finally found a good area that had rubs on trees the size of my leg, and a lot of trails funneling toward a small lake. Still, I had no luck for another day. While scouting for another location, I decided on a thicket with fresh tracks only a few hours after a rain. The next morning, I got into my climber and climbed too high. With daylight breaking, I couldn't see very far under the overgrowth in the treetops. I decided to stay put anyway.

At that magical hour of seven thirty in the morning, I saw a doe standing to my left about one hundred yards away. I decided that with no more than I had seen, I'd go ahead and take the shot. I turned the scope power up to try to see through the limbs and fired my muzzleloader. After the smoke cleared and two limbs waved at me ten yards away, I could tell that the slug from my Optima .50-caliber had been thrown off. Now a little disgusted, I decided to reload and finish the hunt. I called my friend Brian Todd to fill him in on my fine marksmanship. While I was on the phone, a nice buck came out, trailing a doe straight at me. He was thirty yards out and at a trot. I threw down the phone and brought up my gun, but I couldn't find him in the scope. I grunted at him about four times, trying to slow him down, with no luck whatsoever. He was acting like he'd never trailed a doe before this time. When he was about ten yards from my stand, I realized I'd forgotten to turn my scope back down. Needless to say, it was that buck's lucky day, but not mine! Nevertheless, it was a fun hunt on a WMA with some good friends. We ended up with one deer lost, one doe down, and my misses, along with a few more deer and some hogs seen. I might add we had some good food at Danny's Hot Boiled Seafood on Highway 1 in Simmesport.

Anyway, it's February, and I'm going to be busy working on food plots and fertilizing.

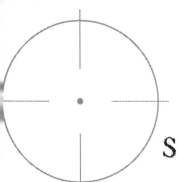

South Africa 2007

Black Wildebeest

August 12, 2007 Africa

Today we flew out of Houston Bush Airport for the first leg of our journey to South Africa. We spent last night with Debbie's sister, Kim Brown, and her husband, Larry. We had the pleasure of devouring some large T-bones before bed and playing with their children, Colton and Lynnsey. Kim drove us to the airport at five in the morning, and I felt my anticipation grow almost as though it was 2003, the first time I hunted in Africa. The flight from Houston to Washington, DC, was about four hours long. On arrival, we had to claim our luggage and recheck it for the flight to South Africa. My gun was checked all the way through to Johannesburg.

The layover in DC was five hours, so we passed the time by

visiting with some very nice people we met from the Houston area. Their names were Jerry and Linda Rubenstein. Jerry is the owner of Texas Pipe & Supply Co., and Linda is a former model. They were so interesting to talk with because they have traveled and hunted all over the world. Jerry was recovering from a broken back after falling off a mountain in Spain while sheep hunting. He's also hunted in Africa numerous times, as well as Mongolia and Spain. Hearing his stories got my blood pumping even more. He also gave me hope that I might make more hunts if God should bless me to make it to his age.

Once on the plane to Johannesburg, South Africa, we settled in for a very long flight. The trip was fifteen hours long and as miserable as you might think. I had a hard time resting, but Debbie fared okay, getting about seven hours' sleep. I slept for about seven minutes. The worst part was how bad my back, legs, and bottom hurt after sitting cramped up for so long.

After arriving in "Joburg" on August 13, we cleared customs and were met by Bruce. He was working for the Afton Guest House, where we would be spending the night. He helped us through the police station, claiming my gun, and then drove us and another couple to the guesthouse. Even though it was late morning to us, it was actually about seven in the evening there. We were hungry, so we went to eat seafood (prawns) and then decided to head back to our room for some rest. By two in the morning, we were both wide awake.

August 14, 2007

We were back at Joburg airport by ten in the morning and were soon flying to Port Elizabeth, which is on the coast of the Indian Ocean. There we were met by John Barnes, our PH. In Africa you have to have a licensed PH in order to hunt. John loaded us up in his Land Rover safari truck, and we headed out to our lodge, which was two hours away, near Grahamstown. The drive was nice, with a landscape of low-lying mountains that looked sort of like South Texas mixed with lower elevations of the Rocky Mountains. We saw exotic animals everywhere we looked. There were kudu, warthogs, ostriches, zebras, and lots more. Debbie had never seen most of these animals in her life. We arrived at Kikuyu Lodge about three in the afternoon, and let me tell you—it was gorgeous. The main house was a massive stone building with a thatched roof, and the guest cabins looked the same but smaller and were set on the edge of the cliff, overlooking a small river surrounded by beautiful mountains. Our cabin was nicer than most people's homes. This was right up Debbie's alley, which made me happy. The lodge owner is another story, but was not the man with whom we booked our hunt.

We met Gary Sparrow that night, who runs Bundu Hunts / African Cape Safaris. Gary had set up our safari for us and booked us at Kikuyu for the week and a half we'd be hunting. That evening, we went out and shot my gun a few times to check it out after the flight. Just at dark we saw a group of hunters looking for caracals but had only gotten a jackal. The caracal is a lot like our bobcat and lynx at home. About the only way to take one is with hounds. We had a delicious dinner of bontebok lasagna with all the trimmings and got to know the lodge managers, Ken and Marlene. We were in bed as early as possible that night so we'd be ready for our first hunt in the morning. I was raring to go!

August 15, 2007

Today was our first day to hunt in South Africa. We drove about an hour to our first location through diverse terrain that included cacti and mountains. The temperature was about forty-five or fifty degrees, and as soon as the sun came up, we were treated to very strong winds that lasted all day. Early on we started seeing black wildebeests, black springboks, and some mountain reedbucks. After a while, we caught a glimpse of the animal we were looking for—a lechwe. The lechwe were in a group of about twenty. We stalked over extremely rocky terrain for three and a half hours. Finally they went into a swampy area thick with thorn trees. I positioned myself near the opening of a water hole and waited for them to come out. After about forty minutes, two bulls came out, and I picked the best one for my shot. I made a heart shot at about 250 yards, and he literally jumped five feet high, hit the ground, and ran fifty yards before collapsing.

Later that evening, we headed up a mountain and hunted for mountain reedbuck. We saw only a few does and small bucks before we called it a day. We headed back to the Sparrow Ranch, where our tracker, Nahoy, would skin our animal.

August 16, 2007

The wind was slow during the first half of the day, but it was still very cold. We were again looking for a nice mountain reedbuck. While working the edge of the mountain, we found the one we wanted. Eventually we caught him in a group and made a running shot that ranged at 160 yards. After getting him skinned, we stopped to eat the lunch that had been packed for us. Debbie and I had to laugh at the contents: shredded cheese and lettuce sandwiches on white bread, and crispies (potato chips).

After lunch, we decided our next trophy would be the black springbok. We rode on the safari bench on top of the Land Rover and scouted with our binoculars. After an hour, we spotted a group of about eighty scattered along a hillside. We sat under a small tree while Nahoy went to try to flush them out. Luckily, seven of them were trotting toward us and stopped about 185 yards away. About five of them were horned, so I picked out the best one and squeezed the trigger. We all lost sight of him immediately and weren't sure where he went. When we went out to inspect, we saw that he had dropped in his tracks.

August 17, 2007

Today we drove for an hour toward the coast of the Indian Ocean to Port Alfred. The terrain was completely different than where we'd been hunting. There were rolling green hills and pineapple plantations with the ocean in the distant background. We started the morning by hunting for nyala. We were lucky enough to find one early that morning having his breakfast in a pineapple grove. I made a good shot and bagged our first animal of the day.

Enyala

We spent the rest of the day searching for a bushbuck. We drove over hills and valleys, and along the Fish River, and saw many different animals, such as zebras, waterbuck, and impalas. We had one bushbuck jump out in front of our truck and then run into the bush. I got my gun ready, and Nahoy went to try to flush him out. He ran out quickly enough, but I wasn't able to pull off a shot. We were then headed out for the day and thought our chances were over. But we then caught a glimpse of two bushbuck bedded down near the road. I took my shot at 130 yards and put one down in his tracks.

On the way home, we stopped at a taxidermy studio and were given a tour. We were all impressed with their beautiful mounts—especially the lions and baboons. That night, Marlene treated us to dessert using some pineapples we had brought back to the lodge for her.

August 18, 2007

There was no hunting today. John, Debbie, and I slept a little late and then headed out to Addo Elephant National Park. We wanted a chance to see as many animals as we could—especially those we weren't hunting. The park is huge, and we were able to drive through only a small portion of it in one day. We immediately found a herd of elephants grazing on small bushes and playing at a water hole. We snapped pictures of zebras, kudu, warthogs, impalas, land turtles, and red hartebeests.

This place was nothing like the zoo. There were animals roaming free everywhere, and we knew there was a certain level of danger—especially for those dumb enough to get out of their truck. We were disappointed that we didn't see the lions. They're apparently hard to see during the day because they mostly hunt at night. The highlight of our trip was having a monster cape buffalo fifteen yards from the truck. The cape buffalo is the second most dangerous animal in Africa, and here one was, staring us down. We finished our trip by eating lunch at the park restaurant and buying a few gifts. We drove home down some quiet village roads, spotting and pointing out different animals. John pointed out a lodge that was well known as the place where Tiger Woods got engaged. Back at the lodge, we shared a glass of wine and then took a walk down by the river. Apparently the baboons didn't like our presence; we had them all barking like crazy on the cliff above us.

For dinner we had a *braai* (barbecue). Actually, Marlene grilled lamb kebabs and sausages. By the time I was done, I looked like a pregnant armadillo. We pitched in on the cleanup and then headed off to bed to prepare for another day of hunting.

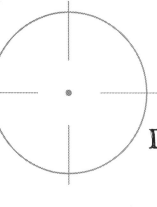

Dallas Safari Club
Convention 2008

Howdy, sportsman!

Looks like we have time to rest a spell before turkey hunting and fishing. I spent a little time at the SCI Convention in Dallas with more than nine hundred vendors. Please take a look at SCI on the internet. They are a valuable asset to sportsmen across the world. The desire for a fair choice hunt has put a value on animals across the globe that once was never there, thus leading people in these regions to protect them and allow them to reach full maturity.

The trip to Dallas took five and a half hours and about thirty-five dollars in fuel. We got a very good rate at Hilton Anatole because of the convention. We spent the first half day working our way through booths, talking to vendors, and making friends. Then we were off to the silent auction area to place bids. The items up for sale ranged from $5 to $50,000. There was something of interest for any sportsman's budget. Later we make it to the banquet.

Our dinner was an appetizer of open-face shrimp ravioli, mushroom cream, and pancetta caviar cream in pistachio oil. The main meal was chicken stuffed with Boursin cheese and prosciutto, wehani rice with maple bourbon-glazed pecans, and vegetables. Dessert was molten chocolate cake.

After dinner, awards were given, and there were speeches from people like Larry Potterfield. We learned that the NRA has acquired millions toward protecting our gun rights and uses five percent of that, each year, to pay lawyers. The NRA will be starting a shooting team in every high school and college in America. We met a young lady that shoots on the US Olympic team while having dinner with Shelah, who owns an online clothing and accessory store for lady hunters.

We spent day two at the Dallas SCI show with a lot of walking and talking to artists, taxidermists, gun and scope makers, and people from other countries while watching bids on our silent auction. It looked as if we were holding our own with a bid of $800 on a $3,600 dove hunt for two in Mexico. We had also bid on a fully paid hunt in Ireland for $1,200. It was like playing cards. I'm a simple man, so I was just gambling on luck, hoping some ole rich man didn't decide to bid against me. I determined that if I were to win a hunt, I would pray God would deliver me the jobs I must work to be able to go. I believe God helps those who help themselves if they truly believe. My desire to see new things in new places propels my life like no other. This is the case with most big game hunters. Some of the success stories I hear from these hunters never cease to amaze me.

We walked our legs off and turned in for a rest before supper. We got a table to ourselves this time and had Bibb lettuce with walnuts, goat cheese, and raspberries, topped with champagne dressing. That had me eating more salad than usual. We followed it with thick-cut grilled rib eye steak as big as our plates, caramelized onions, and roasted fingerling potatoes with asparagus spears. Dessert was raspberry crème brûlée in raspberry coulis.

The ladies' luncheon raised $171,000 to go toward the SCI Convention. The young jungle boys working as servers must have helped. A world-famous philosopher gave a speech about conservation and its importance to the USA and the world that made about eight hundred people shut up for the first time. There were many commonsense issues he spoke of, such as the lack of water. In the fifth grade I became so troubled about trash starting to accumulate along Anacoco Creek, which was pretty much my home that I was finally brought to a counselor Mr. Stokes in Anacoco. I still think they thought I had a problem.

That evening, we showed up at the suit-and-tie banquet. We had lobster bisque with puff pastry crust, beef tenderloin steak with foie gras hollandaise, truffle mashed potatoes, mini carrots, assorted breads, and chocolate decadence torte in burnt rum sauce, and we sipped Canyon Road Chardonnay and Canyon Road Merlot. During the dinner, some awards were given along with some well-deserved praise to a few military members present and gone. Then there were more auctions, with the most surprising being a bull elk hunt on White Mountain Apache Reservation in Arizona—a thirty-five-day hunt. In 2007, it sold for $77,000; this year it went for $71,000. There was also a black bear hunt for two people, two bears each, for $5,000 in Alaska. These were just some of the great opportunities for anyone with drive to save a little money and make it happen.

Take a look at SCI. For thirty-plus years now, they have been the leader in protecting the freedom to hunt. No other organization works with legislators, governments, and state and federal agencies while partnering with other conservation and political action groups the way SCI does. SCI protects the hunting rights of more than fifteen million Americans and forty-five million families worldwide.

With the recent merger of HSUS and the Fund for Animals, hunters face their biggest challenge ever. Our foe has assets of over $100 million, with annual revenues of $90 million. HSUS president and CEO Wayne Pacelle has promised to take hunting out-state by state. SCI has fifty-two thousand members, and HSUS claims to have seven million against the hunter and conservationist. Please write or call your officials and ask for more to be done to protect your right to hunt and own guns. We have to stop talking and start doing things about our problem, or life as we know it will fade for us and our children. If you don't agree, please study it with an open mind before you decide.

God bless you, and don't stop till you drop.

Hunting and Cleaning Boar

Hello out there. It seems a few things changed for a lot of us because of the storms. Mother Nature always seems to reclaim a lot she has given. Though it's not a good thing in most cases, it is something we must accept and live with as best we can. I can tell you God has helped me weather many types of storms.

It seems that this will most likely affect the 2008 and 2009 hunting seasons. Gustav definitely knocked most acorns off the oaks. I think wild muscadines were also blown off. This will probably make deer move more for food, especially during archery season.

Use binoculars to search the trees for acorns. Of course, corn will help you see deer too. Most hunters feel buying high-priced corn is not feasible, with fuel so costly and hunting land continuing to get more expensive. Food plots are the most feasible option. Of course, none of this can be done in a WMA or National Forest. These are always best hunted during the week, and as the season progresses, you must get deeper where it is thicker. Also, be extra careful about your scent everywhere—how far you ride your four-wheeler, which way the wind blows, etc. I hope you will get all your stands ready, except maybe your late-season food plots.

I have already gotten to hunt a few days. I have about 250 acres on Highway 28 East near the river. Going to my stand for my thirty-day camera check didn't take me long. Some hogs moved in, chasing acorns blown off by the storm. I don't mind a little pork taken from the wild.

That evening, I quickly mounted myself in a climbing stand hanging off a pine a little wider than my body for cover. About ten minutes before dark, I heard a few squeals in the swamp behind me. I followed this hunt to lay eyes on any animal other than a coon and a few doves.

The next morning, a long time before daylight, I settled at about twenty-five feet. It wasn't long before I heard them either bedding down or bedding up. Daylight broke, and everything quickly became a hog or sounded like a hog. After an hour or so, my head began to turn back and forth, searching. I had forgotten my pad to sit on, and it left my butt feeling as if I had been on a park bench all day. It is hard to hurt and be still. Suddenly, to my right, a single hog quietly appeared in the fire lane nearby. Immediately I saw him—an ole boar! He was weary. I didn't waste much time spanking him with my Marlin .30-30, my favorite gun for hog hunting and hunting in the brush. He ran about forty yards and cleared the brush, falling to his last breath. He weighed about two hundred pounds and had white and cream-colored hair with an average set tusk. He would have made an ugly mount. They must mostly look mean mounted. I think the hogs must have already been there when I got there, and they split at my arrival. This boar was only trying to get back to the group, late. He should have paid more attention. Ha!

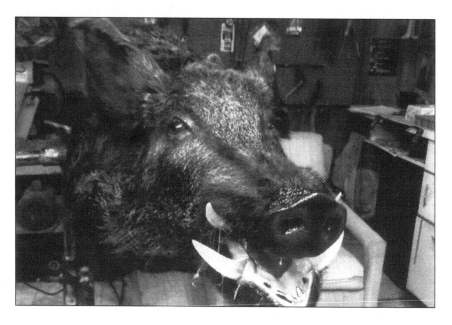

I can tell you that if you know how to clean a boar yourself and prepare the meat, you can eat nearly all of it. Most of the time, the time it's shot and the time I get home determine the way I clean it. If the hog can be gutted on the spot, be careful not to burst his piss sack or split the glands that must be removed. Cut him all the way up to the bottom jaw, removing his throat, which carries a lot of bacteria. Prop his chest cavity open with a stick, and get him to the house. Hang him, cooling him immediately with a water hose, hair on. Skin him, cutting the hide into strips if need be to make it easier to peel the hide off. Continue washing him and keeping him cool as you go. Cut off all the fat you are able to. Debone if you can, cleaning each piece well. Soak the meat in saltwater and ice, changing the water every day, for about two days. Try to cut up the meat so that there is nearly no fat. After freezing, soak the meat again before cooking.

Oh—just another little note. Don't waste your time hunting hogs with a shotgun. If you must, keep the shot distance under than twenty yards, and try to shoot the animal quartering away slightly to get a pellet behind the adult's shield.

Till next time, good hunting, and tell God hello for me in your prayers. Being able to hunt and enjoy the outdoors is most definitely worth giving thanks for.

Preparing for Bow Hunting

Hello, folks. Looks like we're down to about two and a half months till we can pull out the old stick and string for archery hunting in some areas of the state. A lot of people don't get overly excited this early. Mosquitoes and heat steer folks to stay off their stands. I love this time, since their reasons leave me alone out there a lot, and the deer are still settled and aren't as leery.

The first thing I do this time of year is try to find what kinds of food sources that are left in my area. I start by looking for pin oak acorns along the edge of a hardwood bottom. Sometimes I use the best way I know to see deer. I bait them in. Some say this is not hunting, and I agree and disagree. With a bow, you still have to get them in close for a good shot to produce an ethical kill and not leave the animal wounded. Please never take a shot you are not capable of. Even the Indians used water holes, animal carcasses, etc. Now, back to the best bait I know—freshly turned dirt.

I have a small food plot site with some structure left in the middle for cover and a stand on each end so there will be shade given only at morning or evening. I'll disk and plant iron clays, whole-bag soybeans, and whole-bag corn. I use the term "plow," but all I do is drag over all the seeds. Some will establish a food plot, but my suggestion is to have food everywhere. Give it a few days and then sit on it for a week and see what happens. The deer smell freshly turned dirt and are just darn curious. Also, do it during a cool snap compared to the usual weather, usually in late September or the first week in October. Try it. You just might see more deer than you expect.

Also, put a little OFF! on before getting in your stand. When you cool down, respray yourself so you won't sweat it off again. Always shower prior to your hunt if you can, and watch the wind closely if you're an archery hunter. Hunt the edges of different terrain types. I find that I photograph and see more bucks in the evening hunts of early archery season than at other times. But I still hunt in the mornings when the moon is straight overhead, and in the evenings when it is completely underfoot. I never miss these hunts, no matter how the weather is.

Leave the things that make you smoke and drink by finding yourself a challenge. Try to get a 100-class whitetail on his turf. And God bless you.

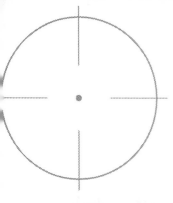

Youth Hunt

Well, howdy ho! Have you all been hunting? My bow season is not what I wished it would be. I have been caught missing a lot of hunts. The storms taking out about 80 percent of the acorns hasn't helped much. Some of the weather has been nice. Have you ever seen those mornings when you just knew everything should be moving, yet the crows were not hollering, the squirrels were not moving, etc.? Look at the moon on those nights.

There are still a few acorns to come. I scout trees, looking for acorns on the ground, rather than use my binoculars to see if there are enough left in the trees to last a week or so. If there is some deer sign there, I try to see if a stand site is there. Sometimes I'll find six or eight trees within a quarter mile and move around on them. Deer soon find these trees too, usually early on, and especially in area three. This is where you see some early scrapes because the deer are spending a lot of time in some areas; it tends to excite them a little early. Nine out of ten times, the deer making these scrapes are young bucks. My camera actually seeing them work their hooves confirmed this for me over the years, though not always some older bucks would pass by.

My bow season ended with a no-kill. I managed to send an arrow through a young doe, leaving her gut shot, thanks to a sweetgum limb. I'm very sad to say I couldn't find her. Animals that have been gut shot with an arrow can travel a long way. I once followed a mule deer within my sights for about one and a half miles.

I got to pull back on a few small bucks, with great luck. I've had fun, and most of all, I'm very ready for coming seasons by being out there. I'll tell ya, with all the small things needing work—my stands, feeders, hunting truck, four-wheeler, etc.—I can't imagine trying to be ready if I started a week before gun season. I've already photographed four nice bucks. I plan to still do a little bow hunting from October 19 to November 8 in Kentucky and Ohio, with some friends.

The few days I tried to get out there for the youth hunt weren't so great either. The club next to us came in for a work day. They were talking, riding around at seven thirty in the morning, and pulling stands off trailers. I still haven't let them know how much I appreciated it. I intend to show them what it's like before I speak with them. You know, if it were me, it would be one thing, but when a kid has been awake since two in the morning to get on a stand and someone's lack of respect kills it for them, I become a little bloom-butted. That's ten thousand degrees hotter than red ass. People, please respect your fellow hunters. Also, I would like to let you know the youth season is for those seventeen years old and younger now (not fifteen years). Bobby Jindal brought this on. I think it is a good thing.

I guess we'll see how muzzleloader season goes—or primitive weapon season, as the Department of Wildlife and Fisheries calls it now.

The best advice I can give you, of course, is to keep your powder dry. Remember: a muzzleloader is not like your 7 mm after one hundred tries. Try waiting for a good shot, since one, most likely, is all you're gonna get. Shoot your gun enough to be familiar with it, and always use the same amount of powder and same weight of bullet, of course. I usually stick to the same powder that I sighted the gun in with. If you choose to use a scope use a low-power scope like a one to four. Most likely don't want to try long shot over about one hundred fifty yards with a muzzle loader. Keep a few extra percussion caps close in case one doesn't fire. That seldom happens. If it does, keep hold of your gun with the muzzle in the same direction for a few minutes. Misfires can happen with any gun or ammo.

My stepson's, Jessie Strength's, .410 fired a slug about two minutes after a misfire on his first hog hunt. Two other people saw it. Oh, by the way, he was nine years old when he killed his first deer with a bow at Fort Polk. I believe that makes him the youngest ever in a lot of places. I was one thousand yards from him when it happened. I could hardly believe it! I'm as proud now as I was then. I had spent six months preparing his stand for him.

Well, stay alert out there. At any moment, you might just get him before he sees or smells you. Your desire to chase and hunt goes way back, so get in there. Climb high and shoot straight. The most important thing in hunting is to stay with it every chance you get, no matter what the day is like. The days of hunting as we know it are numbered, because as I always say, there are too many people and not enough world to go round. It seems a lot of things are changing fast lately. Good luck, and great hunting.

Ole Cap and Ball Hunting
Season 2008

Hello out there. It's time for ole cap and ball hunting season beginning October 11 in area three. We headed out early. My wife finally got to go. She's a nurse at Beauregard Hospital full-time and is going to school to become a nurse practitioner. She was ready for a break. We also had Brian Todd from Hornbeck with us.

We were on our stands early, though Debbie didn't like it. I enjoyed the sounds of the night while waiting on the sun to pop up. The moon was full, so my expectations weren't very high till late morning. We saw the usual animals but no deer. At ten in the morning, I was thinking of a second breakfast and maybe a midday hunt.

The midday hunt never happened, but a good nap did. The evening hunt got culled as a result of the waterline project at the RV park.

Sunday, October 12

The morning hunt went very slowly. I got on the stand about six o'clock. First I heard a wood duck fly over, and then I was very surprised to see a small group of mallards fly by. Finally, at 11:18, I saw some legs moving, then more body, and soon a full-fledged ole doe.

The evening started with a rabbit coming out, and then a couple of squirrels, an armadillo, and not long after, another ole doe. I got on a different stand. I put my doe decoy out for the first time in about three years. I couldn't tell if this ole doe was trying to warn the decoy away or play. About thirty minutes later, a nubby came out of the thicket from behind me but was not willing to come out into the open. He just wasn't in the mood to take a deer yet.

Monday, October 13

I planted my butt back on the stand about six in the morning after a few minor limb adjustments that were messing with my view from my stand. It was rather slow as far as anything moving. At 8:46 a.m., I finally saw a spike with about three inches showing on each side. He turned a few yellow acorns into lollipops and then moved on. I spent the rest of the day meeting my obligations to the bill collectors.

Tuesday, October 14

The moon was very full last night. I wasn't sure if it would really get dark. I slept in this morning and headed out about ten in the morning and sat till one thirty, hoping to see ole' big boy stretching his legs. I went down to the swamp where it was dark so it would be cool. There were a lot of squirrels moving about on the ground, gathering acorns, but that was all I saw.

The evening hunt turned out half good and half bad. I was still and comfortable. I had felt good about the hunt. Right at dark, a squirrel started barking making noise to my left. I was so sure something had alarmed him, I cocked my gun. Several minutes went by before, out in front of me, a deer appeared. It wasn't a doe; it was a buck! It was no mounter, but was a nice one. As I raised my gun, he turned and walked straight away. I grunted at him, finally getting him to stop, but he was barely quartering away. I took aim but had turned my scope to 1× power, expecting the deer to come out close to the left. I squeezed the trigger, and when the smoke cleared, no deer was on the ground. I wasn't confident in my shot and probably shouldn't have taken it. I came down and couldn't find any sign of a hit. Too bad I can't eat this story—ha! But I was right; the deer took off to my left after I shot.

Wednesday, October 15

I was right about the time for a hunt. It was cloudy and just cool enough to keep the mosquitoes down. The deer had made a scrape right in the fire lane. I walked down to my stand. Too sad, too bad. He didn't come back. I tried some doe bleats, and then, ten minutes later, I gave a really soft grunt call, and I lightly rattled my antlers. Still no deer. About nine thirty, I decided to stalk.

Thursday, October 16

The morning hunt ended without some meat. For most of the day, I got rained on off and on, and more rain was expected that evening. I decided that was too bad up at my RV park on Highway 28, but I thought I would try my box stand, since that's why I built it. Sure enough, the evening brought drizzle and cooling temps. About ten minutes before dark, a three-pointer came out, and I downed him so that I could use his cape for a deer I was mounting for a young boy. Unfortunately, the boy's father had ruined the original cape. That helped me decide to take him. Also, I was ready to have some jerky made from Soileau's Meat Market in Rosepine. They can throw a Cajun twist in it to taste make you say, "Oh it's so good."

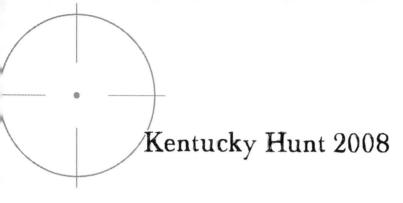

Kentucky Hunt 2008

Well hello. I hope that if you haven't downed a big one yet, you're like me—still having fun trying. I made a trip to Logan County, Kentucky, on my own this year. The 715-mile journey wasn't too bad and my TomTom was a lot of help. I made a stop in Nashville at the new Gander Mountain store and spent a few Benjamin Franklins. I got in just in time and sat in the camp and froze my butt off the first night (it was thirty-four degrees). The coyotes did a good job keeping me awake, raising sand most of the time.

The first morning, I broke out in an oak flat with my climber and was a little late getting up the tree because I'm so picky. I have been known not to hunt at all when I can't find a tree that satisfies me. It was a cold morning. I stood up about every thirty minutes, trying to keep my blood moving. Finally, about 9:46 a.m., I heard something in the leaves behind me. I knew not to turn and look, and soon a deer passed just to my left. He looked perfect but was only a small spike.

That evening, I sat in a lookout I put up last year, and I saw another spike, this one bigger, and three does at different times, though none of the does presented a good shot for me to drive an arrow in.

Day 3

The morning hunt was cool—about thirty-four degrees with a light frost. I took a long walk in to warm up for a hunt. I went into a long, narrow flat in between two large oak ridges where three trails meet. As soon as I put my bow in the bow holder, I heard something in the leaves behind me. I could barely make out anything. Managing to stand up and move around, I could see a deer. When I drew on the animal, I could see fine and was confident it was a deer. I released the arrow, resulting in a big thump. It sounded like three rotten trees had fallen. I stayed in the stand till about ten in the morning, and then I came down. Quickly I saw that the deer must have run into three strands of barbwire in the canebrake and that I had put the arrow all the way through her body from behind the shoulder to her back leg bone. Yep. It was a very big doe that will make some big jerky sticks, which will make my gut happy. The evening hunt got a little messed up from a brush-hogging job nearby.

Day 4

It warmed up a bit and got cloudy—a slight change already since I went out. A lot of leaves had fallen, and the hues had changed a lot. I spent a lot of time nodding off, and all I saw was two dogs.

The evening hunt turned out to be an awesome one. For seven hours, the bucks weren't within sight. The does were fighting; the yearlings playing. Just at dark, I think, from the shape of its body, that a buck came out. I could even hear him eating acorns about twenty five yards from my stand in the thicket near me. It's okay. I plan, if possible, to be in a better place come tomorrow evening. Right now I'm battling the food I ate at a Mexican restaurant with Shelly, Mrs. Bonnie's daughter.

Day 5

The morning hunt was windy early on, and the birds were lively. Ten squirrels were moving. I heard a few turkeys in the background, but no deer were to be seen. I sat till ten thirty and came down to scout the area a little more to be sure I was in the right spot. I must have been, with acorns abundant, the scrapes I found, the rubs on trees as big as my leg, a few does, and deer dung everywhere on trail after trail. I was getting a little more respect for the deer in Kentucky. They had been harvesting some big cornfields not too far away, and I was scared the deer had moved farther back to an area I couldn't hunt. I moved my climber and spent an hour trimming vines and limbs off the trees to be able to climb.

That evening, it was windy right up to the last thirty minutes, and I felt I was sure to see a deer. I even sat on the bottom part of my climber to be able to stand up easier for the shot. All I saw was a doe and yearling that passed in front of my truck on the road.

Day 6

I slept wrong last night, leaving me feeling as if someone hit me between the shoulders with a hammer. After getting up and down three or four times, I just slept in for the morning, waking late to get a big breakfast at Webb's Café. A front was moving in with some rain. I thought the bass might bite in the ponds on the property. Sure enough, I called it right. I caught several, each weighing about two and a half pounds. I quickly went out and set up a ground blind in case of rain, though I felt I probably wouldn't use it. I checked my camera but saw no sign of big bucks.

I hit the stand for the evening hunt about four o'clock hoping to make up a little time lost this morning. I went ahead, wearing my slicker gear, thinking it might rain. I climbed to about twenty-two feet, took my arrow holder off, and set an extra arrow aside in case I got a second shot, as I have many times. I pulled a little piece off my cotton ball and checked the wind about four times during the hunt, to be sure of its direction. I always do this again about thirty minutes before dark. I want to know exactly where the deer have the best chance of scenting me. I try to make a shot before they get there.

About every hour, I stand for five minutes to stretch, and sometimes I stand for the full last fifteen minutes of the day. I was altering the call every ten minutes. I learned on this trip from watching does way out in the cornfields that the doe bleats could be heard in most cases on still evenings for about 150 to 200 yards. After that, I could never get them to look up. The wind never slowed, the rain never came, and it never cooled back down. I started second-guessing my location and strategies. Although, the reason I wasn't seeing any deer could have been due to a weather change. I never did see a deer.

On another note, I thought I'd mention a few things about the gear

I like. One item is Shines White Oak Acorn Scent. It has an appealing smell, and combined with my scent-lock clothes, I haven't had a deer wind me with them all around. I use this in conjunction with Dead Down Wind Terminator field spray. Another item is my Mr. Heater. It has been good for my tent.

Day 7

The morning hunt never happened, as there was rain from ten at night to ten in the morning and my tent went from weather resistant to what could be called halfway rain proof. I mopped two buckets of water off the floor with a towel. I spent most of the day sightseeing, and then I dried everything out.

Ohio Whitetail Brute

Hello, folks. It's almost time for the big Ohio Whitetail Brutes to want and choose an ole doe. I had about a seven-hour drive from Kentucky, and the majority of it was different to my eyes. I was going to meet a friend I met at the Safari Club Convention in Reno, Nevada. (Scott Bagi). We planned to hunt public land. We would also meet another friend who's an outfitter from Alaska. We planned to work hard for about ten to fourteen days. I figure it will take me a few days just to think about getting satisfied with a spot.

October 29

I did not hunt that morning. I did some scouting and set up stands. That evening, I got my first glimpse of a deer. Later that night, I went in for some groceries.

October 30

It was eighteen degrees that morning. I thought someone should watch the camp since it was so cold. That afternoon, I did a lot more scouting and changed my setup with a few fresh scrapes to watch over with three connecting trails in their path. I had to go to town and get a bigger coat. That evening, it was easy to see it was well worth the investment, though it did not bring any deer in.

October 31

What's called deer camp here in Ohio? There are about eight campers and tents, and most everyone knows everyone. There are no ladies in sight—just a bunch of good ole boys yacking about this and that around fifty-five-gallon-drum burn barrels while cooking up some awesome grub. No electricity here. A lot of good ole campfires smoldering here and there. These men all help each other in any way they can by getting deer, pitching in to retrieve deer, picking up things in town, etc. It's really nice when the dinner bell goes off at the cook tent. That's when about thirty men start making it look like a family reunion in the woods. I can't help but keep a half roll of toilet paper with me at all times.

During my morning hunt, it was still twenty-four degrees with heavy frost. I was sure glad I had covered my stand with my camo umbrella. I got still just in time; about thirty minutes later, something was moving around behind me. After another thirty minutes, I couldn't help but look back, fearing I'd be spotted, since a steep hill was behind me. It was a nubby buck. I watched him feed all morning till ten thirty, learning what they eat. He even spotted other deer for me: two does downhill and later a smaller six-pointer. When he got about eight steps away under my tree, I photographed him. I saw he could smell me then, so I thought I'd teach him what he was smelling as a good lesson. I spooked the fire out of him, sending him into a slipping, crashing frantic run the hell out of Dodge. He pooped on himself while racing away. That ended that hunt somewhat interestingly for me.

My evening hunt started out about fifteen degrees cooler and as windy as can be. I wasn't expecting much more than maybe getting wet from a rain later, but very late, at the end of the day, a deer came down the hill in front of me. I knew it was a deer from the sound; the wind had calmed down quite a bit. I drew my bow but stopped. I was let down. A few minutes later, he came on down. A good buck at least out to ears stood fifteen yards below me. This was a buck anyone would have pounced on in Louisiana. I decided to wait awhile with nine days left.

November 1

This was the official first day of deer camp. This group has been meeting here for over thirty years. In the last two days, six deer had been taken, including two nine-point bucks. One of these was a young man's first. There were about six young hunters. All of them seemed to be into it.

My morning hunt turned out to take a good two hours of hiking in and out. I came up empty-handed, but the nap I took in my climber was well worth it.

That evening, I did a lot of what I always do. I dusted the insides of my boots with a little scent-away powder, sprayed myself and all my clothes with Dead Down Wind spray, and started up the mountain making as little noise as I could, trying not to touch anything on my way in. I did spray the very bottoms of my rubber boots with fox piss. That's the only place I use it.

When I got to my climber, I sprayed a little doe pee on the side bags and under the seat, and about twenty yards out I hung my tarsal gland that I had cut off a buck killed in the camp. I kept my Doe in Estrus bottle close by. I climbed up, got settled, and then checked the wind with my cotton ball to see where my kill-before line was. About twenty minutes later, I rattled lightly for about five minutes while grunting at the same time; then, ten minutes later, I used my estrus bleater. I usually try to call lightly about every fifteen minutes up until the last forty-five minutes or so.

After about an hour, I stood up for ten minutes, and it had cooled enough to add a small shirt. During those last thirty magical minutes, I slipped into my coveralls and traded my mesh mask for my scent-lock head gear. Unclean hair can be the worst spot on you since it gives a strong detectable odor to a deer. I let the bottom part of my climber down a little more to ease my standing to shoot.

Allow me to fill some folks in on how a lot of hunters prepare—some more than others. About every hour, check the wind. You will be surprised to see how much it can change. The lighter the wind, the smaller the piece of cotton you use. It won't always be in your favor, but knowing where it is will be.

Well, as much as I hate to say it, after all that, all I saw was a chipmunk getting slower with each piece of corn he was toting back to his crib. Each time there, he would spend a little more time eating some.

November 2

Well, hell-bent and dead set today, I was determined to see a deer if I had to walk ten miles to do so. Besides, I needed to work off the cow tongue sandwiches I ate the night before with three bowls of spaghetti. I spent my morning hunt wearing my neck out investigating every sound I heard. I spent my evening hunt about the same way, except now my eyes hurt because everything looked like a deer coming toward me. Back at the camp, three deer were down. We found all of them. It takes about four to eight men and a cart to get a deer out of most areas in the mountains.

November 3

Today was a lot like yesterday. Two deer were brought into camp. We spent some time trying to find a farm to hunt on, with no luck. We wanted to get off public land. The highlight for the day, I guess, would have to be the cow tail soup.

November 4

We actually had a frost. It was a little better, but still no luck. Almost all the leaves are brown now and almost fallen from the trees. We started hearing large flocks of geese here and there. Overall, the sighting of deer slowed way down—especially on public land. Nevertheless, I laid eyes on some different country while hiking. That helps me feel like life is going on for me. Something new—something different.

November 5

This morning's temperature was around forty-one degrees, and I moved my climber back down the hill about three-quarters of a mile. I hiked in and climbed to about twenty-two feet. And when I cooled down from the hike up, I slipped my coveralls on for the hunt. I did this very carefully, especially because I didn't have a harness. The Magellan Camp Pillow for a seat cushion worked really well. Take a look at them. Unfortunately, the weather was still not good, and the moon was rising more and more. It looked as if it were snowing leaves. The flakes were falling fast.

This morning I saw no deer, and the same was true of the evening. I pulled off the mountain and plan to move to a new area. There are only a few days left, and it is not looking good. Now I'm having trouble with keeping up the want-tos.

November 6

This morning I went in blind with my climber. I spent a little time looking from atop a tree just before dawn for a decent shot off a trail I came across. It was just a perfect morning—still, and about forty-two degrees. Shortly after daylight, a small four-pointer idled down the trail but turned uphill just too far off for a shot. I tried to turn him by grunting, with no luck. I was meat hunting at this point.

About thirty minutes later, having come from out of nowhere like they can do, a doe stood on the hill dead in front of me, about eighty yards out. She loped down and stopped fifteen yards in front of my stand. After some time, a six-pointer followed. I checked the wind with my cotton piece, and it fell right where she stood. I thought to wait on the buck, but she was about to bust me and head straight to him. I decided any deer was better than no deer. I sent the Maximo 350 Carbon to her with a good hit. The buck just stood at about fifty yards, so I restrung my arrow and tried to take him, too. It was too bad, too sad, though. He left the country fast.

I sat out the evening hunt in the rain.

November 7

That night, we went to a place called the Shack, where a lot of hunters gather to grill some big steaks, have a few drinks, play cards, and see what other camps have taken. We packed up camp and drove three hours to a different location. We got to bed down about one in the morning and were up at five o'clock, planning to hunt on the ground. Now here's where it gets unbelievable. While we were slipping in, we spooked a few deer. We then decided to hunt there so as not to spook anymore, because daylight was coming on fast. I nestled down, and Scott went ahead. He had encountered a good buck going in, as I found out later. Now me, I had just sat down and hooked my release to my string loop when I saw coming straight to me, ten yards out, a good free-roaming whitetail. I got my bow drawn, and he was in a squat, duck, and run position. I took the shot and knew I hit. I was feeling an emotion I'd never felt. I think I said ten prayers. I waited an hour and then had to look at where I hit him. I found my arrow; it had completely passed through. I was still excited, but yet scared, because no blood was anywhere within the first twenty-five yards, and that was as far as I wanted to push. I was guessing he dipped and ducked and the arrow got into him behind the front shoulder and came out in front of his back leg.

I went back and sat down. Five minutes later, I hammered a doe and heard her fall. About thirty minutes later, Scott came along, and we whispered and started discussing what had happened. We then began tracking, my buck, by his running hoof prints. About forty-five yards into it, I inhaled a breath loudly because to my right, at maybe eight yards, there stood a 185-plus deer. Scott looked at me, wondering what I had inhaled about, and then he saw him too. His crossbow was loaded, so he raised it and nailed him. We were immediately just freaked out with disbelief to the point of shock. He'd killed about five deer already at 150 points, but this was his best. We were on a very, very unusual high.

We decided to get my doe out and wait a few hours before we looked for our bucks. On the way back out, riding the four-wheeler, I noticed an arrow lying in a field. Again we were shocked, because it was Scott's. We followed the blood trail about thirty yards to an island in a cornfield. About the time we saw it, the buck jumped out of it really slowly, headed across the field to the edge of the next section of woods. We spent a few hours following very little blood until it ran dry. We didn't see any that evening.

November 8

Rain came in about three in the morning, and at five thirty we decided we were rained out. We skinned my doe and then decided to goose hunt till the evening deer hunt. We got decoys out, and a half hour later I had my first goose hunting experience—and my first goose. I liked it.

Later, Scott's dad came out to help try to find the big buck. We first made a drive in a small patch of woods, resulting in Scott slinging an arrow at a running buck. We then split up where the blood trail ran out, and an hour later or so, to my surprise, I jumped him—but I didn't have my bow! I watched him lope off again. This was good and bad news, I guess. We looked even more later that day but had no luck. The only thing we found while looking for Scott's big buck was my very nice ten-pointer. Scott's dad found him about twenty-five yards from where I shot him in some tall, thick willow not ten feet from where we had already looked. I was as happy as a coon in a corn patch.

The next day, we set a few traps and I got ready to make the twenty-two hour drive. I drove straight through. This trip was a really nice, new experience with a good new friend. Thanks Scott. Another good part was that I hunted for twenty-seven days in Kentucky and Ohio for $780.

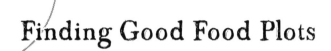

Finding Good Food Plots

Hey, folks. Thank goodness and God Almighty for this rain. Ha! I don't think most realized how dry we were in June. It will help us, I hope, watering up the root systems of the oak trees so many acorns will drop.

If you have a few good oaks around your stand, try clearing under them; cutting all brush, trash trees, etc.; and fertilizing them about September 15. This will help a lot of times with how many acorns are produced if it's a good year for it. I fertilize everything: honeysuckles, trees, blackberries, huckleberry bushes, and young oaks coming up. I don't fertilize around every stand, but a few now and then.

I don't care when you plant, but you must have rain to get your plants up and started. If you see a good forecast around planting time, get 'er done. Of course, nothing will help one more then brush-hogging and then spraying. Wait a week and then go at it when you think you will get more rain shortly thereafter.

With archery season coming in mid-September, don't wait too late to run out to Star Gun and Archery and get Mickey to hook you up. Practice and learn your limits, and stay within them when shooting at a deer to avoid losing one, although it will happen. Try to set stands that will allow you to have deer roam in close while bow hunting. Just think a little differently than you would if you were rattling up to gun hunt. Practice at your stand and in your hunting clothes, and shoot at unknown targets if you plan to stalk some.

Well, good luck.

Getting Ready for Hunting Season

Now is the time to tape an extra pin for your climber in case you lose one and oil your feeder motors (3-in-1 is best). Clean the solar panel and run your wires through a tube like one used for your water heater (greenfield, flexible conduit), or a water hose. Use shelf brackets to brace under the solar panel to keep the coons from rolling them over to face the ground or breaking their brackets. Place a varmint guard or build them around spinners. You get the picture. This time of year, I also give my guns a good cleaning.

Time to brush-hog the food plots, use a weed eater on them, and spray them with Roundup. I usually lime them at this time as well. This will really give you a nice plot free of grass and weeds. Disk the grass- and weed-free area about the first of September after spraying. Wait about ten days, and spray the area again. Disk after the last spray, deep and rough. Sow seed and drag the plot, and then plant on September 15—or, better yet, October 1 or whenever there is a good chance of rain.

A lot of times when you disk, you turn dormant seeds up. There is no need to disk real deep because most the food plot seeds are to be planted one inch or less anyway. The second spray will kill all the little secondary new grass coming up. This kind of work is well worth doing on private property.

Meanwhile, catch a smile and go hunt for that big buck this fall.

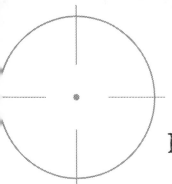

Hello, Everyone!

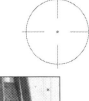

Debbie Thompson

I 'm Debbie, C. H.'s other (not better) half, and I provide all the backup support in our relationship. I don't even try to keep up with him. He's just like my dad, Lynn Thompson. They both wake up in the morning and immediately start working on something and don't stop until their heads hit the pillow at night. C. H. attacks everything he does with gusto, and that includes hunting.

This time C. H. wanted me to share the story of my first deer. I've hunted with C. H. for three years, and I have to tell you that I was getting pretty frustrated until this year. I have soaked up and applied everything C. H. has told me for three years, but it just seemed like I *never* saw any deer. I used scent cover, estrus bombs, doe bleats, grunts—you name it; but my luck was bad.

Well, this year I finally started seeing some deer. During bow season, C. H. and I went to one of our new hunting leases and used our climbers to set up our hunts. On the first day out, I had a yearling come out and bed down near my tree. Of course, I would never shoot a yearling, but it was exciting to actually see a deer. On another occasion, I had a doe and her yearling walk around me within shooting range, and again this boosted my confidence that there really were deer in the woods. I was beginning to think there was a conspiracy against me!

In September C. H. took off to my cousin Shelly's place in Kentucky for more bow hunting. I chose not to go this year, because I didn't want to take any more time off from work. I had bought a new muzzleloader, so I stayed home with plans to try out my new gun.

On opening day of muzzleloader season, I got up bright and early and made coffee for me and my hunting partner. C. H. had asked his good friend Brian Todd to come and accompany me on a hunt. Brian and I took the Rhino and headed over to the lease. We decided to head way back in the swamp, where C. H. had some good stands set up. My spot was a ladder stand about five minutes from the Rhino.

I got set up quickly and made sure everything was ready to go. Not long after daybreak, I started hearing a few shots on neighboring leases. After not seeing anything for a while, I pulled out a James Patterson novel to pass the time. C. H. hates when I do this, but it keeps me calm, and I check my periphery quite often. At about 8:40 a.m., my cell phone vibrated. It was C. H. calling from Kentucky. I answered in my lowest whisper and found out that C. H. had just killed a four-pointer. He also had food poisoning and had managed to use a climber while throwing his guts up. Talk about dedication! I told him that Brian and I were coming down at nine in the morning and that, no, I hadn't seen anything. We got off the phone, and I thought I surely wouldn't see anything after talking on that blasted cell phone. I went back to reading my last chapter, and within a few minutes I saw something out of the corner of my left eye. I slowly lowered the book and put my hands on my gun. At first I thought it was a doe, but I then decided it was a spike. I watched as it walked around out in front of me, but there were a lot of small trees between me and him. I had him in my sights and waited for the shot. I thought he was a goner for a second because he trotted back the way he came, but then he stopped and looked in my direction. I was aiming right at his heart, so I pulled the trigger.

It was the oddest thing when I made that shot. My heart was racing, and I couldn't see for a few seconds because of the smoke from the muzzleloader. When the smoke started to clear, I saw my deer, and he dropped right in his tracks. Honestly, I was shaking while trying to come down that ladder stand. I met Brian back at the Rhino and was excited to report that I had killed my first deer. When we went back to retrieve him, Brian pointed out that my spike was actually a four-pointer. I can't brag about that, because those extra points were small.

Thank goodness Brian was with me! He helped me get him back to the skinning rack and showed me how he skins deer. I think everybody does it a little differently. I doubt if I'm strong enough to do it by myself, though, so I sure did appreciate Brian. It took us a while to get hold of C. H., but when we did, you can imagine how Brian ribbed him about sharing this experience with me. C. H. was just tickled I'd finally gotten one. I also had to call and share my story with Daddy, and he, too, was proud for me.

If I have anything to share with other hunters, it would be to tell you girls to get up and go hunting with your men. The same thing goes for you men folk. Encourage your girls to go hunting with you, or take them with you when you're just out in the woods looking for deer sign.

C. H. will be back with you next time to share our stories from Reno, Nevada. We're attending the Safari Club International Convention and plan on visiting a wedding chapel while we're there. Take care!

Kentucky Hunt with Ryan 2009

Hello, folks. Finally that much-anticipated time has come for many of us who share the passion of archery hunting. I now sit in my Montana Lodge tent, writing this article with Ryan, the son of my friend who is like a brother to me, Pete Dowden. At four thirty in the morning, we'll be walking through the woods to a stand here in Kentucky.

We left for a 750-mile trip a few days early. On our first day, we set camp, hung stands, and did a little baiting. The first night brought heavy downpours that wet a good bit of our supplies. We spent the next day visiting and going to town for food and extra supplies. Later that evening, we watched over a few soybean fields. We both saw deer, though the bucks we saw were small ones. We were turkey hunting while we hunted deer, but we didn't see any turkeys either.

We found out that two dangerous convicts had escaped and were running loose near where we were hunting. We never saw them, but we had some good broadheads ready just in case. The moon was full, and it would be for the next few days, but I didn't think it was gonna be a big factor based on what we were seeing. Some coon hounds were on a ridge by us, which I thought might keep us awake a little while longer.

Saturday, September 5

Opening morning was about fifty-two degrees and slightly foggy. The moon was high and bright so I didn't need a light to find my stand. As the morning slipped by, all I saw were some birds I had never seen before and a few squirrels. Around nine in the morning, I had a few does come way out of the soybean field. As they had ninety directions to choose from, it was doubtful they would move my way. Then, as if I were a magnet, one broke away and beelined straight along the woods to me, up to within ten steps. I hammered her, leaving her belting off making a loop through the beans and then darting into the woods.

I sat still, giving Ryan time to finish his hunt. A young six-pointer came out, but he was much too far for a shot. Ryan did get a shot off at the buck I saw but missed. He saw a fawn and a tom turkey as well. We made it to Webb's Café and then came back to bake in the sun. It was a little too hot during the day for anything. The worst part of the afternoon was dragging my Ozark blow-up bed out of the tent door and popping it on a tent stake, which I knew would probably cause me to have an interesting night of sleep. Also, the solar shower valve developed a leak. It was one of those just lovely afternoons.

I decided that, with no bed and the fact that it was raining, we needed to go to Lake Malone to stay at a friend's lake house—but not until we had a nice dinner with Jerry and his wife. Our evening hunt was just one of those where you get into your stand and then right back out, mostly because of a lot of thunder and lightning. One reason I don't like to plan less than twelve days of hunting when out of state is because of the weather.

Day 2

I started out wet from the rain most of the night. We hoped it would help with hunting, since the moon was full. I settled in at break of daylight. It wasn't long after that I heard some turkeys come off their roost. I tried to call them. Calling is not very effective this time of year.

It's really like you just hope one comes along as you deer hunt. I usually get one chance each year.

My calling did draw some attention. A coyote came running in, and then a lot of crows. Morning drew by to the point at which most of the heavy rain had dripped out of the trees. A light breeze blew now and then, a touch of sunlight peered through the clouds, and then the birds and squirrels began to move. When nine o'clock started to roll up on me, I decided to put one leg up on the front of my stand awhile to change positions. Soon I caught myself wanting to doze off.

Suddenly I heard something that sounded like a squirrel does just before he starts to bark at you when he realizes you're there. I bent right and then left very slowly, looking behind me, trying to see what it was. Five minutes or so went by, and I finally decided to ease my leg down so I could turn more. When I did, right dead behind me, a buck loped off and stopped under some brush about forty yards off. Now standing up, bow in hand, I waited, hoping this deer would decide that he only thought he had seen me about twenty-eight feet high in my climber. Several minutes went by. He just walked straight away. The bad part was that if I'd trusted my first instinct and put my stand where I wanted, he would have been twenty yards dead in front of men—and then dead on the ground, probably.

Ryan spent the morning trying to keep a big red fox squirrel out of his lap and listening to turkeys. Heavy rains broke out shortly after the morning hunt again, so we went back to Lake Malone and had prime rib for brunch and we then went to the lake house for nap time. Sometimes I love to feel my eyes roll to the back of my head as if I were dead.

Our evening hunt was spent butt wet, sitting through rain. Just at dark, there was rain heavy enough to wet us good on the walk back. That night, we went to Walmart to get another bed and a banana split. Just as we lay down, extensive rain and lightning began, and it continued all night. I was a little worried I might become a piece of molten sleeping bag.

The next morning, the rain was quiet at daylight. We got to the stands late to go ahead and make a hunt. Ryan saw some hen turkeys, and I saw two squirrels. I spent the day baiting up and checking cameras. I went to town and bought a twenty-two-foot ladder stand to set tomorrow.

The evening hunt for me ended with me having seen nothing at all. Ryan, sitting in my hunting chair on the ground, slung a broadhead through both lungs of a big doe for his first deer down in Kentucky. The night was cool and calm. We got a little sleep.

Day 3

It was a cool morning, but the moon was high and dawn was just starting to break. I sat until about nine fifteen and then came down and walked out to the edge of the soybean field. There were two groups of turkeys way out. That was all I saw that could have been eaten. Ryan saw a tom, but it was at over fifty yards, so he passed on the shot. That afternoon, we put together the ladder stand we bought to leave it for Jared and Jerry, and then we went and stood her up. We ate a little lunch and tried to nap a little.

That evening, I went to the new stand we had put up, fairly reluctant because of all the noise and scent we had left on location. About thirty minutes into the hunt, a cat squirrel got within two feet of me and never showed one ounce of fear while it scratched its fleas. A short time later, I saw a deer in the distance. Soon it was within ten yards under my stand. It was a spotted fawn, and then I saw its mama. She was leery but came in also for about fifteen minutes. It reminded me of trying to get a child who has wandered away to come back and follow you. Ryan saw two deer way off in the distance. He tried a new location.

Day 4

I woke up to a much cooler morning with everything wet, as if it had rained again. I went to the new stand again, and shortly thereafter the spotted fawn showed up to entertain me. But that was all I saw.

That afternoon, we ate brunch and then took the deer out to some Amish for processing. We came back and reset the stands in better locations. For the evening hunt, Ryan went to the fawn stand and I moved over to the backslide stand. I didn't see anything except a few birds and a lot of acorns crashing through limbs by me. I just knew the two pounds of roasted peanuts I put out would lure one in. I was just experimenting. I'll have to let Ryan tell you his experience with white toes.

Well, folks, I crawled into what C. H. calls the fawn stand now. (He calls it this because every time he sits in it, he sees a fawn.) It wasn't but about fifteen minutes after I got good and settled in my stand when I saw a little reddish fawn, still so full of spots that it looked white when it fed around my stand at only ten yards away. I saw its mother coming in really alert. I would say she was about a four-year-old doe. Finally she relaxed and started feeding alongside her little fawn. I was filming the fawn this whole time.

When I realized how caught up I was in the fawn learning how to be careful, I heard a limb crack, and I slowly turned and looked. I saw what seemed to be a cow-horn spike. As I put my camera up, I got ready for the shot. The fawn nailed me and began to shake like it wanted to run off but its legs were stuck. When the buck offered me the perfect shot, I drove the arrow a little high, but the buck fell in its tracks. Later, after I brought the buck into the field next to me to get him out of the corn pile, I spotted the same little fawn trying to find its mom, who ran a different way after the shot. I settled to film the fawn again. As I was filming, the fawn bleated, sounding identical to a young goat. As we were skinning the buck, I realized that its front legs and hooves were solid white. We realized that the deer was a piebald buck—the first one I had ever seen. That closes my favorite evening hunt I ever experienced.

Day 5

I woke to the moon being a little less than three-quarters full about five o'clock. I made some coffee and scarfed down a peanut butter sandwich. I lit out on the four-wheeler for a while and then made the ten-minute walk to the backslide stand. It was cool enough to wear a light coat again. I wasn't too excited about the morning, since I already felt evening was best during the decrease of the moon. I soon heard a little noise by me. Yep, there he was—a big chipmunk. He was commencing to gorge himself on the roasted peanuts I put out. I spent the rest of the morning just trying to keep myself in the stand. Ryan slept in. We both spent the afternoon walking, stalking, and scouting. We also managed to cut each other's hair with a pair of old horse trimmers we found in Jerry's barn. We thought that might help us with seed ticks, since we had already gotten two good doses.

We went to the high side stand for the evening. It was about thirty feet high. I had two spotted fawns come and lie down about twenty yards in front of me. About every ten minutes for one and a half hours, they got up and walked around, and then went right back to the same place. The bugs never gave them one second of relief. Their tails were steadily twitching, and they were continuously biting at themselves, all over their bodies.

I never saw any other deer. The fawns waited until I came down out of the tree with the light on. Then I walked to within ten feet of them with the light in their eyes, and about that time I stomped at them, hollering "Boo!" I probably gave them something to have bad dreams about for a few nights. That night, we couldn't stand it. We rode around some roads to see if any deer were out there. We saw plenty, including one good buck.

Day 6

I broke out of bed to a cool morning again. All was very still, and it felt just perfect not to see even a squirrel. I heard a few clucks from a turkey in the distance. Ryan slept in again. We spent the afternoon taking camp down and showing Jared how to turn his property into a better hunting property. I slipped back into the stand about five thirty. After about ten minutes, I caught some movement out of the corner of my eye; it was two big toms. I reached over to take my bow out of the bow holder and raised it to draw, waiting for two more steps. Their heads popped up, stopped, and were still for enough time. I couldn't hold anymore. Just before I let down, they turned and walked away without giving me a shot. They walked uphill until out of sight. I was waiting to cool off before I slipped my head net on. I think they saw my face. This happens every year; I get one chance every time. They just don't respond to calls at this time of year.

Evening was as good as one could expect. It was a little warm. A good bit before dark, a gobbler roosted about thirty-five yards dead behind me. I just couldn't win. Turkeys up here seem to roost much earlier than the ones in Louisiana. I managed to stand up. I drew my bow, and at that time another flew up wide open, too far out. Of course, the one I shot at was behind a few limbs; though small, they were big enough to deflect an arrow. I slung one at him anyway. Nothing but air, but very close. His head popped up, and he gave a few clucks. I slung another. I missed but got his attention. I thought at first I had made a hit. Fifteen minutes later, two more birds roosted about one hundred yards away. There were no deer anywhere.

Day 7

I slipped in early during the morning for our last hunt in Kentucky. This being the last hunt, I worked all the water out of my eyes by rotating them, hoping to see something. I saw turkeys come off the roost—a few birds, and that was it. Ryan slept in. We packed up the cook shack, tent, four-wheeler, and bows and headed to West Virginia to scout for a spot to hunt next year along with the Kentucky hunt. We saw a lot of deer and came across 350 acres very near where the movie *We Are Marshall* was made; the plane carrying the football team crashed between Huntington and Prichard.

My boy had a blast once he made it through missing his girlfriend. Killing that first buck with his bow manned him up, and this made the trip for me.

Well, go make your own story.

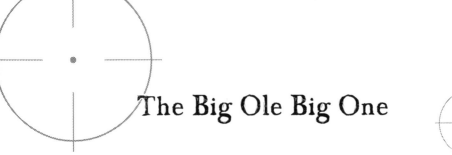

The Big Ole Big One

Hello, fellow outdoorsmen! I got a good ole good one about a big ole big one! It's kinda short and sweet. I've been hunting the edge of the swamp off and on since bow season opened, and I hoped a few hogs would show up as they usually do for a short spell on this stand each season. Sure enough, I saw a track in my food plot, and I was very surprised as to how big it was. A few days went by, and I saw only a few deer, all of them too far for a decent shot. My game camera revealed that the tracks were made by a very large hog, a boar, and that's what I figured he was, since they travel alone a lot walking roads, fire lanes, etc., searching for sows. Now, I've put arrows in three hogs that would be considered super trophies in a paid hunt situation. I'm excited I still have a chance at a free-roaming trophy boar. I've shot many with guns, but it's not the same. I seem to never get a break on these big boys.

One night it rained harder than a cow pissing on a flat rock all night long. My alarm sounded at five o'clock, and I was pumped to go, but there was still a slow rain. After always staying soaked in the oil field years ago, I don't much care for it, so I stayed in bed. About a quarter to six, the rain stopped. I jumped out of bed, dressed, and lit out, hoping to get a shot at anything. I jumped into my little camo Toyota and drove out, and when I got there, I realized I couldn't find my four-wheeler key. After much frustration, I took off on foot for about a mile to my stand. It was light enough out that I could go without a flashlight down an old road, walking quietly, listening to frogs holler after all the rain as I went.

It dawned on me about eighty yards from the food plot that the boar might be there. I had baited it a good bit. As I came to the first corner, I saw a black image at the plot's edge. I knew it must be my boar. I dropped down, pulled a cotton ball out, and checked the wind as best I could in the light I had. I was good. I crawled, walked on my knees, and closed in to about thirty yards, looking through the thicket. I thought he was facing away from me. I drew my bow and eased out. I was wrong; he was facing me. I knew to take the shot now or never at all. The arrow hit him behind the shoulder as he was facing me, which I knew was not good. "But I wanted a chance at that boar!" I said. I knew he would never come back after seeing me. He sprayed his scent everywhere and took off with my arrow in him. Immediately I wasn't excited.

I went on ahead and sat in the climber for about one and a half hours, and I then came down to scope out the situation. Quickly I realized it wasn't good. No blood. I spent a while looking for him, all the while looking for snakes too. This area is very snake infested. Soon I realized I needed a dog and should have just brought one in the first place. This was not the way I wanted to take the boar.

Down the road, Robert had some dogs, but at that time, he had only one at home. We went back into the swamp for a while, but the dog left us eventually. We suspect he ran the boar too far away for us to hear him.

It quickly occurred to me that all I was going to get was this story I am writing now. I can tell you I saw a boar in that plot that was over 250 pounds, two feet wide, and four feet tall or better. My adrenaline was rushing for sure. I truly hate that I lost that boar. Some animals are just meant to be the ones that got away. There's always a chance he made it. Well, I hope y'all's next shot leaves your animal lying to fill your fridge.

Happy hunting!

Colorado 2009 Lion Hunt

On Friday, February 20, about noon, my wife, Debbie, and I pulled out for the 1,034-mile trip into Model, Colorado. It's between Trinidad and La Junta, near Pinon Canyon Maneuver Site. We were hunting mountain lions between five thousand and eight thousand feet on several ranches. One of the other ranch owners was the world-renowned saddle maker Jessie Smith. My outfitter was Eagle Trackem Outfitters with Johnny Hamilton and Jay Waring. The drive up took sixteen and a half hours.

Saturday the twenty-first was the first morning out, and it was sixteen degrees with a wind chill of zero degrees. A lack of snow was already making it very hard to kill a lion. It's very hard to cut a trail without snow. One trick used is to drag the roads to see tracks more easily. To make matters worse, we lost our best dog. We tried to run a bobcat, walked a few canyons, looked over a few creek beds, etc. We saw no pussycats this day, though.

On Sunday the twenty-second, it had warmed a good bit. We set out and were lucky enough to catch Cowboy, the dog we lost the day before. Johnson is a good dog trainer. His wife's grandpa was Bobby Davenport. He trained Black Beauty; Gus, the kicking mule; Rooster from *Best Little Whorehouse in Texas*; the horse Silver that the Lone Ranger rode; the black horse Burt Reynolds rode in *Smoky and the Bandit*; and many more.

We broke up into two groups, working the ridges for tracks with dogs. We found a couple of old digs where tomcats had marked their territories. The area was rocky with a lot of scattered cedar. There is a nice creek that runs through the canyon; along it are a lot of big holes backed up by beavers. The state record bass was caught in one of those holes. We have seen a lot of ducks, bighorn sheep, mule deer, whitetails, and loads of turkeys—at least thirty in one group. I'm serious! I'm talking thirty gobblers! Johnnys Merriam's hunts run $800 each; that includes the turkeys, meals, and accommodations.

On Monday the twenty-third, we went out early and headed to high country along the side of Ted Turner's ranch. He's a media mogul who owns TNT and CNN, just to name a couple. He was married to Jane Fonda. We also skirted Hill Ranch and then an old coal-mining town, which was really loaded with game. I have never seen so much sign. We took a nice four-wheeler ride, looking for tracks. The drifts were too much to ride through, and the dirt between them kept us from using a snowmobile. The weather was just too bad to find a track. We did see some nice six-by-six bulls and a group of two hundred cow elk, along with several small groups.

After looking over about three areas, we stopped for lunch and then made a hike, trying to call some coyotes and bobcats. We didn't have any luck. We later went back to look for prairie dogs but had no luck there either. The wind was about thirty miles per hour all day. I walked out in front of the outfitters house with a .223 to try to see a coyote. Again I had no luck, but I did find a decent mule deer shed that I hoped to add to my lion mount.

On Tuesday the twenty-fourth, it was rise and shine about four o'clock for coffee and muffins before lighting out. It's about a one-hour-and-twenty-minute drive to the canyons on the other side of Comanche National Grassland. We broke into two groups. Johnnie rode a four-wheeler out, looking for tracks along the road. Debbie and I went with Jay, working rim rock and crossing dried creek beds, trying to cut a track and trying to get the dogs on a trail. We had treeing Walkers and bluetick coonhounds. Most already had very sore feet torn by rocks, gravel, cacti, and burrs, and their noses were full of cactus needles, bloodied up with raw skin.

We finally found a track, but the dogs couldn't pick it up. I think it was about a day old. Not long after, Johnnie found a track while walking the road, so we went to him and followed it in the dirt as far as we could, and then we tried the dogs. Again it was still too old or the scent had disappeared because of the sun and heat.

We loaded the dogs and drove farther down the canyon in hopes of gaining ground. Again we found a track, but it was old. We went to look in a couple of caves nearby. We saw sign that a big tom had been there. We unloaded the dogs and thought it was on along a creek. They trailed out into the grass and sun and just lost the scent. At this point, we decided the weather was just about as bad as it gets to hunt lions. Dry tracking is very tough; lion hunting is best with snow on the ground. We decided to give it up till the next morning. We also decided that if we didn't run a lion by eleven in the morning, we would end the hunt three days early and spend more time looking over my old stomping grounds in Pagosa Springs and visiting friends in Colorado. This would be easier done than normal, since Johnnie was a fair and good enough man to let me come back later on till I killed my lion. He'd taken over two hundred in the past fifteen years. He said he could count on one hand the number of people who hadn't taken one on one of his hunts. It was just my luck that I'd be the one making him break out the other hand.

It was seventy-five degrees but should have been twenty degrees at night with a fifty-degree high during the day. He promised that with some snow it would take two and a half days at most to get my lion. I want to mention that he outfits for everything. I'd seen so many turkeys on this hunt. Well, it wasn't over yet.

On February 24, we struck out a little earlier and split up again, looking for tracks along road ditches. We saw a few mule deer but no tracks. The dogs struck one time, but were never sure what they hit. Then we made a long loop through a canyon for a nice hike, but we still found no cats.

We decided to end the hunt and take it back up with the big cats in December 2009. Johnnie took us out for a nice steak lunch, and then we came back home to pack up and leave. Debbie had never been to Colorado or New Mexico, so we went to Pagosa Springs, Vallecito Lake in Bayfield, Durango, and then Carson National Forest in New Mexico. From Chama to Taos, Debbie got her shopping in, and we made our way back home, sightseeing along the way.

Eagle and Trackem Outfitters have areas for all ages to hunt. Well, we all work for what we need. If you get a chance, slow down to speed up to work for what you want, and go on that dream hunt. And thank God you can.

Colorado 2010 Lion Hunt

Howdy, y'all. Looks like I was blessed to try again for my mountain lion in Colorado with Eagle Trackem Outfitters in Model, Colorado. We tried last year, but the weather was the hottest and driest since the eighties, and that just killed my chances. But Johnnie's hunters always get their lion.

It cost a little money, but I decided to fly up for the hunt. I got a rental car from Colorado Springs for the two-and-a-half-hour drive. I want to inform y'all to do plenty of research on your rental cars and book them online for the best deals.

I had a little fun on the drive through grass flats, cruising at between 100 and 120 miles an hour for about thirty-eight miles on Highway 305. Sometimes I still think I'm a teenager. The day before, about two in the afternoon, Johnnie called and wanted to know how fast I could get to Colorado. A storm was brewing, and I needed snow for the best chance of taking a mountain lion. Twenty-four hours later, I was there.

The first evening, we got settled, studied the weather, loaded the dog box, and discussed a game plan. Waking up at daylight on the first morning was tough, considering the sleep that I lost waiting to hunt. The bad part was that the snow had not yet hit, leaving me with a letdown along with some worrying. Johnnie was a little sickly on top of that. After watching the weather, some hope was brought back, as snow was still coming. I found it hard not to think that this could be the first animal I might not get. I rarely don't get what I'm after. Also, I found myself thinking of what you have to look past, sometimes, to do anything worthwhile—such as the $1,500 I'd already put into my second trip to Colorado. The plane was about $750, other items were around $300, and the rental car was $400, which was hard to swallow. I try to keep in mind that anything worth doing or having usually isn't cheap.

Soon we went out to feed the animals, and while we were there, the snow started. We then trucked on down to town to get my license and supplies. I soon figured out the license machine just couldn't recognize me in their system. We had to go to Johnnie's wife's place of employment to retake the lion hunt certification online, and then we went back to get the license. For the rest of the day, we prepared for the first hunt and rested.

About two in the morning we rolled out of bed and had a cup of coffee and a bowl of Raisin Bran. It was eighteen degrees with light winds and a full moon that illuminated the mountaintops out across the Comanche Grass Flats. Sometimes the wind would carry a mist of ice with it across my neck.

Now, you can't turn dogs out on a cat until daylight. The drive down to Hill Ranch took about one hour and twenty minutes. There were several thousand acres that had burned in a lightning storm, leaving a lot of open range with the Rockies in the backdrop, plain to see. About three thirty we cut an old cat track, but it had been snowed in a good bit. We knew it couldn't be much older than twelve to fifteen hours. Our guess was that he couldn't be more than fifteen miles away. We drove around every road and split we could find, looking for another track. The whole time, I was trying to keep my head up and eyes open. Soon we saw four or five bull elk in a group. Right at daylight and about the time I fell completely asleep on Johnnie, he yelled out, "There's a lion track and some elk!" This resulted in another good chuckle for Johnnie at scaring the poopoo out of me.

"Some elk" was an understatement. There was a herd of about one hundred or so elk filtering across the burn on the mountain. Right down the middle of the road, a lion track ran for about half a mile. It was a much fresher track, showing a full point, immediately revealing that it was a big Tom. Now that was music to my ears. We figured he was hunting the elk.

Johnnie had one of his guides on an adjacent ranch trying to cut a track in case we didn't have any luck. We wanted them to tag along, but we needed to get started and hoped they could catch up. Cowboy, Johnnie's top dog, lit out right after him with two others following. All this was after putting on their shock collars and tracking collars. Of course, they weren't about to put him up a tree fast. A few times during the four-mile hike through canyons and thick oak bushes, and then alongside snow-covered hillsides, we thought we lost him, no longer hearing the dogs. Many highs and lows ran through my emotions. This was my second try for a cat. The weather had not been so good in 2009, and Johnnie had let me come back at a better time with three paid days left. That said a lot for him as an outfitter. He outfits most everything with many private ranchers, but lion hunting is his passion, and he's good at it. For the reward of such a magnificent animal, the price can't be beat.

Now, for those of you that don't like the taking of lions, each one taken must be checked with the Department of Wildlife and Fisheries, the GPS location given and tagged. They keep up with how many are taken and where they are taken from. When the quota is met, hunting must stop. Lions have large territories, and the presence of too many in one area is devastating to the other animals, such as livestock and even humans.

Now back to the hunt. About every mile, we could tell the lion print was getting more pronounced, and we found a territorial dig along the way. He had a jump on us. For about the last mile, we weren't hearing the dogs much. But to our surprise, here came the dogs back to us. This rarely happens. At that point I just knew it was over. Johnnie gave them a little spanking and sent them back down the trail. About twenty minutes later, they treed the cat. All this took about five hours. We didn't think the dogs had treed the cat already and thought he wasn't going to show. I hurt my knee about this time, so God was on my side in having the cat treed now.

Upon seeing the cat, my eyes popped out of my head. He was a big tom for sure. We had dogs climbing the tree, spinning around mad as hell, and power circling the cat at the treetop. The cat was antsy. It was thick under the tree, so we could not regain control of the dogs on the leash. Neither of us wanted the cat to jump, for many reasons. In order not to harm the dogs, we decided not to use my bow. I shot him with a .357 magnum pistol at about twenty-five yards. The hit was good. The cat tumbled through the limbs and hit the ground with four dogs on top of him, and he was still giving them a fight back. We had to shoot him four more times in order not to lose a dog. Unfortunately, one dog still got cut, one had its leg broken, and there were teeth punctures through their legs. It takes about three years to train a decent lion dog, so protecting them is top priority.

After dragging the lion down the canyon through a small creek with dog leashes, Marty met us with the truck. (Thank you, Marty.) The walk back would have been hell.

When we got home with the cat, after meeting with the game wardens, we measured him from tip of nose to tail. He was at least seven feet five inches long and weighed in at about 175 to 185 pounds. And it was the biggest cat, so far, checked by the game warden. His head was bigger than mine, and he had a paw to match. His skull supported teeth that could easily cut down a deer or kill a man. He had claws to match and muscles to use them. He was definitely in his prime. Skinning the lion took about an hour. We saved the meat to eat. Yes, people eat them. The meat looks like pork and has about the same texture.

For me this was another dream come true. Though one lion is enough for me, I hope to go on another hunt with someone else someday to film the hunt. Folks, you don't have to be rich to experience this hunt. Just save a little money and work a little extra and put it aside. For about $5,000, this could be your reality. I am a taxidermist and could do a nice rug for about $750 to $1,000. Full-body mounts differ somewhat.

Till the next hunt, at another time, may the Lord grant all your dreams. With a little work on your part and a lot of faith, I tell you, He will.

Turkey Season Done Cut Loose!

Eastern Turkey Hunt

Hello, folks. Looks like turkey season done cut loose. I wasn't sure turkeys would cut loose with the gobbling on opening morning, what with the cool 40 mph winds. Nevertheless, my wife and I went to our traditional spot in Kisatchie National Forest. Again it seemed there were no other hunters around. I hadn't been out there to look, so we were hoping for some luck.

Soon after it was daylight, we realized the wind was only gonna get worse, so I called as loudly as I could. We never heard anything. About half an hour later, we just lit out walking, and I hit my call now and then to try to get a response. I think it just wasn't their morning. I seldom don't hear or get one on my hill.

After missing a day or two, I was bouncing off the walls to feel spring air and plant my butt firmly behind a big pin oak I knew about for another round. I think I was a little too ready, as I got into the woods very early. It was a good thing I did, though, because I went in differently than usual because I couldn't cross the creek as a result of all the rain. By doing so, I spooked what sounded like one bird off the roost. I went on in anyway and became as one with a big pin oak. Shortly after daylight, while having a hooting contest with two owls, I made a tree call and heard a gobble across the creek at what I estimated to be about 650 to 800 yards away. Slowly I blended in my different slate calls, trying to sound like more than one hen. After about thirty minutes with no more gobbles, I was about to give up when the crows and hawks, raising cane at my decoys, about twenty-five yards away, got him to gobble. He sounded as though he was not moving. I assumed he was henned up; having two or three girls is better than having one across the creek. I called a few minutes more with no response, so I decided to try to move on him.

I walked about a quarter mile. Still standing, I hit my slate loud. Seconds later, he gobbled back and was close. I immediately found a tree to get against and threw out a few soft yelps and sat my gun on my knees. Five minutes later, I heard a thump. He drummed. Now I knew I was about to see the bird. Sure enough, his blue-and-red head was bobbing toward me—but from across the creek. I eased my gun up and took aim and slammed him in the head with my Beretta using a three-and-a-half-inch no. 4 turkey load. If I'd had this gun fifteen years ago, about fifteen more turkeys would have been run through my gut for supper.

He was a twenty-nine pounder with a ten-and-a-half-inch beard about two inches thick at the bottom, sporting spurs that were two and a quarter inches long. I was proud to put him in the freezer and thank God for having been able to take a good gobbler. Man, get a call and get out there. You don't know what you're letting slip away in your life. Just spending time in the woods is worth the time. Mother Nature always has been my favorite lady. Take her on a date and see what I mean.

Alaska First-Phase Group Hunt

Hello, folks. Thought I'd share another dream come true for me with you. Well, I finally got to go to Alaska. I left from the house about a quarter after five in the morning and arrived in Ketchikan, Alaska, about five in the evening, their time. There is a three-hour time difference between Louisiana and Alaska. I ran into three guys going with us in Seattle—Scott, Jade, and Brian, from Cincinnati, Ohio—at the airport in Houston, Texas. Also hunting with us were Scott Bagi and Joseph.

We stayed at the Best Western. Scott Bagi stayed with Jody, who lives in Alaska, and helped set up the hunt for Sitka blacktail deer. The next morning, three guys took a float plane out with food and some supplies to a cabin we arranged from the forest service—Red Bay Lake Cabin. It's on the island of Prince of Wales. We drove about one hundred miles to a trail head after a three-and-a-half-hour ferry ride. The road was very windy. I felt as if we were on a roller-coaster ride. It was already very dark and raining, but we lit out anyway for an hour hike to the lake. We all had more than a load. According to the airport, my duffel bag tied on my pack together weighed 157 pounds. With my gun in one hand and another bag in the other, it was a job for everyone.

On our way down the trail, we spotted some eyes. It spooked us a little, as we thought it was a bear, but it turned out to be a deer. I had gotten a black bear tag just in case we came across one. Sure enough, our 5½ × 14–foot aluminum boat was at the end of the trail. Scott had toted our two-horsepower Honda engine in from the truck. At first we weren't sure it was going to start, but after jerking until our arms were ready to fall off, she fired. Paddling to our cabin would have been a nightmare.

The first night was fine, except I realized I had forgotten my socks, and the batteries for my air pump for the Coleman inflatable mattress had been run down. I guess the pump had been turned on during the flight. We were exhausted because of the travel and time change.

We woke early and had some coffee, eggs, and sausage, and then we lit out. Everyone left in the boat, and then Scott Bagi and I headed out from the cabin. Early on we saw two does at twenty yards; and that was it. Halfway through the day, we split up. I had almost killed myself walking. It was very thick, with fallen dead trees that three men couldn't reach around. But a beautiful carpet of moss covered 90 percent of the forest floor. The trees stood two hundred feet tall in some places. Tongass is a lot of rain forest. I'm telling you there are some huge trees in Tongass National Forest. Most are cedar, and they don't rot fast. Needles cover everything. The forest floor is full of dangerous leg and foot catches, holes to fall into as deep as your waist, and hidden water pools under the earth.

We did see some salmon held up in some of the large pools in the streams. We saw some swans and a few ducks. On this trip, I realized hunting in these extreme conditions is coming to an end for me. It hurts me already. The first night in, we ate steak and baked potatoes.

Day 2

We all loaded up in the boat and cut across the lake for a hunt in different areas. I walked myself through about three different terrains. I still didn't see any deer. I watched a few eagles and ravens soar by some nice scenic areas. I met some other hunters on the road. They were locals and said it wasn't right yet and that it had been the worst on the island that they had seen in years (just my luck). No one shot a deer today, but Jay shot a six-point yesterday. We had some Halibut burritos for supper. We ended the night talking and making fun of Joey's rock that he killed when shooting at a deer. We punched up the wood heater and crawled into our sleeping bags.

Day 3

About three in the morning, I got up and put a few more pieces of wood in the heater. Shortly after, the bottom fell out of the sky and the wind was gusting. It wasn't long before we all rolled out of our bags. Quickly, a lot of sarcastic comments were made as to how nice the day was for hunting; we were trying to laugh ourselves into feeling better about shoving ourselves into the Alaska elements. The four of us, sure enough, loaded into the boat—our packs covered, wearing full rain gear—and went off. Scott and I hung back, staring out the windows, waiting for a break. Later the wind broke a good bit and the rain slowed. Cabin fever was setting in, so we lit out, paddling across the lake, one of us going left and one right. I had just sat down and hit my deer call once, about an hour into the hunt, when Scott shot. That was when I realized my scope was fogged from keeping my cover on. I inched along through devil's claw and brush, hopping, crawling, and jumping through the landscape, while at the same time trying to spot an animal. The devil's claw is like a cactus with millions of very tiny stickers.

Soon I happened to spot Scott, but he hadn't seen me yet. I slipped up about two hundred yards behind him, to within twelve inches behind him. I braced, ready to possibly get the h—— knocked out of me, and proceeded to scare the poopoo out of him. I didn't know it, but he was watching two does. After a very short talk about what had been going on, I saw a deer heading straight up the mountain—a buck. It was a big buck all the way around for a Sitka blacktail. I threw up my gun, and sure enough, water was all over both ends of my scope. Doing my best with God Almighty helping me, I landed the kill shot. Scott had taken a four-pointer.

Now the fun part started. We decided to attempt to quarter and debone both deer in the dark and take them out that night. Scott forgot his headlamp, and all I had was a Walmart book bag for a day pack. With the temperature dropping, though we ended up soaked, we managed to get both deer cleaned. We packed our packs, tied all we could into them, and, with guns in hand, started shoving our way through the brush, moving downhill. About fifteen minutes later, I tried to cross a log that was about chest high and fell straight back, pinned to the ground by at least two hundred pounds of meat. I tried getting up when one strap broke. This wasn't good. I tied what was left all over my body and held about fifty pounds in my arms, as if holding a baby, and I tried again. Quickly into it, I fell face-first. The only thing saving my face was the meat in front of me that knocked the breath out of me. Scott was battling a similar situation. Luckily it was toward the end of our crossing streams when our feet met snowmelt water coming off the mountain. At one point, Scott's leg got stuck about up to his crotch in mud, and we weren't sure we were ever gonna get his leg out in one piece.

"Adventure" isn't the word. I'll tell you—you must be ready to hunt in Alaska. If you are not sure, never go without an outfitter or experienced person. A self-guided hunt like the one Scott and I were doing will save money, but it won't save your life. We were exhausted. Thank God we made it without shattering a leg, falling without a stick driving through our gut, or stepping into a hole big and deep enough to hold three people inside, with a twelve-by-twelve-foot entrance and a stream running under it. I just can't explain the dangers up here. One step can be life altering.

We managed to get our share of chicken at the camp. The other guys were just about to send for search parties on the satellite phone. We gave some high fives and got some shut-eye.

Day 4

Everyone went hunting the next morning after breakfast except for me. There had been a good bit more snow last night. I washed dishes in the creek and pumped some water out of the stream through the Katadyn water-filtering pump. It is not recommended to just drink water out of the streams. I chopped some wood for supper and our last evening. Then I prepared some venison backstrap. After cooking the backstrap, I wrote this story, debating on another, final, evening hunt. I am tired for sure.

I couldn't stand it. I lit out till about three forty-five. It gets dark at four in the afternoon. I found a good place, but I didn't try too hard, because I really didn't want to pack another deer out on the night we were going in. I just took in the sights. It snowed quite heavily most of the time. It was interesting packing our gear out a mile or so to the truck and then hoping to find a place to sleep until the ferry came back to Prince of Wales Island for us.

Everyone made it out. They had taken three good bucks. All had been quartered and packed out. We didn't even change clothes till we had loaded six deer into the boat, along with our gear and butts. As soon as we started across the lake, the bottom fell out of the sky, with snow and sleet falling. We hoped to be out before the trail froze over through the morning hours. We had to be on the large ferry at eight in the morning. After finding the trailhead in the dark, we started packing everything up to the truck for a one-mile hike. After the first hike up, Joey realized he had left the truck key back in the cabin. Scott volunteered to make the trip back in the boat, alone. Conditions had changed on the lake.

By now, our so-called wet gear had left us wet with one hundred miles to go to Hollis, where the ferry was. I made three trips, for a total of six miles, carrying no less than one hundred pounds—fifteen or twenty of those in each hand. Joey did the same but in four trips. Scott made two trips and doubled up on the boat ride. "Tired, cold, and exhausted" doesn't describe how I felt. For the last thirty minutes, I broke out a survival suit.

Now on the road, we soon realized we were gonna have to plow our way out. The snow on the road had already gotten deep. It was about seventy-five miles to the blacktop. It was about two thirty in the morning when we got to Hollis. We could not find a place to stay, so it was truck camping for us until eight in the morning, when the ferry left.

None of us slept till we were in Hollis, about twenty-eight hours from the time we all left for a hunt that day. Now on the ferry, we went straight for the galley and got a twenty-dollar breakfast. Everything is expensive in Alaska. About twenty minutes into the trip, it got rough. Seventeen-plus-foot seas are hard to deal with. It wasn't long until most everyone was running for a trash can. That made the second time I got seasick. We stayed that way for four hours. It was a bad storm, and several locals said it was the worst ride they had ever had. It took me the rest of the day and all night and part of the next morning to get over the dry heaves and headaches.

Day 5

At Joey's house in Ketchikan, we took our first showers in seven days. Joey has a friend, Boyd, who is a biologist, and he said our deer were the biggest he had seen anywhere since the season opened on August 5. If we had entered the big buck contest in time, Scott would have been first, I second, and Joey third. We worked for it in the dense rain forest most would not go to just to kill a deer. We spent the evening recuperating and washing clothes. The bad part was that the rest of our party—the other Scott, Jade, and Bryan—was still at the cabin. The storm wouldn't let the float plane come in, and they had only enough food for the rest of this day and one more.

Day 6

We slept a little late and then set out across the bay on a little ferry to an island behind the airport, looking for black bears and more deer. We hunted over six miles but didn't see a deer. It was the first day it didn't rain and snow on us the whole time. We headed to Micky D's for an Angus burger, went home, and put some thought into the rest of the trip, since another spot with another cabin had already been taken.

Day 7

We decided on a flight to Ohio for the remainder of the rut. Our flight home was a big mess, starting right off the bat with a two-hour snow delay.

All is well. Alaska and the friends I made on the adventure we had will never be forgotten.

Hunting Down South in the Basin

Hello, hunting buddies, I made a little hunting adventure down south in the basin with a few friends: Jodie and Jonathan White, of Slagle, Louisiana, some of my new family of one year; Lynn and Curtis Thompson, and Flip, who just opened a machine shop in Rosepine; and Jason Above from Broussard, Louisiana.

At about one hundred miles from my house, it's not that far away to be and feel like I'm in another world, compared to the piney woods of Hicks, Louisiana. We have a lot to offer as far as sights to see along our rivers and swamps. Please adventure into them if you get a chance. I plan to explore all our WMAs a little at a time and write about them.

The rut usually starts in late December down south. We all saw deer, but only Jodie saw a good shooter; however, he didn't have a good shot. I could have taken a few hogs but decided not to. Every camp had a little meat hanging—mostly small bucks. A lot of geese and ducks were smacked right at daylight. Just seeing a lot of different wildlife was a nice change.

Do something different close to home. You might be glad you did. There is a beauty and peace of its own kind deep in the Louisiana swamps, and at different times of the year, it still draws me in. I hope all the hunters out there haven't gotten all the hunting they want. I'm about halfway. I've ended up with nine between three states, including six with bow, and a nice eight-pointer worth mounting.

During these last few days, your best bet, probably, is to go deep in some thick cover, such as pine plantations. Find a well-used trail and sit about sixty yards away, watching one spot. Or pick spots along the edges of thickets where you can see longer toward dark. You've got to remember that the deer are very spooked by now. They spend a lot of time in good food plots at this time of year at night. Hunt somewhere they might be as dark approaches and when they might be leaving to bed up in the mornings. Even though the season is ending, you still need to fill your feeders for the months leading up to spring to help them along through the cold. It's a good time to get them used to one scene. They will be looking hard for food out there. Even a few seconds a day will help them, and you'll see more deer next year. A metal fifty-five-gallon drum with one hole cut in it about the size of a quarter does well shoved back up into brush along a trail. Plastic drums tend to get holes chewed in them by coons and squirrels and such. Well, good luck!

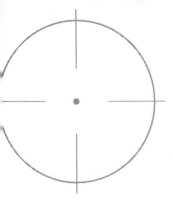

A Typical Hunt

Hello, folks. If you are a hunter wondering what a typical hunt might be like, or a hunter who can just relate, this story is about a typical day's hunt.

The morning started with me getting out of bed about 4:20 a.m. with a cup of coffee and a world-famous blueberry Pop Tart. This usually sustains me till I or my lovely wife, formerly Debbie Thompson from Rosepine, cook some deer meat with a couple of eggs sunny-side up, two pieces of toast, coffee, and milk. This is usually enough to push me through lunch as well.

Dressed for a two-mile Rhino ride into Calcasieu River swamp by my house, I struck out, pushing through a lot of water, and slipping and spinning in the mud. Mother Nature had just recently given the swamp a good house cleaning with a flood that took four deer cameras, the underbrush from all my deer stands, the ears of my deer decoy, and about sixty dollars' worth of corn from me. I knew this could happen, but not well enough, since my cameras apparently still weren't high enough.

I parked my Rhino and stayed beside it till a half hour before daylight, at which point I began walking through the woods as quietly as I could, being careful not to touch anything as much as possible. I like to be like a ghost as much as I can. Good bucks are well equipped with experience to know you are there and have been around. If you forget that, then there's a lot higher chance you won't bag one.

I slipped up into my box stand, got my cover scent out, and sat in my chair, face net on. I nestled into the sounds I love hearing so much—the sounds of the swamp waking up. Soon owls hollered, and then I noticed the vague sound of automobiles traveling down Highway 28. That's usually my signal. With my bow in my hand, I thanked God for being blessed not to be in the shoes of those drivers at this moment. Now, I love to work, but not so much as to miss out on all the magical mornings God can give me here in the swamp.

Soon it grew a little lighter out, and then I heard wood ducks coming off the roost and flying by. A few minutes later, the sound of birds chirping started getting louder and louder. Crows began arguing in the distance, and it wasn't long before two big swamp rabbits were chasing each other around on the patch of rye grass I planted, only to be interrupted by a red fox squirrel hustling up fragments of corn.

I sat gazing out of the stand, and hues of colors continued to change before my eyes, painting pictures on the water-filled holes around me. Thankfully, the sky was clear, the moon was full, and there was no wind at all. This made for a nice forty-seven-degree morning, which in my book is perfect. I began continually easing my head around, using my eyes like radar, gazing as deep as they would go into the shadows between the trees, hoping to see a five-to-eight-year-old mature buck with a respectable rack of antlers. While hunting, I try to make myself half like the animals out here and half like myself. This is something I probably couldn't explain to many people, but serious hunters probably can relate.

A while passed, and I started to feel really comfy and relaxed. I heard leaves moving around under my box. I looked down and saw a field mouse whacking the ground around me, looking for something to eat. Later, a coon was walking the edge of a ditch line, most likely hoping to collect a crawfish before the sun got too high and it came time to bed down. The sun was up now, and in its light I blew fog, as we called it as kids, out of my mouth. It always looks sort of mystical. It also helps me check the wind direction. A very small piece of cotton helps too. I like to know in which way the deer are most likely to pick my scent up.

Sometimes periods go by and you are just as one with the knots on a log by you. Most opportunities in life requires patience and desire. Then you actually need to try to have a new experience while hunting. These are moments I refer to as "getting my mind right for the hardening task of human interaction." Folks, we have to get up and make our government wake up! The liberals are killing us. We can't keep giving everyone everything. If you're feeling a change would be good in your life, the peace of Mother Nature works, given along with Jesus Christ. You see, it's more than just killing the animals to hunters; it's the bond of being part of nature for those brief moments in life. Being out there can sometimes take you to a good place for a spell.

Later the sun rose and the wind started to blow, and the trees danced in it as if happy it rose. I didn't even see a deer, but I was out here. I'm living. You all should come dance with the trees when you get a chance. Mother Nature loves everyone. Take care of your environment; we only hurt ourselves when we don't.

Country Competitive
By Jody White

Here is a fishing story that started about eight years ago when C. H. and I decided we were going to go fishing, and I had another friend with a sweet honey hole south of Pitkin. Well, I guess it really started about a year before that, when he would take me to his places on the lakes, creeks, and rivers. I thought I was a good fisherman, but we always ended up kind of even or he would get the better ones more often. Being the competitive person that I am, I decided to seek out some of the best fishing holes and get the jump on him. After hitting about five of my best fishing spots, I settled for this honey hole of mine on a friend's property south of Pitkin. Loaded with my knowledge of what they were biting on, where they were, and what kind of fish were there, I challenged him.

On the morning we met up to do this fishing, he showed up with a twenty-inch inch Snoopy pole from 1969. Being the good friend I am, I ridiculed him, laughed till I cried, and had the confidence of a gold medalist against a high schooler. We went on to the creek and down the middle of the property, and I gave him the choice to go north or south, as I knew where good spots were on both sides; he took north, so I went south. Here we were, alone, fishing competitively—and I mean *competitively*. In my mind, the media should have been there covering it, with crowds of people on the banks and vendors selling hot dogs.

It took about two hours of fishing before we finally met up in the middle. Having a stringer of fish and feeling pretty good about them, I decided to meander over to him and ask, "How'd you do?" Being that both of us have a competitive streak a mile long makes for half the fun when we do something together. His response prompted my ego to deflate quite a bit when he said, "I got one or two." Now, if any of you have competitive friends like this, you know this answer could either be a bluff or the truth; it could possibly mean that he was whooping my butt. I thought it was more than likely that he was whooping my butt. So I proudly displayed my stringer of four or five good creek bass. He just smiled and said in a low voice, "Is that all you got?" That was when the rest of my ego deflated.

Now I wanted him to lay his cards down, which he did not. We just continued to fish around each other, me watching him and him watching me. But after about thirty minutes of that, I found that I was fishing pretty nearly on top of him, and he was just grinning. By now I'd tried all of my bait tricks and techniques and could only manage to pull two small ones out in front of him, which did make me feel good. Unfortunately, him being the sly fox that he is, armed with only his Snoopy pole and a small box of jigs, he pulled two bigger ones out right in front of me. As you can guess, by now I was ready to break his Snoopy pole and leave him at the creek. Well, he finally showed me his stringer of fish. To my surprise, we were about even. I heaved a sigh of relief for my ego. But he still had the biggest and the most, so I live to fight another day.

That fishing trip started an even more competitive nature in our upcoming adventures. Fast forward five years; we were on another creek on our deer lease, and nothing had changed. Here I was with about three bass in my basket, and his stringer was full. You might find this next part of my story a little cruel, but you gotta understand country boy friends. To put this day into perspective, it was very hot. We were both sweating, watching out for water moccasins, alligators, ticks, and thick brush briars to get to these fishing holes. It's kind of hard work if you don't like it, but a competitive streak is still there, just as when you are fifteen on the baseball or football team, trying to win the championship game. So we took a lunch break around noon on the creek bank and began talking about hunting, fishing, and just life in general.

Eager to get back to fishing, he got up and started down the creek, and this was when I noticed he had made a fatal fishing error. He had walked off and left his stringer by me! Since the events at the beginning of this story, I'd gone through five years' worth of almost beating him and getting beaten or downright whooped in the fishing competitions between us. So I did the only thing I could; I let his fish go.

About an hour went by, and I heard him walking around in the woods. I saw him through the trees, looking for what I guessed to be the spot where we had lunch. I walked over to him while he was mumbling and asked him, "What's up, bud?" Of course, I had a grin on my face.

He said, "I know for darn sure this is where we had lunch."

Right about now I was thinking about how I could be more mischievous, and I said, "I think it's over there, around the bend." But after a little thought, I decided to join him in his detective work in the sand of the creek bank, the whole time smiling and sometimes laughing under my breath. Finally we got to the speculation part, and of course our number-one predators where we live are alligators, so I jumped at the chance to agree with him and said, "That looks like an alligator dragged your stringer away." Now feeling a little guilty, as I should have, but still enjoying the moment, I decided to tell him.

Right as I was going to tell him, he caught me laughing and put two and two together. No, we didn't have a fistfight on the creek bank; it was more like satisfaction in knowing what really happened. His face went from bewildered and angry,that the fruits of his labor had been taken by something else, to satisfied that he now knew the fish were not on a stringer in a gator's belly. I think he was more worried that they simply jerked the stringer out of the sand and were gonna be hung up on a stick or something underwater and die. But that's really one of the best mindsets of a good country boy: to have fun and not waste the harvest if you're hunting or the fish if you're fishing.

Needless to say, he doesn't leave his stringer or baskets around me anymore, and I don't try to beat him at fishing anymore. We just have fun—with a slight competitive nature, I guess you would say. These are just a few of the good memories with my good bud C.H. that we both talk about, and we always look forward to the next ones. By the way, that damn Snoopy pole of his finally broke a few years back; I guess it really was from 1969. I felt a little bad, as I was with him when it happened. And I know he thinks I fiddled with it, but I didn't; I promise.

South Mexico Turkey Hunt

Ocellated Turkey

Hello, folks! Looks like it's about to get hotter than a firecracker on the Fourth of July. Sure enough, we're in it now. I and my good friend Trent Johnson, with N-Time Inc. Mobile Home Movers in Rosepine, Louisiana, have lit out to Mexico City. We're staying in Campeche for tonight on our way to the jungle seven and one half hours away. We hope to bag an ocellated turkey and maybe a forest cougar. The flight was $680.

We lucked out and got a ride with some fishermen to the motel where we were staying, saving us a taxi. Soon we saw we were definitely in another country. The contrast in the surroundings between the United States and here were striking. At least until we made it near the coast along the center of the city. We unloaded our gear in the room, hid our money, and hit the bar across the road for one cerveza. Then we broke out walking along the beach for a long ways, then back through a less desirable part of town on the way back to get a better feel for the place. Dark fell, so by now we were headed down in the other direction to a more touristy area and had a good meal: roast pork in banana leaves and shrimp cocktail, with coconut cream cake for dessert.

Then we noticed a big crowd and went to investigate the scene. When we reached the second gate, there were some dancers. It turned out to be the governor and president of Mexico. I'm not sure they knew what to think when I broke out in front of the stage with a little dance of my own, leaving Trent acting as if he didn't know me. We then moseyed on back to the motel for some sleep.

The night's sleep was good, thanks to AC. The second day in Campeche, we had breakfast at the motel and then lit out walking to explore in a different direction to find a city market with meats, fish, and many spices and fruits. I can tell you there's no need for lawn mowers and Weed eaters here. The simplest of yards are gardens compared to the ones here, although throughout the city are nice red, yellow, and orange flowering trees. We spent a short time arranging a tour of some Mayan ruins, and then we went back to rest and wait on Alfredo to drive us into the jungle. After a few hours watching dance performances, we finally met Alfredo for the seven-hour ride down to the jungle.

Along the drive, some interesting things we saw were military men at checkpoints about every fifty miles, as well as concrete posts every ten feet or so in the fences along the highway. The posts were there for the burning of fields and land to make more cattle pasture and farmland. (Using concrete is the only way to ensure posts won't be destroyed in the burning process.)

When you order a Coke in this area, you won't get much ice, if any, and if drinks are in a cooler, most are not even cool. Also, there are not many washers and dryers; you see clothes hung outside everywhere. Water is kept in plastic drums above houses, and about half of the houses appear to have electricity. Very few have TVs. We saw a lot of adobe-type homes with curtains for windows and palm branches for roofs, similar to what I saw in Africa. Around most homes there are chickens, turkeys, pigs, cats, dogs, and cattle, all living together, without pens or cages most often. We saw young boys herding and watching livestock along the highways to get every inch of green stuff they could find. The bad part is that the wooded habitat is being destroyed rapidly, and a lot of trash is scattered about.

We took a four-hour jeep ride back to camp. The ride was like one of those you pay fifty dollars an hour for in Colorado, except it is through the jungle, outside of civilization, with a lot of insects bombarding you along the way. It was dark when we went in. At camp, we had a very late supper about one in the morning, and then we got into our screen-covered beds.

Day 3

We awoke about four thirty in the morning, had coffee and a light breakfast, loaded the jeeps, and headed out for about a one-hour trip to our first hunting destination. Shortly out of the gate, I realized my backpack was not with me. (My bad.) I went back to camp for a short spell. Needless to say, I wasn't happy, thinking I might have lost it crossing the river in the jeep. Along the way, we were stopping and listening for turkeys (ocellated) to sing for a stalk. Near us in a big tree just up the road was a crested guan. Trent lit out of the front seat, ran up the road, and unloaded five rounds, finally taking him down. It was a long shot. Soon we split up, and just after Alfredo stopped the truck, killing the engine, the monkeys went ape! The call of these monkeys was a very loud growl like a holler. If we hadn't known what they were, we most probably would have left the area.

About two hours into the hunt, we stumbled on a guan for me that I took out of a tree. We went back to camp for a late breakfast and a nap. We woke later, with it being about one hundred degrees. It wasn't long before Trent and I were sitting in the river, cooling down like boar hogs. We had a snack, and then headed out. A few hours later, we heard a turkey, but it didn't make the sound you would think a turkey would make. We knew not to try to stalk the bird, so we sat for two more hours. He was still in the same spot at dark. He roosted nearby, so we slipped out until the next morning. We saw a lot of different birds, insects, and a large bird flying while carrying a snake. It's funny how hanging out with a person who speaks a different language, makes you end up playing Pictionary a lot. And you also end up looking as if you're doing sign language, and you find yourself using a funny tone of voice as well.

For the evening hunt, we headed out after a long drive to hopefully set Trent up on a gobbler I saw this morning. Rosealina and I slipped on down three quiet steps, paused, listened, and looked for a few minutes. We ended up in a dried lagoon that had a lot of javelinas and white-lipped peccaries in it and sat on a log. We were watching millions of bees scattered throughout the vegetation, as well as doves and hummingbirds. A crested guan showed up. We tried a predator call, but with no luck. On the way back, we found a small croc that had died, most likely trying to find water.

Shortly before dark, we heard a bang. We knew Trenton Johnson had gotten his chance, and hoped for the best. We eased down the road and parked, and after ten minutes, a turkey flew off its roost in the dark, in a tree that was right over us, and we never knew it. (What are the chances? Ha!) Soon Trent came out with a nice ten-and-a-half-pound tom turkey with large spurs.

Heading in for a two-hour drive, we were casing the trees for coatis. The coati is an animal that looks like a cross between a monkey and a coon. (The tail is much longer). We spotted a female curassow, and Trent busted it straight over our head. We had an awesome supper, eating some of the animals we killed. The night was windy, thank God!

Day 4

We were up at four o'clock with a fast breakfast, and then we hit the trail for a long, rough ride to where we had seen a turkey roosting. I was hoping he had been able to stay in the tree despite how windy it had been through the night. It was a little cooler, which had helped me get a decent night's rest. After walking in halfway to where we had seen the gobbler roost, we shut the lights out altogether, and began inching our way to where we hoped to see a black silhouette. And we did, at about eighty yards. When daylight was getting closer, he gobbled in their way (which sounds like drumming). Now we were up and down, moving between our bellies and knees, through brush and grass. I got to within a decent range, but not as close as I had hoped. I decided I was close enough, and it turned out I was, because after my shot, the turkey slammed to the ground. At that moment, with the sun capping the edge of the trees, I realized God once again had blessed me by fulfilling another dream.

Giving Trent more time to hunt, Rosealina and I slipped along the road. We came upon some toucans (the type of bird used as the mascot for Froot Loops). Then a bunch of mad monkeys came at us, entertaining us well. We heard another tom and slipped in to see if we could have taken him and we could have. I shot him with my camera but not without trying to call—which can't be done, Rosealina says, but by slapping my belly and growling with my mouth, using my foot to make noise in the leaves, I think I did. It was fun anyway. We ran across some massive elm trees for pictures, and then some gum trees they use the sap of for the gum (zapote). The roads here are from forestry logging around 1940 to 1980; now any logging occurs on a very small scale.

Day 5

Now that we don't have to listen for turkeys, we got a couple extra winks of sleep. We left on foot heading upriver near camp. Everything was very lively and green near the water's edge. We came across a lot of mesmerizing pools, which left me gazing into them through sunlight, looking at fish, leaving me wishing I had some of my scuba gear. We saw a few places where fish were fighting over rocks and logs like salmon going upstream. We also came across a few large trails ants had left as clean as a whistle, up to ten inches wide. Amazingly enough, I hadn't gotten a single mosquito bite yet. However, there had been a lot of insects on me that I'd had to knock off, as well as a few seed ticks now and then. This was nothing like what I was expecting from the jungle, though. As with any area, there were plants that could do more damage than the insects out there. There were long, thin thorns up to five inches long on some vines.

About one hour into our hunt, we heard a sound like a cell phone going off when lying on a kitchen counter. It's almost like you feel the vibration as well when you are near a male curassow. We had walked on a log across the river, and shortly after, we spooked a good one. This bird weighed between seven and ten pounds, just smaller than the turkeys here.

A little later on the trail, while looking up into a tree with full of vines and fruit, I saw a male coati. He was close, and I wanted one really badly. I aimed over to the side, hoping to make the kill without tearing the animal up too much to mount it. It busted out of the tree, hit the ground, and I popped off two more rounds, ruining my one-shot kill on this hunt. We found very few small drops of blood while cutting our way through the vegetation. No luck. It left me feeling as if I had lost the trophy of a lifetime.

Soon we heard that vibrating call again. Now, moving very slowly, trying to spot the curassow, we saw the senorita, a female. I dropped her. The females are prettier than the males. We bagged her up, had a banana and some water, and started to hike back to camp. When we were almost back, we heard something tearing through the trees up the trail. We thought it must be monkeys, but I ran up the trail, and a coati was running through the trees. I released a round out of my Italian-made Fabarm Lion H368 twelve-gauge and dropped it. It was a female, but I was still happy to get this unusual animal, which was light colored with somewhat reddish hair.

Trent was shooting a camo twelve-gauge with a modified choke. We had brunch and then bathed in river water while washing clothes. All the while, a four foot croc was just upstream. The water was cold enough to put a little life back in us, for sure. If having fish nipping at you bothers you, you might want to use a shower made from a fifty-five-gallon drum of water up the hill when you come on this hunt.

For the evening hunt, we had a young boy ride out on a Honda 250 dirt bike to cover some ground, checking water holes for white-lipped peccaries. We rode about forty-five minutes in the jeep before Trent and I split up. We ended up in some jungle so thick it felt as if we were walking through a cardboard box. Soon we spotted a tinamou, and after a little stalking, I peppered him to death. The tinamou is like a quail but three times larger. But wow, when I say it was hot, it was a rough day. It felt as if a blow dryer was hitting me.

Right at dark, Trent's gun rang out behind us. Soon they walked up with another nice turkey. He couldn't help himself, and we saw why. It was a twelve-pound bird with one-and-three-quarter-inch spurs and nice feathers.

We did get entertained by a large group of saraguato aullando monkeys, or howler monkeys. The large monkeys were as big as we were. These monkeys are the ones that make the hair-raising sounds you can hear from two miles away. We had a nice pork dinner that evening.

We pulled out of camp in a direction I hadn't been. This time I and the other person in camp, Roger, were going together to sit on a water hole. Roger runs a charter service in Cedar Key, Florida. He also does a lot of bird watching. This water hole was where they had seen jaguars and filmed them a few weeks back. We hadn't seen any though. There had been a lot of signs of pumas, or mountain lions. I was looking for killer bees but hadn't seen those either. Maybe that was a good thing.

Well, we had been there for about an hour when we heard them coming in. Now we had planned on the old one-, two-, or three-shot deals. It didn't work, and they had grouped up well with about fifty-plus there; and after Roger shot, all I had left was to shoot among them. That is not what I really wanted to do, for fear of killing two. I could have killed one but was waiting for Roger to creep up so we could do it together. I did manage to slam down face-first after tripping in an attempt to get a clear shot. It was a good hunt, although now I do wish I'd shot, since the white-lipped peccary was there. It's the only place on the planet to get one. They are a lot like a javelinas, but they have bigger heads and the bottom half of their skulls have white hair.

I got a little sick upon finding out they had seven tags left for white-lipped peccaries and we were the last hunters of the season. At the end of this hunt, there will not be any more white-lipped peccary tags issued in the entire country, so I might be the last person ever to shoot one legally. I still have the morning, but once they're spooked, they never come back for the rest of the season.

For the evening hunt, we sat at a lagoon, hoping to see a coati—a bigger and darker one. We did, but the ones we saw were too far off. Most of the time we sat there, it was dead quiet, and billions of flying insects were buzzing about. We saw several birds through binoculars. Trent took a hen to add the other sex to his turkey mounts.

Day 6

We woke up a little later since the moon was kind of high during the night. I had some fruit and one cup of coffee, and I then headed back to the hole where I had let the peccary slip through. The back woods were lit up with noises I had never heard—those of insects and animals. Every half hour offered something to entertain me. First, two big male curassow birds slipped in. I had decided to go ahead and take one, but it was too early, and I didn't want to spook the pigs if they were out there. But I knew I should have shot, because you usually get only one chance on a hunt. Then the monkeys went to swinging about and some didn't like where we were. They came up to about thirty yards away, shook limbs, and threw sticks toward us. Then we saw several kinds of pigeons, hummingbirds, hawks, and female curassows. I then saw a coati, which I had been trying to find. He slipped by me, and when I saw him, I unloaded my buckshot and changed to bird shot.

About four hours into the hunt, it was really heating up, with no sign of peccaries. Later I saw a good monkey fight. I saw a scaled pigeon and would have liked to have taken it, but he sat just long enough for me to look at him through binoculars to be sure. Six hours later, I was very hot and had had enough. For the evening, Trent and I set up on a water hole and saw many different kinds of insects, lizards, birds, and butterflies—but nothing else till we were slipping out.

With about ten minutes left, I heard some movement up the trail. With some luck, and to my disbelief, I spotted a big male coati with black coloring and a silver face about ten yards out on the side of a tree. I figured that if I saw one, it would be close, so I loaded with bird shot. I followed him up the tree as much as I could, and then he stopped with his belly on the back side, so I shot for back of his tail, knocking him out of the tree and onto the ground. It was a good way to end the hunt.

We spent another night in the jungle and then headed out for the drive back to civilization and then to Campeche for the night. On the way in, we checked out some Mayan ruins. We had an awesome mixed seafood supper and then went to bed and flew in. All I can say is that I thank God for the chance to have made this trip. Till next time, I hope.

First New Zealand Hunt, 2012

Day 1

Hello, my friends. Looks like I'm out to live another dream hunting trip with my brother from another mother, Scott Bagi. I left on the sixteenth of April for Alexandria to visit my cousin, Frank Bruynix, and grill a little dead deer. The plan was to catch a flight to Houston from AEX in Alexandria. About the time I was thinking to bed down, Scott called and said all seats were booked. *So here we go* … After a four-hour drive to Houston, I pulled in about three in the morning and caught a nap in the back seat of my truck in the parking lot of the Hilton Hotel, all along watching four does. No joke. Every time I'm around that airport, I see deer—often some nice bucks.

After getting my boarding pass and having a little trouble with my

Visa, I limped out to what I hoped would be an 8:30 a.m. flight. Wrong. It was all booked. Finally, at 11:50 a.m., I boarded to San Francisco for a four-and-a-half hour flight. I had been there once as a kid to visit my dad, who worked in the hotel and motel business. It's a pretty well laid out airport. I got there at 3:00 p.m. their time and did not have to fly out till 10:30 p.m.

I spent a little time singing along with the radio to "Town Line" with Aaron Lewis, Justin Moore, and Trace Atkins, and "Every Chance I Get" with Colt Ford. Next trip was to Sydney, Australia, and then on to New Zealand to meet Scott, a.k.a. the Predator, as I call him sometimes. He's almost as bad as I am at wanting to hunt something down, kill and eat it, and then preserve the head to remember it all. The only time I get jealous is when he gets Adam, his son—who I could see as my own as well down the road. I don't have any kids yet. I think I'd better wait till I'm sixty years old—if I can live that long.

Day 2

The flight to Sydney was fourteen hours and forty-seven minutes long, taking me 7,982 miles. The blessing of this flight was that Scott got us into business class through his company for $1,300, while it usually is $22,000 plus. Talk about spoiling you. The seats could be laid all the way back for sleeping and had built-in back massagers. Each had a TV with movies on demand. I had four windows to look out of. It was pretty much like attending the Hilton—all but the flight time. There were big compartments to store things in, pillows and blankets, and piles of snacks and liquors to try. There were chilled appetizers: vegetable spring rolls with ginger soy sauce, and shrimp cocktail. Then we had fresh seasonal greens with roasted tomatoes, Kalamata olives, mozzarella cheese, and a choice of dressings. The main course was pan-seared fillet of salmon, oven-roasted fingerling potatoes with green beans and carrots, or a choice of braised short rib of beef or spinach lasagna rolls with rosetta sauce and parmesan cheese. To finish the meal, there was a four-year aged cheddar cheese and St. Rocco triple-cream pie. The midflight snack was hummus and cream cheese sandwiches, breast of chicken, and smoked gouda cheese. Breakfast was a swiss cheese omelet, broccoli-potato gratin, turkey sausage, and tomato with fresh fruit and yogurt. Of course, none of this could beat the packed whitetail deer jerky Garret Soileau made me that I gave to the captain.

The airports in Sydney and New Zealand were both nice. We landed in Auckland, New Zealand, and got our bags. I had planned on staying downtown, but the motels were booked, so I stayed near the airport. We got a taxi and went downtown and walked in the city square and ate roast duck and listened to some live music. We checked out the boats at the port. We didn't stay out too late. Two days and nights of travel had left us both pretty tuckered.

Day 3

I woke up and walked a little piece down the road for an eight-dollar breakfast of toast and coffee. Let me tell ya, it's all expensive here, even though it is not a tourist town. We planned on meeting our hunting partner, Andrew, about noon to pick us up. After a six-and-a-half-hour trip, we stepped into Andrew's restaurant for lunch on a hot rock. We were staying at the old work-center building near the area we were going to hunt. We all fought to stay awake just to get there.

Day 4

We spent the day roaming, looking for paradise shelducks and turkeys, and we saw a spike and a ten-pointer. We had deer sausage for supper. We visited with our friends Bill and Ngati, two gun lovers, in the Mangatu National Forest along the Waipoua River.

We broke out of bed with Andrew having a nice little breakfast ready. We were staying in free-range land within the Mangatu National Forest on the Waipoua River. The river was wide and sandy but not very deep where we hunted. We spent the day peeking over canyon edges, roaring and trying to get a bull to roar back. We glassed a few nice ones. That evening, we spotted a nice bull. Scott and Andrew tried to stalk it but had no luck. The brush was very thick.

Day 5

I woke up to an early morning and a nice day. Right off the bat, along the river, I saw a few nice pheasants. I decided, since we weren't having a lot of luck getting stags to roar back, we would break out for a long stalk, looking over ridges. About an hour into it, I sneaked up on a small fallow doe. A little later, I found about nine pigs bedded, and Scott tried to stalk them but got busted. Soon thereafter, we stalked three sheep that had been transplanted here. Again Scott slipped in and took a shot. The shot was a little low.

After getting back to the truck, we drove awhile to another location. Soon I was stalking four tom turkeys and got a shot but had no luck. Twenty minutes later, Scott was stalking a group of hens but did not shoot. After calling up some steep hills, we started through tall timber. We had seen some fresh mess and tracks and saw two hinds, female red deer. We sat awhile watching them and then roared, but we had no luck.

Slipping along later, I spotted movement way down the hill. I gave a little roar, watching, and soon saw some movement toward us. Then we saw a small spike. It took the little guy about fifteen minutes to come up to within about forty yards of Scott, and he slung some Easton fiberglass at him. At that point, we thought he missed. It bolted down hill about eighty yards and stopped. I stalked it very slowly. I got a shot and let loose an arrow from my Mathews Drenalin. I got a hit, and it ran only twenty yards and folded up. On getting there, I noticed Scott had hit it as well, in the gut. While we were fooling with it, Andrew came up the hill and told us that he had seen a bull that was on the spike about thirty yards away. I had been making my way to wash my hands in the water nearby. When I got to Andrew and looked through the scope, I saw it, but it was kind of blurry.

Andrew had the scope turned way up. About the time I found it in the scope, it took off. It busted Scott down the hill. So I did the only thing I knew to do—run after it. With a lot of luck, I hit it on the third shot, running, with a bolt action. It was a nice eight-point. We had to drag it a few yards uphill to be able to get side by side with it. This nearly killed us, and I had already been suffering with my sciatic nerve to the point that I almost did not even want to go on this trip. After a bunch of pictures, we loaded up and headed in. I again tried to stalk some turkeys and got one decent shot. I was glad I didn't take it, because it was too far.

Day 6

I woke up to a peanut butter sandwich and a Red Bull to supplement my coffee, took a long drive through mountains, and unloaded the Polaris for another long ride. Walking down into the canyon, we saw some goats standing in the near opening. Scott tried to get a shot at a big billy with no luck. Soon I spotted two hinds, so we quickly got up to a high point and roared some. There was no answer back, so we headed on down. Doing this makes your legs shake and the ends of your toes hurt. It was some fine country, for sure. Sitting on a hill in some thick country, we called a young spike close. It was an awesome moment.

The hike back out was rough. We got the AR-15 out and spent most of the rest of the day calling goats gone wild. The wild goats were easy to find because of all their colors and their spending so much time out in the open and roaming trails and roads.

Later Scott hammered a big billy. They tracked it a long way but ran into some terrain that they could not move through. That afternoon, we cleaned the stags and mopped up some spaghetti. Bedtime couldn't come too soon.

Day 7

The nights were right as well, as all the days had been here. We slept in a little later and had cheese and bacon for breakfast. We loaded up the Polaris and headed down the river. We rode awhile, having to cut limbs out of our way to slip around bends, looking for stags and turkeys on all sides. Soon we spotted a female duck and about eight turkeys all in a meadow. I looked over the turkeys with binoculars, but there were only hens. We bailed out, stalking along the river's bank, and shot a few rounds with a .22 rifle. I was sure I made my shot because the bird would not fly but would only run. I thought it was wounded. It turned out they go through molting and can't fly for a short spell. I ran it down and got some good pics and let it go. There just aren't any predators here besides hawks. There were tons of rabbits all about.

Later, around another bend in a small pond, there was a pair of mallard ducks. These birds are beautiful. I slipped through some tall grass and knelt down and got a picture of the female before I startled them and they flew off in separate directions. I saw them land about eight hundred yards down the river.

About eighty yards shy, I saw a male fly up, so I moved on in. The male began circling around, looking for the female back in the field, near a pond. Almost always, if you shoot the female you will kill the male, too, because it won't leave the female. These birds are very loyal. I was lying flat on my belly, facedown, hoping the male would land, and sure enough, it did. At about eighty yards, I was able to get a picture of the male as well.

Later we saw two groups of turkeys high up on the mountain and decided to see if there was a tom. Scott and I together, moving up the hill, eased over the hill, bows drawn. Scott released an arrow but had no luck. We started toward the other group—same deal. Scott was on the left, and I was on the right. This time we split up, putting about sixty yards between us. We eased over the hill, bows drawn again. Andrew and Thomas were following Scott with camera gear. We were gonna be on the New Zealand TV outdoor channel. Andrew is a stuntman and has appeared in the Lord of the Rings movies, *The Hobbit*, *Yogi Bear*, and other films.

Soon I heard Scott release an arrow, and it sounded like a hit but ended up being a fence post. Seconds later, heads popped up over the hill; there was one tom—a jake. I drew and released an arrow, slamming it. Man, was I pumped. I had gotten a turkey, even if it was a jake, with a bow in open country, stalking. Later, back at the camp, we decided to pack it all up and head down to Gisborne for a hot shower, a hot meal, and some rest for the upcoming tahr and chamois hunt in the Christchurch Mountains—much harsher country.

The New Zealand hunt was more than I expected—more than a trip of a lifetime. Made some lifetime friends and made memories with Scott. This trip wasn't really made with money as much as it was made by my being blessed by Andrew and his friend Bill, along with Thomas—a.k.a. Sharp Eye, as I call him. Most of all, I have to give God thanks for this blessing. Well, string your bow and go when ya can.

Second New Zealand Hunt, 2012

Day 1—April 2012

Hello, folks. I got my red stag in New Zealand and am now resting up in Christchurch at a motel for a few days, recouping and preparing to head back to the hills to try to stick an arrow in a tahr and a chamois, and maybe another stag. It's gonna be very challenging with my sciatic nerve problem.

We left Gisborne about one in the afternoon and flew to Wellman on my first plane with a propeller, which took about an hour. The sight out of the window of mountains and ocean was awesome. They say the seas between North Island and South Island are the roughest in the world. It looked it even at twenty thousand feet. In Wellman we boarded a jet for a forty-five-minute flight to Christchurch.

Day 2

Today, on South Island, I slept late at Argyle Hotel on Park. Then I hit the streets for some last-minute gear and supplies. The weather was perfect. I managed to get a good haircut also. I found one man on all of the island of over four hundred thousand people who could help me with more arrows. Christchurch was the second-largest city in New Zealand till a recent earthquake.

I'll be taking my last shower today for five to seven days. I showered, packed, and repacked gear, and then Scott and I set out on foot to look for some grub. A few miles later, we picked a spot. Then we headed back to the motel for some rest.

I think it was April 27. We were up waiting for John McGinley and Craig D. Hamond to pick us up in a car for a four-hour drive to where we would get on a helicopter. We stopped along the way for brunch at a small-town cafe. Along the way, everyone's place was kept neat, and the land was full of fields and livestock. There was a lot of green, and streams flowed all about. We saw some stag farms along the way. Then, slowly the mountains grew bigger with each few minutes as we drove. Then we hit the edge of a glacier-fed river that was half a mile wide in some places but not very deep. We arrived at Double Hill Station, which is owned by Tim Hutchinson. He's a big farmer also. As soon as we got there, a storm started brewing. We managed to get loaded after getting scolded by John about how much gear I had, limping up to and into the chopper, and putting headphones on. With me in front seat, we took off in the rain. At that point, I double-checked that I had my information on me from Global Rescue in case something bad happened.

Flying along the river, even in the storm, gave us a whole different view along the mountains. It was still beautiful, and we were seeing it better than we ever had from the ground. Our flight was about an hour. It saved us three days of hiking, and we all split the cost. After landing, as quickly as we could, we started humping gear up for about four hundred yards up a hill, and already I could feel the pain in my back. The cabin we were in was Lyell Hut, built in 1933 on Rakaia

River in the Southern Alps along the Mount Cook region, about twelve or so miles from the ocean. The rain was coming down pretty good. We were already glassing slopes for tahrs while trying to get settled in the cabin and figure out where and how to sleep around the leaks without sleeping in rat and mice crap.

The hut had a makeshift fireplace that was about three by three feet, though there was no firewood; we found only twigs that burned in seconds. The cabin was really just a shed about ten by twenty feet or so with tin sides, and it was uninsulated, so the later it got, the more clothes we added and slept in. There was no heat at night, and none when we woke up either. On the first night, I quickly realized this stay was not gonna be a walk in the park without even leaving the cabin. We were probably overstocked with food, but we had to be, because we might not always be able to leave when we wanted to. We had a satellite phone but soon realized it didn't work. This would not be good if something bad happened. Thankfully, Craig had a personal locator which was some good if he knows we need it.

The first night, I had to get up in the freezing cold for nature's call about three times, and I realized I would be sticking to this pattern every night till the end. No fun. Also on the first night, an opossum came to eat some scrap food outside the door, spooking me a bit.

Day 2

The next morning, Craig and I lit out down the river through tons of rock, trying to stay out of the water. We soon started up the mountains about one mile from the camp. There was no trail there, just bundles of rock and scrub over our heads. We had to push and pull ourselves up through it. All was very wet from dew, so we were wet right off the bat, but we got cold only if we stopped for more than five minutes. That we did many times, catching our breath. After a few thousand feet, we broke out into the open, but it was still steep. It was grassy there and full of cactus-type plants with sharp points. A lot of small pools of water were scattered about, making for a view that was out of this world.

We continued to inch higher, glassing areas with binoculars as we went. About the time we got to a great area, fog rolled in, leaving us with one hundred yards of visibility. We hunkered down, wet, and shook ourselves into a sort of nap. A few hours later, we were very glad to be moving again, half frozen and happy to feel some sunlight on our bodies. A few more hours later, exhausted but comfy now that we were half dried out, we found a cozy spot to settle in and watch distant mountainsides for tahrs. If I had worn a slicker suit, it just would have been too hot to climb. Changing clothes back and forth is just the way it is.

Soon we saw a tahr, with daylight running out. We tried to close the gap but chose to stop and call it a good day to remember. That night, after grub, we spent a lot of time trying to hang out clothes to dry by a twig fire that lasted about five minutes and gave off about the amount of heat one stove burner would produce.

Day 3

I woke up to a cold chill and got dressed as soon as possible; some of the clothes were still damp. We refurbished our backpacks with nuts and fruit and water bottles. This time Craig and I headed upriver a few miles and then headed up a mountain in the general direction of where Scott and John had gotten Scott's tahr. About eleven in the morning we got high enough to feel we could see some. Resting on vantage points and glassing, we saw some tahrs miles away on the ridgeline. It wasn't long till the sun started to fall, so we started back down through rock and down slopes to call it a day. That night, I cooked some of Scott's tahr, and it was good.

Day 4

Well, I didn't sleep so well and was hurting because of my back, and it was raining a good bit, so I decided to sit one day out and rest. This morning was very cold—eighteen degrees—and snow and ice lay everywhere. Scott and John had packed up and decided to hike a day down the river to try to find a chamois, the second animal we hoped to take. Watching them crossing the river in icy water was something to see. They had to undress and then dress again, and a fall would have been a disaster. Craig went out on his own hunting and hit one tahr but could not find it. There were a lot of holes in those rocks. He got in a good bit after dark, and I was very worried. About the time he came into the cabin, beaten down and worn to a nub, I had supper cooked and a twig fire going. After talking a bit and planning our final day, we turned in about eleven thirty.

Day 5

We knew we had about four hours of hiking before we would have a good possibility of seeing some tahrs. We left just before daylight. I was still hurting but knew this was the time to suck it up or go home sick to death. Slowly but surely, we moved up the mountain, moving across boulders and rock drifts, stopping often to slow our heart rates. We reached a point where we got serious about watching. About a mile away, we spotted some tahrs walking across a ridgeline. Later, in the direction we were headed, we saw two females moving slowly among the rocks. We picked a point for a goal to reach to set up and hunt for the rest of the evening. Somehow we got split up among the boulders, and I ended up going straight up on all fours, pulling and crawling up scree most of the time.

About halfway up, I saw I had made a mistake by doing this and became worried. Craig would show up below me now and then, looking like a spot on the wall. After reaching the point we had picked and sitting a bit, I realized that it had clouded up and gotten cooler also. We had known it was a bold move to try to get to this point. Also, I knew Craig was probably pissed about how we had gotten split up. The farther I went up, the more I knew there was no going back down without a fall to my death—and that if I didn't get down soon, I would die from freezing. For the first time in a long time, I was scared and truly thought this could be a rough night. I was wet and was wearing nowhere near the amount of clothes I probably needed, and a fire was out of the question. Sitting on a knoll, I watched Craig work his way up through the back side, picking his route, hoping it would be a different way down. I felt like a cat stuck up a tree, and my back pain was the least of my worries. About an hour later, Craig reached me, and I wasn't sure if we were gonna fight or talk.

I knew, though, that this hunt had been beyond our desire. We knew they were up there; we just had to get in range. Now we knew it was time for them to move soon, so we tried to dry out and look over some places where if we did shoot, we could get them. By now we would normally have been done and headed down, but I had to convince Craig that I would rather be out all night or die before I left without being there for the last minute of daylight giving me every chance before I traveled on. Every moment was tough as I watched the sun creep down and felt the temperature drop, and I was still not sure about a five-hour hike back out.

Soon we spotted a tahr 164 yards ahead. Perfect, ha. Not! There was no way to get it, and the worst part was that it was a stud; and even Craig got very excited. We were begging for a chance. I was praying. This tahr had a very good coat and was as big as anyone had ever taken. I wished I knew if the chopper could retrieve him tomorrow when we left. Craig didn't think so. I would have hung by my ankles from a rope to put my hands on him. Shortly after, he moved out of sight. I felt as if I had just watched a friend die and as if that had been my only chance. I felt as though I deserved such an animal. We both just sat back and were silent for about a half hour, with only maybe an hour of light left, contemplating days gone by—bone-aching days—while looking across country that we couldn't have imagined. I bowed my head and thanked God for it, with or without a tahr.

I no sooner opened my eyes than Craig tapped me on the head. Two nice bull tahrs stood up some rock to our left about 360 yards away. I was scrambling, trying to get into a shooting position, but I kept sliding down on the mountain. Even now I wasn't sure about how these could be retrieved, but it looked much better than before. Finally, with Craig kinda letting me use him as a foot rest, I pulled the trigger and hit underneath the one I was aiming at. Craig thought I used the wrong space inside the scope. The second shot was a hit, and we both were really on top of the world; I had tears in my eyes and was even happier as it slowly fell in the direction we needed it to. Then, in slow motion, barely moving, it came to the edge of a bad spot, and we were like, *"No!"* With one flip of his body, he fell out of sight.

Now happy and worried, we were knocked down. I was about played out with back pain and knew I could not get to the animal. Craig, glassing the rims of the ridges, felt he could get it. So I said, "If you get that tahr, I'll give you my Mathews bow and everything with it!" Son, he lit out. I watched him in the binoculars, losing sight now and then, all along feeling guilty for not trying on my own and now thinking how I would feel if something happened over this animal and us still not sure about the trip down. Then I completely lost sight of him. Now I began shivering like a cat at a dog kennel.

About the time I was thinking the worst, Craig popped up with my tahr's head, coming down the ridge and rock. I was relieved yet still worried. A few minutes later, Craig whistled, and I saw him pointing at me in the binoculars. I was thinking, *What the heck?* Then he just yelled, "Behind you!" I turned, and down the hill, at one hundred yards, there stood another one, so I plugged him. I knew we could get to this one, and it was right in the path for the way out—or so I hoped. I just realized no matter what my sins may have been, God still loved me. I had no worries—only faith. He has wild ways of showing us things in wild times. "Thank you, Jesus," I said.

We caped both animals, found our way to a safe point out, took a few pictures, and slapped each other's hands off. After a few moments of hugs, we acknowledged that we had just had a hunt we would never forget.

About one in the morning, we reached camp, and we still had to eat, pack, and finish caping the animals before the flight out in the morning. At least, we hoped we were flying out, since the supplies were running low. The next morning we were glad to see the chopper with Scott and John in it. They were so happy when I told them I had taken two tahrs.

Wow! Thanks, y'all, for such a great hunt. And thanks to God for allowing us all to enjoy it. It was the hunt of a lifetime. There is so much more to this story, but all I can say is it's enough for me to remember it all, should God allow me another twenty years to relive it through this story. This is the reason I write these stories, primarily, but I do it also to share my blessings and hope with all who read it. "Seek and you shall find," says the Lord. Go find your dreams. Till then, Swampman is in the woods.

Merriam Turkey Hunt 2012

Merriam Turkey

Again I knew God had blessed me to lay eyes on another piece of his planet that I had never seen. I noticed its unique beauty for sure, with the sun being fairly low. As with a lot of places like this, there were old buildings, farm equipment, etc., of days gone by. Passing through Badlands National Park was definitely unique, and I could imagine times when Indians and buffalo survived together and dinosaurs ran about, and what it might have looked like then with more water and trees. Of course, there was startling evidence that the oil boom was starting.

I arrived at Kyle, South Dakota, just before dark and got checked in and scarfed down two big plates of spaghetti, unpacked, and laid my hunting things out. I had not met Randy Pucket, the guide yet. Kenneth Gardner was already there and was out with Randy trying to roost some birds. Kenneth is the designer of Strutn J's Game Calls. He was raised in Louisiana but lives in Nebraska, and soon I will be lucky to have him for a neighbor, not just a friend. The first night's sleep went well, other than us worrying about the clock going off at the right time, so as not to be late.

Day 2

We busted out of bed at a quarter after four and brewed up a little caffeine in the pot. After moving through several fence gaps, we finally ousted ourselves from the truck into the twenty-nine-degree temps. It wasn't long before we heard some gobbling while going down the creek out of a small canyon. We set up a couple decoys and backed into the cedars, standing and calling. At first we thought they were coming in. After my hands had gotten to the point at which they felt as if they were frozen and the bottoms of my feet were killing me from standing, four jakes came out near Kenneth, but I never saw them. Soon we moved on.

After working down the canyon and past a windmill, we set up again, and I could see toms and hens. It was plain to see they didn't care about our calling; they continued to move about in all the wrong directions. We decided to try to just stalk them, so each time they crested over a hill, we moved up on them. Finally the gobblers began chasing and fighting each other, and soon tail feathers and heads were moving about right at the skyline on the hill, about twenty-five yards up. Soon I saw feathers down and heads up, and I knew the jig was up. Out of the corner of my eye, I saw Kenny busted in the open.

Looking back up, I saw a good one move by and then disappear, and then I saw it again and took aim, hoping it was the same bird. I drew a bead, pulled the trigger, and slung three-and-a-half inches of BBs out of my Beretta twelve-gauge. Instantly I had a bird flopping about in front of me. Cha-ching! One Merriam turkey down. This was another bird I needed for my world slam. A sense of relief came over me. It turned out to be a nice bird for the breed, with about one-inch spurs and an eight-inch beard. Beards hardly get bigger than that, as the kind of terrain they move through continually keeps them trimmed down. The bird appeared to have a much thicker group of feathers than Eastern birds, probably to cope with the cold here. This makes them look huge. There is a lot of open country here, and hunting them can prove to be a challenge.

We came in and ate, took about an hour nap, and headed back out. Sitting on a high vantage point, we glassed all about, watching deer, and from out of the clear blue, a tom started coming right toward the truck. And then two hens followed, with another gobbler bringing up the rear. I got down the hill, and hid well enough for us to break guns out of the back seat. We called and waited. Some time went by until we crawled out to peek, and we then saw only two hens. Flabbergasted, it was only then that we realized the gobblers had moved out on us, so we went that way, but they had already gotten one hundred yards ahead of us. They gobbled a lot and moved out of sight. We chased and watched the turkeys all evening. There was nonstop action. Finally I pulled a fast rush on them and got a chance to take my second bird, but they were all too small. I watched them end up where I felt they were gonna roost. Now we had a two-mile hike to get back to the truck and to scout the terrain to determine how to get on them the next morning. We put some hamburger steak down and went to sleep.

Day 3

The next morning was twenty-eight degrees with a slight breeze, and rain was in the air. We had to think a little while going in, as roads run all through the reservation. Last night on the way out, we made a wrong turn, and after going through five fence gaps and driving by a house, we realized we had taken the wrong road. Twelve miles of it.

We had left a bottle in the road and turned around in the sand to leave evidence of where I had roosted the birds. Now somehow we had missed that, and by the time we figured it out, we were late getting close to the roost to set up. Bailing out of the truck and heading down the mountain, we spooked a mule deer and a whitetail. Soon we heard gobbling. It wasn't long until we peeked over the canyon ridge and, with my Pentax binoculars, saw them on the very flat I wanted to be set up on. There were about fifteen or twenty of them. To the right, down the hill from us, were some on roosts, but they were all hens. They flew off toward other birds—all except one of them. With birds in the wide open, getting closer for a shot would be almost impossible. Since it wasn't too far to the right to some washes at the edge of the canyon, Kenny and I started the sideways slide down the canyon to creep through cover.

After another good walk, we discussed setting up and calling, and we both were all about hunting this way, but I decided that it wasn't likely to happen this early, as they already had hens with them. That at least would not work for a big tom. We had seen a few jakes out and about.

Kenny had just had enough of stalking, crawling, sneaking, jumping, hopping, and walking through prickly pear on our knees. We decided to split up, and he broke out over a ridge opposite the direction I thought the birds would most likely go, should I fail to take one down the canyon.

Slipping slowly to give him time to move over the ridge, I scanned every hole before me on my way through, and it was hard to take it so slow since my adrenaline was high and I felt as if this was my last chance to get a good bird, with rain coming soon. I literally crawled over every single ridge. Finally I saw a fan at the skyline from a strutting tom. Lying flat on my belly and watching, I had a shot at a head a few times, but I knew I could not shoot till I saw his beard.

I saw that he had a smooth transition across his tail feathers, meaning there was a good chance he was at least a three-year-old; this is something Kenny taught me. Younger birds' tail feathers in the center are taller than the rest. I knew there was a chance many more were there, and soon a jake walked by, almost blowing my cover in the grass. Soon there it was—a full body, with a beard in plain sight. *Wow! Fun hunt!* My adrenaline almost had me blinded, the pain in my leg and back were gone. I pulled the trigger and saw feathers fly, but the bird disappeared; so I shot up over the ridge, and turkeys went in every direction, but most flew over the canyon toward Kenny. I had a long beard flying over my head. My bird was down. It was a mature tom. I knelt down by the bird and looked around me and was happy and thankful to God almighty to have lived this morning in such a beautiful and unique spot on the planet He created.

I never heard Kenny shoot, so I grabbed my twenty-pound bird and started the long hike through the hills and canyon, stopping a few times to rest and watch the deer in the binoculars and contemplate life gone by and try to presume my future, sure I couldn't imagine the world without these experiences. I got to the truck and drove around the canyon, getting closer to where I thought Kenny would end up hunting. I stopped on a high spot where he would most likely see the truck and where there were a lot of groundhogs to watch as I waited. He didn't do any good. We both decided to end the hunt there, and I saw an opportunity to sightsee and hot-rod my rental car some more.

I buzzed through Rapid City to Black Hills National Forest on my way up to Mount Rushmore and then the Crazy Horse Memorial, all along visiting and talking to folks and making friends. I stayed at the Hotel Alex Johnson, built in 1929. It was old, but a nice place.

I also took a Merriam in New Zealand with a bow. Well, two more birds and my grand slam on turkeys is done. Wish me luck. Till later, get into the outdoors.

Taking Care of Food Plots

Hello folks, Swampman here again. Hope all is well. I've been tearing up a little dirt and slinging some iron clay peas and cow peas for Mr. Whitetail. I am starting to see some nubs in some of my deer photos taken when hanging around in my Whitetail Extreme and clover plots. It's time to mow them high. About a week after the flowers die, mow them back down by just clipping the tops off, where the seeds are at. Don't do this on a hot day or they will die. I did this late one evening when thunderstorms were predicted for a few days, so the clovers would have a better chance of surviving.

I'm feeding for only a couple seconds a day this time of year. You should feed after dark and before daylight so the deer will get a chance to find it and the birds and crows won't get it all. Deer like the clover small and tender.

If you plan to change your stand's location and feeder spots, you should get it done soon so the deer have a chance to become used to it. I don't usually do a lot of brush-hogging until about the third week in August. Then I spray to prep for the fall plots coming up.

For a few years, I have been planting trees and shrubs for wildlife and deer: sawtooth oak, Nuttall's oak, Shumard oak, mulberry, hybrid white oak, etc. If you have property to do this on, get started. It takes a while to reap the benefits. I love this stuff and would be glad to help. It takes the smaller ones about a year to take off. Plant them in good soil with a root stimulator. Keep grass out from around them with a hoe, and mulch them. Don't place too much mulch too tightly around the dirt line. A good start always helps them out. Lime and fertilize in spring and fall; some watering during summer helps if there is a drought.

Mix planting these trees with a variety of food plots to produces something for deer to eat almost year-round. Keep some cover: tall grass thickets, briar patches, etc.

Well, has the government, your job, or taxes been stressing you out? Get in the woods, work on your deer stands, and talk to Jesus. Get up; go harder.

Youth Turkey Hunt 2013

Hello, my friends. Looks like we're back to that magical time of the year to hunt those thunder chickens chasing hens around, all love-struck. Also, it's time to get out and enjoy those few days of weather we rarely get. It's always nice to see spring come in down on the creek bank, down in some woods with everything blooming, birds moving about, and water flowing into streams.

On March 13, youth hunting started. This year I was lucky enough to have a chance to bring my nephew and brother-in-law, Colton and Larry Brown. We don't get to do much together, so I seized the opportunity. I don't have any kids by blood, so for me to take one and give him a nice chance is special for me. Neither had ever been turkey hunting, and at five thirty in the morning we met up, starting toward some old pasture land to set up decoys and give it a first try.

The morning was good but not great, with forty-degree weather. We found turkeys don't gobble as well as usual on cold, damp mornings. We situated ourselves up in a thicket along the edge of a field, covered with camo from head to toe. As soon as the majority of the birds began their daily routines, I made a tree call, but nothing came back at us. Then there were some clucks and cackles. Still no reply. Shortly we decided to move along, "crossing creek" and setting up farther down, but there were still no birds.

Later that morning, when we were about to stop calling, I wanted to go look one more time at a spot. When we got there, there they were, all right; and we were busted. We went down a road out and around the direction of the birds, and, sure enough old tom lit up. After several gobbles and about twenty minutes, which can seem like an hour to an eleven-year-old, the tom began coming in, but he came in to our left at the wrong spot and busted us.

I was let down, yet I was happy we even got to experience it together. Calling turkeys is sort of like sensing part of nature for a brief time when you are talking their language. The reward comes when you eat one, completing the cycle of life on your own terms with God's will. Just shooting a turkey walking about, more like target practice, is shameful and about as nonhunterly and unethical as it gets. Save it for the right way if you are inclined to do that.

The next morning, we had nonstop action. We tried almost every trick in the book, but they would not come in. I was assuming the birds were henned up. I set up behind them but could not see how thick it was between the birds and the hunters. If I had been able to we would have moved. It was just one of those things.

Well, we didn't take any birds, but I got to spend two awesome mornings trying with good family. I hope I was able to set a spark in a young man's eye, prompting him to get into the magical God-given outdoors, which is the closest thing to perfect left to behold. Get a call and give it a try! God bless you, and have a good day.

California Hunt 2012

Day 1

Today, August 17, 2012, I, Trent Johnson, Jacob Waldrop, Josh Warn, and Sami Young pulled out on Interstate 5 for our destination in Klamath National Forest. We were in search of primarily black-tailed deer, and maybe a bear. The truck was loaded down, making it look as if Jed Clampett or a bunch of redneck hippies were leaving town. The night's rest before we left was a good start at Jacob's house with some good cooking. We had pretty much gotten all our gear loaded before bed that night. This trip was gonna be bow hunting only, so as soon as we got off the plane, we started buying supplies and splitting the cost. We went to the local bow shop, tweaked our bows, and dropped in on the local sporting goods store for last-minute supplies and licenses. The town we stayed in was Redding,

California. Along the way, passing Mount Shasta and the lakes was impressive. It was apparent that California actually uses tax money on roads; they were nice.

About four hours from Redding, we arrived at Trailhead Creek Campground at 6,149 feet and started setting up tents. With enough done till later, Josh and I lit out to the hills. He was in need of knee surgery, as was I, and this was added to my just having gotten over having a pinched sciatic nerve caused by a bulging disk. Early on, we knew it was gonna be tough. But I knew that if I could make it through the New Zealand hunt prior to this hunt, this should be no problem—if I was careful.

Creeping about the mountains, mainly scouting, we saw one deer almost back at the camp. It was good visiting and hashing out life during our rest. Arriving back at camp was nice. Josh had caught some trout and grilled them with potatoes. We had a few showers with a solar shower and then did a bit of rearranging of the campsite. After that, we were quick to bed.

Day 2

At four o'clock, we were up and brewing coffee. We headed for Trinity Alps along the Pacific Coast Trail. After an hour, we all unloaded and headed out. Right off the bat, we saw a few grouse and a small buck too far off to shoot with a bow. Jacob and I soon decided to hunt our way back to the truck. It wasn't quite what I was looking for. We headed back down the mountain a few thousand feet, and we looked over a few other areas. The two of us were barely able to walk, with our bad knees. After we'd had all we could take, we headed back to camp and made some salami sandwiches and took a quick nap.

After waking, we headed down to a very small town—Cecilville, California. We went into the biggest building, and it was a store, bar, post office, and restaurant. LOL. The idea was to look road banks over for trails and maybe meet someone in town. Sam had already warned us to stay away from town, and I had assured him, based on my experience with my many travels around the world and country, that this place wouldn't be any worse than anywhere I had been. Blending in and getting along with the locals is all in how you present yourself and the words that come out of your mouth. We fell right in with hippies and local folks that we saw. One old gold miner came in, and he fit the part. We could smell his body odor from twenty yards.

On our way back up the mountain, we saw a small creek running off the mountain, and on each side was a decent game trail. I told Jacob we'd start here and see where the animals were coming from. About a forty-five-minute hike in, we ran into some small grass openings along the slow-moving creek. Thick, dark timber stood all around on steep slopes. There were a lot of crisscrossing trails and fresh droppings. Instinct led us to slow down; we needed to anyway because of our knees. We sat down, and I remembered I had a cow elk call in my bag. I said to Jacob, "I want to try something." I blew a call, and two minutes later, a deer ran to us, coming within twenty feet. It was a big doe.

We sat a bit longer, but we were soon up and climbing. I have always felt the need to go to the top when I am in the mountains. I also like to explore the bottoms. Frankly, I don't like leaving any stone unturned. The climb was tough enough. We stopped about every twenty-five yards to let the old tickers catch up and laugh at each other's pain.

With just enough daylight left to start the knee-shattering climb, or slide, down, we headed that way. Soon we split up where we had called the doe, and we finished out the day still hunting. I moved two times and couldn't seem to be happy with where I was sitting. After I was finally feeling content and had sat still for a bit, out came some chipmunks scurrying around. Then a bird that looked like a cross between a magpie and a blue jay spotted me where I was kinda hidden in some sticks. It landed about ten yards above my head and commenced to raise all kinds of Cain. Soon another arrived, and another, until twenty-five or more had gathered above me, raising Cain to the point that I thought my head was gonna explode. I stood up, slammed a limb against the tree, and got them to fly away.

Suddenly it was so quiet you could hear a chipmunk fart at twenty yards. Now scanning for deer, I felt something on my leg. I almost pooped my pants! Some black cow ants had gone up my pant leg. They left me slapping like crazy, trying to kill them before they reached ole crown jewel area. I finally resorted to dropping my pants to my ankles and having my second battle for the day. Now dark was falling, and I was guessing there were probably some deer sleeping up hill, watching my strange actions.

Down the hill, I met up with Jacob. I learned his hunt had been interrupted by bumblebees wanting to go into a hole at the base of the tree he had sat down by. Back at camp, it was dark and no one was there, so we hoped someone had taken a deer. It turned out, sure enough, that Trent gotten a four-pointer. It was his first blacktail. Jacob and I peeled some taters, fried some eggs, mixed it all up, and then added some sausage for supper that night. We also fed the deer that came up each night at the camp. They would eat almost anything. It was fun experimenting, seeing what they wouldn't turn down. They loved any kind of candy.

Day 3

I was woken up about three thirty in the morning by deer stomping around my tent a few feet away. For real! So, at four o'clock, I got up, hollering, "Good morning, world!" After slamming four Red Bulls down in lieu of coffee and eating four Snickers bars, we headed out to hunt. I eased up the mountain before daylight and got settled in my spot. I liked the spot but not the place I was sitting, so after one and a half hours, I decided to move farther up the mountain to find a more comfy place.

About three hundred yards up, I spooked some quail. A bit farther along, a full-velvet trophy buck stood broadside. Of course, he was too far away. I ranged him at eighty-four yards and had sighted my new Hoyt Vector from Star Pawn only to sixty yards. I drew, climbed high, and released an arrow and missed. It went just above his back.

I moved up a bit farther and saw three more bucks and a doe at 187 yards. After sitting for an hour or so longer, I saw the challenges of the bow. I was sitting in a bowl, sort of, in very rough country with thick trees, making it a good spot to stay hidden from people one mile up, on the Pacific Coast Trail, and one and a half miles down, where other hunters were taking the easy road out to hunt.

Stalking about through alders, slowly, I saw some deer in the next meadow. They were all does and yearlings. I was able to move through without being seen. Then I began seeing a good bit of bear sign. The terrain was getting steeper and higher, and I had to stop many times to let my heart catch up to my body and allow my ankles to rest after being on my toes.

Soon I jumped a small fawn, and I made it to the top about eleven in the morning. It was beautiful, as the top always is in the mountains, so I had to kick back, rest, and just take it in. Peeking over the other side was a fine place to hunt, with some nice meadows full of the things I'd watched the deer eat, surrounded by rough country. I marked the spot on my GPS for the future, in hopes of finding a better way back, and I headed down the mountain in a different direction, through big timber and deadfall. Then it appeared I had found some deer in a "kick ya butt place," like the ones I always find. I never luck upon some easy-to-get-to place.

It didn't take long till I spooked some bedded deer out of deadfall. Then there he was; a nice big buck stood and then ran about forty-five yards from under the big base of a fallen tree. I was able to get a shot off, but he was fast, and I didn't have time to range him. I was shooting about forty-five degrees down. It didn't help that my sling got in the way of my sight and my peep sight needed twisting just a bit. It seemed I couldn't win for losing today, but I was gonna have time to enjoy it. Sitting there, I was having a tough time accepting that I had not gotten one of those nice bucks. They were really nice for blacktails.

Somewhere about halfway down, I had a small log roll out from under me as I stepped on it, slamming me hard on my back and knocking my breath out of me. I was lucky I had my pack on and no limbs had pierced my back. I did manage to skin and hurt my arm pretty badly. I finally got to the road and got Jacob to come pick me up, thanks to Midland radios, and we headed back to camp.

At camp, soon after our arrival, the game warden showed up. It turned out that Trent was not supposed to separate the antlers from the carcass. Sam had already left to go to town with the meat, so they came back to see if our story was the same as theirs. They were respectable, though the first man didn't use much common sense about the whole thing, which is a whole story in itself for sure.

That evening, Jake and I lit out again with a climb. We split up, and I sat in a spot where three trails came together. I moved three times before I was satisfied. I piled some limbs up, and dirt as well, to make a seat. I ended up seeing thirteen deer—one at five yards, which made my day. None were bucks, though. They passed all around me. Jake saw eighteen deer, and seven were bucks. He swore that one at 160 yards was the biggest buck he had ever seen, and he named him "Grandpappy." We just had to sit and watch with binoculars. Can ya say, "Where is the gun?"

Day 4

That night, before the hunt, Jake and I did a bit of road scouting in the truck, using my GPS to try to find a route closer to the spot where we found some deer. We ended up finding a road that went to the top, crossing the Pacific Crest Trail. My GPS showed that we were 1.4 miles from the spot. We went back to camp for sleep and came back the next morning at three thirty for a hike in. It worked out nicely. We worked our way into the bowl, slowly picking our route as we went. Each picked a spot and sat down for a still hunt. Later we stalked about, finding some good places for a few pictures of ourselves, and then we got in the sun for a nap. It was cool.

We headed along the mountainside, stalking in thick timber, seeing a few does. We had heard a bear in there earlier and could have shot one if we had seen it. I can't say it was all fun, however, considering the pain our knees were delivering.

I found a spot where I felt I had a decent chance. I went to work breaking limbs out of the way down the game trail. I built a nice seat out of some rocks. There was about four hours of daylight left. Jacob went to sit at the spot where he had seen Grandpappy.

After bout ten minutes of sitting down, a four-pointer came out at thirty yards, so I released an arrow and dropped him in his tracks. I was happy then, with so much time left that I hoped for a bear. I stayed put to give Jacob a chance, but he had no luck. We skinned and deboned my deer. I used black pepper to keep flies off him till the hunt was over. I always bring black pepper when I am hunting in warm weather. Climbing out of that canyon after all hours of the day is an experience we will remember, and I feel it was well worth the time spent with a man I call my brother.

All in all, it was a good hunt with time spent with old friends and some new ones. I got my eyes on new ground, hunting a new species. This hunt delivered a new challenge, which I so live for and always thank God to have enjoyed—even when I am in pain.

Missouri Turkey Hunt with Tiffany

Day 1

Hello, folks. I want to write a little story about one of my favorite things to do—helping someone else take his or her first turkey or deer and sharing in the new excitement. This time, after some good and bad luck hunting turkeys at home, I was determined to help my girlfriend of two years, Tiffany Edwards, to get her first bird.

Shortly after going to Texas and shooting some nice birds, Kenneth

Manes invited me to Missouri, and that's how this hunt transpired. So off we went, all four of us, in Kenny's new truck. We arrived at the small house of a man who had some land leased for us to hunt. We quickly took turns going to see where we would start to hunt the next morning and to set up our blinds. Here you can't hunt past noon. This I didn't know, or most likely I would not have gone there. I probably won't go back.

The first morning was cool and so windy a turkey would have been lucky to hear us at ten yards. We were hunting in a Conservation Reserve Program (CRP) field. CRP is a government program that provides funds for planting native grasses to benefit wildlife and restore native species. We were on the edge of a wooded area, with a thick area behind us and a freshly planted and disked field next to us. We had seen a gobbler in this field while setting up our blind. I already figured this was where they would be. I assumed we would see one later in the morning, after the gobblers had done their business. That evening was killing me, as we were sitting idle at the house. We passed some time with a movie and ended up meeting a man down the street with some souped-up muscle cars. I managed to talk him into burning some rubber down the street with Tiffany in one of them.

Day 2

We were up early for a forty-five-minute drive to the hunting location. The first word out of my mouth was "crap." It was cold and windy, with a light rain—all things that made me feel like it would take all the luck God gave me to get a turkey out of a tree. We were in a blind, and I was darn glad for that. I managed to let my back get damp, so I was about to freeze to death. About nine thirty in the morning we heard one fly off the roost right in front us. Then, later, another came by close. Both headed to the field next door. I figured they wanted to stretch and feed on some seed. We sat together till noon, dozing off now and then. We didn't see any other gobblers, but we did hear some way off in the distance. Then it was back to the house for torture until the next morning. We did ride out to try to hear some turkeys roosting in another location and to look a bit for morel mushrooms. Then we went and had a good steak in a nearby farm town.

Day 3

We were up really early again. The day was cold and much calmer, darker, and gloomier than the previous day. We had moved the blind to an area closer to where we had heard the birds gobble. Sure enough, there were a lot of gobbles close by. It seemed we might stand a good chance. Not! The tom we heard gobbled his way in the opposite direction, toward the planted field that we were not allowed to hunt. We stuck it out and saw a lot of deer. It ended up being a nice morning, and it's always good when you hear some gobbling.

With ten minutes of legal hunting time left, we decided to stalk to where we had seen two gobblers. We had a small creek running through the middle of the CRP field for cover, so I felt we had a chance. We slipped slowly through high patches of grass. About halfway down was an old house that had fallen in, with some old trucks nearby. We squatted down, and I tried to call them up. I knew they had to be within fifty yards. After several minutes, I determined they must not be interested and moved up the hill unseen. Still totally convinced, we inched our way back to where they stood. After a few minutes with no sign of a turkey, just like that, we spotted them fifteen yards away, just behind some brush and tall grass. Seeing us as soon as we saw them, they lit out. I hollered, "Shoot!" and Tiffany did, but she missed. Man, with the pressure of the end of the hunt drawing near, time spent, and the fact that I knew she wanted one badly, our hearts were broken—more hers than mine.

Hunting is firstly about the hunt and the experience, and sometimes it's a learning experience. I needed to be much more patient, but in this situation, we didn't have the time, legally. The property owners nearby most likely wouldn't appreciate a one-thirty bird. So again we moved the blind back to the original spot for the last morning.

Day 4

Well, this was it—our last chance. We were in the blind with a cold, light wind to start and the sun coming and going. Sure enough, we got some birds gobbling way off in front of us and back where we had been. We were trying to head the gobblers off from going to the plowed field where the hens were gathering every day. I called until I about wore the call out, without overcalling. Decoys were out, and I produced every sound I could. No gobblers. So I decided, as I have many times before, to get out and move. Stalking and calling a turkey can be almost impossible, but not totally. Slipping along in the fields, we saw three hens. We had pushed them off their nests. I don't really like doing that, but it wasn't intentional. They come back, but they are more vulnerable to predators, and low temperatures can cause problems for the exposed eggs.

We decided to go back to the blind and finish the last half hour. We were almost there when we I saw three toms strutting, as we call it, and a half dozen hens gathered in a nearby field. I knew it wasn't going to work with them being all henned up. Now it was around 11:43. We decided to stalk in, but about one hundred yards in, we were busted, and they all lit out as if they had seen us a hundred times.

Back at the blind, with less than an hour left, I told Tiff to hunt it out. I went to get the car and come back to pick her and the blind up and call it a good try. When I topped the hill on the road, I could see about two hundred yards to where we went in, and what did I see but a big tom coming off the neighboring property, heading right down the line toward where Tiff was sitting. It was about twelve forty-five now. I stopped the car, killed the engine, and sat and waited. Five minutes later I heard *boom!* Down the hill I saw that Tiff had made it happen in the last ten minutes of the hunt. Wow. We were stoked and kind of in disbelief. That definitely made it a memorable high-five moment. It was a good bird with one-and-a-quarter-inch spurs and about a nine-and-a-half-inch beard. That's why I almost always hunt it out. Kenny and Bonnie saw some birds but couldn't seal the deal. But we all were happy the trip saw Tiff get her first bird. And I made friends with a great man—Mr. Kenny. I ended up making a nice wing, fan, and beard mount for Tiff.

Mexico Turkey Hunt 2013

Gould Turkey

Day 1

Hello, folks. May 5, 2013, was Cinco de Mayo in Mexico. I was headed there to hopefully finish my world slam for turkeys. I flew to Tucson, Arizona, where I planned to meet Joe Bittner from Los Angeles, California, at the airport. From there we planned to drive down to Douglas, Mexico, and meet Jay, Scott, and Coburn, and then drive over the border and ninety-six miles south into the mountains, up to an elevation of about five thousand feet. After leaving the road there, we drove about forty-five minutes down ranch roads using Polaris Rangers and one truck. We were hunting where Steven Rinella from the MeatEater series hunted his bird also. One guide from here became his cameraman.

Soon we split up and headed out. The wind was kicking, and soon we saw a few Coues deer—does. Every second of that ride was like one you pay for down at the Grand Canyon—rocky and rough. At the first stop, we got out of the Ranger to see if we could hear a bird, and we walked about eighty yards from the Ranger and hit a call. Right by the Ranger, a few hens lit up, and then we saw two jakes on the other side. This was a good thing, because all we could do was sit and watch and hope they would go by, because we didn't have a gun in hand. I wasn't really wanting a jake yet.

Later, farther up the mountain, we saw two gobblers out near the road so we sped through and jumped out about five hundred yards up the road, hiked up another two hundred, and set up, cameras and all. At our first call, they lit up with a gobble downhill, and soon there were some hens behind us also. About thirty minutes into it, we still could not get them to come in, and when darkness set in, they roosted across the canyon. We slipped out and headed in. Coming in, we saw two birds hanging out at camp. Joe took both with a longbow at twenty yards near our blind and decoys, and he got some awesome video footage. One of these completed his royal slam, leaving one needed for the world slam. He got off four shots on first bird, which was fighting the jake decoy. We watched some footage and ate spaghetti and salad and hit the sack (which I was ready to do).

Day 2

We were out of bed a few hours before daylight, sucking coffee and a snack down. We started through the gates and up rocky roads to where we had roosted the birds. We put plenty of time in before daylight. We sat under the stars and counted nine shooting stars while we stared at the moon as it rose above the mountaintops with binoculars. I call this "stopping and smelling the roses" in life and "acknowledging that life and God are good!" Sure enough, right at daylight, he gobbled! We set up and started the game and got one more to gobble while on the roost. Then we heard birds fly down, and hens were clucking in the distance, but nary a bird came in for about an hour. So we made the roller-coaster ride all about through the mountains, looking for more birds, calling now and then. We then came back to again try the ones we had seen at daylight. This was still no good, so we shot in for a burrito and a nap. Upon waking, it wasn't too good. We had really high winds. For evening we elected to try a different spot, and Joe came with us. We stopped along the way, and right off the bat we got a gobble. All together we set up, but the bird just gobbled in the other direction! I guess we didn't sound sexy enough, so Joe, the primitive bowman, went on down to his blind.

We stopped along a meadow and got the dogs out, set up the camera, and let out some yelps, clucks, cackles, purrs, gibble-gers—anything. But we heard nothing until about an hour passed by and, across the way, one gobbled! About twenty minutes later, there he was, slipping through the trees and eventually right up to the decoys. About forty yards out, he stopped, drummed, spit, and strutted all about, and I wanted to get some video, but he didn't come close enough. He ended up cutting up the hill. Now I was really bummed. I swear I will never do that again until I take my first Gould's.

Time was slipping by, and we went to some different places. We split up to try to roost a bird. No one ended up with one roosted. Joe called one in also, but he didn't get the shot with his bow. We marked the road where a bird roosted, and we headed in for supper. After killing a few scorpions, I slipped into my sleeping bag and slept like a baby.

The next morning, we found our marker in the road and slipped very carefully down toward the roosted bird as best we could without lights, hoping not to spook him. We settled in—with good timing, because it was about five minutes till he gobbled on his own. It was the first time without us giving him a check call. From that time, I think he gobbled at least one hundred times in twenty minutes before he flew down—sometimes five times in a row. It sounded as if he was checking himself against every little sound in the mountains. Unfortunately, the hens were with him, and they came down first, about two hundred yards away. Of course, he followed.

We could see them, with him gobbling now and then, strutting, and drumming. We had only one hen decoy out, and Garth called well behind me, about twenty yards, and I helped now and then with my slate. Between us and him, there was a fairly deep dried-up creek bed, and luckily we got him to commit and move in our direction until he hit that creek. I think he just didn't want to come out and start to walk down. Finally he did, and the creek bed was about fifty yards from me. At this point, I used cover to raise my gun and I vowed to take the next shot, if presented, with or without camera footage.

He went down and did not come up, and I was afraid he had walked down the creek. Garth did as well, so he tried to get him to gobble, and it worked. I gave a sigh of relief, because soon, there he was—out and strolling. I let him move up to what I hoped was a good range for the gun and shot. He went down, flopping all about, so I went after him, trying to hold the big boy down. Awesome action for the bird I needed to complete my world slam. He ended up having an eleven-and-a-half-inch inch beard and another beard about four inches. This was my second ever double beard, which is rare with any species. But he had small spurs; these birds don't get very big spurs, though they have very long legs and huge feet, compared to other species. We took some photos and rode in for lunch and to skin my bird for a mount. I also cleaned the meat and prepared to cook later with Jesus Daniel Hernandez Mollini, owner of the ranch in Sonora, Mexico, across the border. Elbruto was a town close by.

I didn't rest much after cleaning the bird before we were ready to go again. With one more evening and one morning left, all the other men went to separate locations to try to roost a bird for me, as did I, up the canyon. The wind was just horrible; I set up anyway and called every way I could, but there were no birds. Soon my butt, back, and legs had had enough and wanted to move, so we did, all together, slowly. I went and tried a few locations in the area every fifteen minutes for one and a half hours or so. Then it was back to my decoys and stool. I changed the location a bit and reset the decoys.

About one and a half hours later, I called up a jake and two hens and got a bit of video on my camera. The wind was so hard it blew the birds around. Soon two does, Coues deer, were feeding about one hundred yards down—one of them about thirty yards to my left. All of a sudden, they started blowing downwind of me, so I knew something was up. I saw that they were looking to my left. I saw a mature mountain lion fifty-five yards or so behind me, coming my way. He dipped into a low spot, so I got my camera up and on video mode, all the time debating on taking him. I decided just seeing him would be best this time, since I had taken one already. It was an awesome encounter—and a rare one.

Soon I heard a gobble faintly down the canyon, so I decided to sacrifice the rest of the evening to try to roost this bird, and I did so. I saw him in the tree. Back at camp, we grilled turkey over the fire pit.

Just as a note, Joe took one with a longbow on the first day, and I thanked him for making me feel bad for having a gun, but I mentioned I wanted to shoot a bird with five or six beards and said that if I saw one, I would take it any way I could. So we decided all together to go after my bird.

We slipped along the canyon's edge in dark—all four of us. Just before daylight, he gobbled on his own, plenty. We all set up fifteen yards or so away from each other, and Jay started calling. Soon we heard him pitch down, and then another was gobbling. I was waiting, and soon my heart dropped when I saw that he had pitched to the other side of the canyon and I could see him. I figured it was over. After Jay spit out some good calling with his mouthpiece, none of us could believe they had both flown across. Soon it was up to the decoys. He thumped the jake decoy and knocked it over and commenced to pounding it. After sixteen minutes of video, I put lead to its head. It was a nice finale for my second-to-last bird I needed to finish my world slam. Then, during photos, we almost fell apart when we saw that he had five beards—the longest being about nine inches—and some actual spurs! *Thank you, Jesus*, was all I can think, and I again felt overwhelmed with my experience and luck.

Hey, as I do, try to save a few bucks and go after one of your dreams. The Bible says man can do anything he imagines, and I believe it.

Setting Up Gun Sights: Don't Take a Chance to Lose a Chance

Hey, y'all! What I'm talking about is something that happens to a lot of hunters every year. Say you've been sitting for hours on your deer stand and the deer you've always wanted steps out. You take the shot with a clean miss. It is so important to take the time to sight your gun in before you hunt—and not just off the hood of your truck. Build or buy a shooting table, because you're going to need it every year. You need to shoot your gun before the season starts and make sure your scope mount is tight before you sight it in.

Learn what you can about the ballistics of the caliber of bullet you're using. You should also give your gun a good cleaning and check it a couple times during the season to make sure that it's still on target. Keep your gun in a soft gun case or anything that will protect it while in transit and keep it from moving around and possibly jarring your scope. I don't like to let anyone even hold my gun. Also be sure to keep your bullets very clean, and avoid rusty casings.

Your gun, whether it cost $150 or $5,000, will most likely take the animal you're after, but your scope is a different story. Unless you hunt out West, where there are a lot of clear cuts, you don't need to have a scope with a high power. I personally prefer a lower-power scope such as 1½× to 1¾× power. With a lower setting, I can get especially close while stalking and shooting at moving targets with both eyes open. Most importantly of all, just wait for a clear shot.

What I'm trying to get across is that if you do the things I have mentioned, you'll feel better about your hunt. You'll have the confidence to make a good shot and not go home to hear your buddies say, "Yeah, right! You missed the big one." Worse yet would be to see someone else bag the deer you shot at and missed.

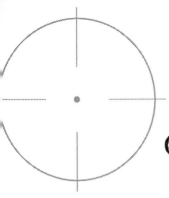

Coues Deer Hunt

Hello, folks! On December 27 I took off to start a new quest for
Coues deer and then mule deer in Chihuahua, Mexico, across
the border. We flew from Alexandria, to Dallas and then
went on to Mexico. It wasn't too bad! Once there we went through a
pretty thorough check of guns and bags. They ran mine through three
times and pretty much unpacked me. They made a big deal out of the
fact that I had only forty rounds of .300 WSM ammo and not the fifty
rounds allowed by the permit.

We got a few supplies, and after picking up a cook, we made the
250-or-so-mile trip to a ranch at 6,500 feet elevation. The ranch was
about forty-seven thousand acres. I hunted with Steve and Scott Esker
from Ohio. One of these guys held the number-five largest deer taken
with a bow in Ohio, and both had taken two deer over two hundred
inches. They would run over forty cameras to find the big one, and

then they would gang up on him. We were also with Bill Farley, another taxidermist from Missouri.

We got to the ranch and built fires in fireplaces, grabbed some grub, and visited for a short while before we hit the hay. Now, one of those ranch dogs, I think, was loco. That dog was determined to bark right outside my window, messing up the sleep I needed so badly.

Day 1

On the first day out, after getting fuller than a pregnant armadillo, we headed up the mountain. It was thirty-two degrees and windy. The heater quit on the truck—about a 1980 model Suburban—and we couldn't see out any of the windows. A few minutes into the trip, we smelled gas. We had knocked a hole in the darned truck. I was thinking, "Oh Lord, here we go." We were all out—binoculars flying and spotting scopes slinging—looking for antlers as though we had never seen a mountain before.

Hugo and I soon split up, and we spotted a shooter about a mile away. We put on a stalk, stepping now and then to make sure he was still there. We were below him so we wouldn't get spotted. We ended up about sixty yards shy of where we believed we could get a shot when Hugo stepped on a rock that rolled. Next the deer was up, going over the ridge right about time I saw his old ass in my scope. I felt sick, because that was a good deer. So then we hunted till our knees popped and our feet hurt, and we felt like sleeping every time we stopped. One time we called in two coyotes and took a shot at five hundred yards. Missed.

Hugo said he doesn't get too many that hunt like me. He said it had been about three years. Well, we ended the evening with nothing planned for the next morning and scarfed down our groceries. Shoving my feet down into my sleeping bag felt like a Chinese foot massage. The night's sleep went fairly well, though there was one staff member who snored so loudly the dogs barked at him. Then I woke up to what felt like someone blowing cold air on my butt. It seems that I managed to get my sleeping bag zipper down a good bit farther than I wanted. I also did my usual spider killing. I found only one black widow. When you add heat to an old ranch house, sometimes critters come out. I don't like sleeping with insects.

At four o'clock, the cook and I were up, and at five o'clock, I woke everyone else up. They said that in twenty-three years, they never had a hunter wake them. We tore up some coffee and an omelet before day two.

Day 2

This morning we made it in just before daybreak. We were glassing a hill about a half mile high and two miles long. It wasn't too long before I spotted two deer, and even with 22×50 binoculars, it was tough to tell how big they were. At a half mile away, even big antlers can look small. I knew I would have to get closer, so I watched a while to make sure no other deer were nearby. Then I decided to make a stalk.

After lining up an approximate vantage point, I headed up. Quickly it became a challenge. I knew cows were near, so I skirted out around, trying to keep the wind in my favor as I went. Then, looking back for my spotter across the hill, I laughed because there was no way I could see him in his camo. Down the hill in the other direction, I saw Scott and Javier coming in my direction. At that point, I assumed they had seen me some deer, and they had. I quickly put my hunter orange on and felt as if we could get in a fix. As it turned out, the deer went behind me. So I guess one could say we all got skunked.

Then came the huffing and puffing walk, and we glassed the ridges for four hours to no avail. We didn't see any exciting sign. I was losing heart, since I had worked so hard for a shot at a deer, only to not get it. That's not like me. But it could have been him this morning. Scott said it was a good buck that they saw run.

Driving in with a fuel leak in the truck, we stopped for a lunch of fish. We regrouped and headed to a location one of the cowboys told us about, but none of us saw a deer. I almost got a shot at a coyote. The ironic part of the day was that I told them we would get rain while I was here. Bill said that it hadn't rained but once in the twenty years–plus since he had been here, and that was just a few minutes one night. Well, it rained and sleeted on them today. Supper looked like thick slices of ham and potato soup. Javier owns a restaurant but comes to cook for the hunters for a break.

Day 3

After breakfast, we headed out, and this morning and it was cold with heavy frost on the ground. It wasn't too long before our socks were wet, and each time we stopped for glassing during most of the morning, our feet were cold. We stayed out all day and had to cover ten miles. It wasn't like ten miles of walking down the highway either; we were glassing ridges, areas under trees, and canyon crevices, all while rolling rocks aside to look for fresh tracks. This led me even more into the excitement of a killer, because of the kind of deer here. Both guides said it was worse than they had ever seen it on the ranch. This was beautiful country, no doubt. We went dead to the top and soaked up the view. Hugo said it was the longest walk he ever made with a hunter. We didn't see a single deer, but it was a fine day in the mountains.

Day 4

We awoke with a burrito breakfast, coffee, and orange juice, still a bit tired from yesterday. I always overdo breakfast for hunts—especially when in the mountains. On another note, I always bring an extra pair of socks, and yesterday I took my extra pair out and needed them for the heavy frost. They are also good if you feel a blister coming on. It's best when you are hunting the mountain to keep the what-ifs in mind and prepare somewhat. Don't overdo the pack you are toting around, though, because it will slow you up.

I knew that if I didn't get a Coues deer, at least I would still trek the hills. It's hard to gather the desire to keep hunting when the guides say it's the worst ranch they have ever seen. This is as close to hunting a needle in a haystack I've seen yet on a deer hunt.

After we unassed the truck, we got to where we planned to sit and saw a few deer—three does. We waited, but there were no bucks. We even counted every hair on one deer's head. The terrain was a little more hilly and easy to walk today. And walk we did—again. Today we got a couple of quick fifteen-minute naps, but Hugo got thirty minutes. I lost fifteen minutes because of his snoring! The hardest part of today was that I was not informed that we would be staying out all day, so hunger was my friend all day long. We saw a few deer this evening again.

Back at camp, I flopped my butt at the dinner table and quickly let them know I wanted two steaks and two of everything. So, for the New Year, I was fuller than a gray dog tick on a hound dog.

I was a bit worried when the owner of the ranch came by and left a big bottle of tequila that I wanted no part of. I hoped the rest of the guys felt the same. Tomorrow morning would be the last hunt for Coues deer. This was one of the two deer I still needed to have taken one of each deer species in the world. Tonight's sleep was going to be interesting, with my legs having been cut and poked to death by briars and thorns, and my belly being the size of a basketball.

Day 5

Well, New Year's night for me was spent wanting to crack the skull of a ranch dog's head for barking into 2014. I ended up telling them that one more night with no sleep just wasn't an option for me.

It was our last morning for Coues deer. We went out to hunt and ended up not going where we had scouted all the day before. We went back to a spot we had already hunted. Yep, yep—no deer, no deer sign, no anything. It looked like Coues deer wasn't in the plan for me in 2013, but starting 2014 in the mountains, in a new place, hunting, still was not bad for sure. I hope the money I spent serves others well in some way. At the very least I had made some new friends along the way.

About three in the afternoon, we decided just to ride around roads with the truck and glass along the hillsides for whatever. We tried to call in a few coyotes a few times. About twenty minutes till dark,

I spotted four juvenile coyotes in an opening on steep cliffs way up high. I went after them; I couldn't see why I shouldn't. I pushed myself to climb and was soon getting hot, breathing so hard my chest was popping and my legs were burning. I was within 250 yards—plenty close for a shot—but I decided to get a bit closer for a spot among the rocks. They had dropped into crevices, and there was no shot there. Dark fell really fast, and I had no light. So it was a hell of a workout and an even better attempt.

I had shot a few javelinas before and it wasn't the end of the world, but to not take a Coues deer was tough! It's not always about the kill. However, since this was the only time I had ever paid to hunt, it was different. It didn't hurt to wake up and go to bed with a cook, for sure. I guess I will have to plan another try for their deer. The most damaging part was that we missed the rut. Either way, I thank God I was here or I was still able to climb the mountain. I wish you all a good day in the woods, mountains, lake, or whatever. Just go spend the day or month with Mother Nature.

Desert Mule Deer Hunt—Mexico

January 2, 2014

Day 1

Hello, folks. Well, I came up empty on Coues, so we headed down for a three-hour drive farther for a desert mule deer hunt. Fifty-six miles of the drive was on a dirt road to the ranch.

Matae has been managing Gemelos Ranch for ten years, so we are feeling good about the hunt. On the drive down, we had to pick up a few more groceries and get some flats fixed. The ride was slow at times when we were stuck behind some trailers loaded with horses, plus we banged our heads on the truck roof a few times while going down the dirt road. When we got to the ranch entrance, the gate was locked, so we had to take the fence down farther up the mountain to get through.

To add to the day, the cook, along with the guides, took a wrong road. We stopped, fired off a few shots, and then a few more, and luckily got to the ranch in the afternoon. It wasn't long before the cook had a meal ready, so we ate and headed out to the hills with about two hours left to hunt. I quickly saw the need to wear brush chaps, with the cactus and bushes resembling rose bushes and prickly pear. We hadn't been sitting long when we heard a shot; we then heard another twenty minutes later. I didn't see anything, and Hugo was about ready to get in my lap, since he needed to wear more clothes. We walked back to camp and saw Bill, who was back from his hunt with a coyote. Soon Matae, Steve, and Scott showed up. Steve had taken a great dark-horned buck that scored 154.7/8. It was an awesome evening for a start, and they got it all on video. It was a 312-yard shot straight through the body. The buck had been bumping four does along the mountainside. Our sore butts ran out, but we made it through.

Day 2

Well, after the orchestra of snoring, coughs, sniffs, and, well, you know, from burritos, I managed to get a few winks in. Up early, we ended up on the mountain before daylight in a 20 mph wind creeping through shale rock and ocotillo, which gets over ten feet high and six feet wide in places, with thorns up to three inches long. We settled in, and it got cold fast. The sun soon broke over the hills, and we could no longer see in that direction, so after about forty-five minutes, we decided to move up a couple of hundred yards for a better spot to glass. I did not really like it though.

Creeping along to about the sixty-five-yard mark, we spotted deer coming right at us. We knelt by each other and became still in the wide open. It was a spike buck. Hugo said "shoot," but I wouldn't. I didn't understand at the time that they cull the spikes. Soon Hugo said, "I hear something behind us." I saw in his eyes the surprise about the time he looked back and said, "Grande deer." I turned and was shocked to see a 5×5 standing there eating on a bush at twenty yards max. As soon as he turned his head, I stood up and aimed but could not find him in my scope. I had turned it up to look at the spike, so I ran it down to 4×, and then the sun blocked me. I finally figured it out and took a shot. I got a hit! After resighting my gun dead on at two hundred yards and being ready to shoot as far as six hundred yards if need be, I ended up shooting a buck at forty yards. I decided that my last few prayers had made me a believer in the power of prayer. Now I really did believe! I looked up, and Hugo said, "I really want you to shoot that spike," so I did. It was about 125 yards away, running up a hill. They cull all the spikes on the ranch. I was on cloud nine for sure!

Hugo and I both felt as if two hundred pounds had just come off our backs, and a great feeling of relief came over us. The buck wasn't 200 inches but was every bit of 145 or so. I'd find out tomorrow.

We gutted both deer and hid them in the shade. I cut the head off, tied it to my Sitka pack, and lit out down the hill for a three-mile hike back to the ranch. We didn't have a truck. I gave the cowboy my Magellan raincoat and some gloves, and Hugo my chaps. I then convinced them to take horses to go get meat for them. When they got back, they spent the entire day cutting up and hand washing meat in a five-gallon bucket of water and then salting it to hang. It was a forty-five-yard jerky hanging.

Hugo worked his butt off while an eleven-year-old boy and I went out for javelinas. We soon came up on three javelinas, and I tried some long-range shooting with no luck, so we slipped within about 175 yards and thumped one with a Ballistic Tip in the head. We tried to get the boy a shot at something; we even called coyotes, but none came in. We sat there till dark and ended up with nothing for him. He was upset. We "no comprende" for sure.

We came back to the ranch at dark. Bill Farley had seen a good buck but passed because it was only a 4×3, "but it was big," he said. Steve and Scott Esker and Matae had seen one and chased it for a mile hike–plus. The Esker boys had taken five bucks over 200 inches since 2009. That's 2,710 inches of antler total for the record book between them. I am proud to have hunted with them. Maybe I can pick up on some of their hunting secrets from the Midwest and now call them friends. That goes the same for Bill Farley.

The international owner of the ranch finally showed up with a generator to help with light and hot water for our weekly showers. We scored my deer at 151.2/8 and headed to bed.

Day 3

It's amazing how lazy a man gets once he has achieved his goal. I got up and ate with everyone and then headed back to bed for a bit. I finished working on deer capes to give Bill a bit more hunting time, and I let Hugo use my gun to go hunt javelinas on his own. He was excited; he said no one had ever let him do that. After pillaging around the camp, the twins came in about lunch time with four javelinas. They wanted two shoulder mounts and two full-body mounts, and the cook wanted meat for supper, so we went at it, skinning till just after dark.

Day 4

After a night of practically no sleep, I broke out of bed anyway and walked up the hill to see the sun come up, saying a few prayers and asking just to see a few deer. I set up three spots and tried to call coyotes with no luck, but it was an awesome morning. It was my last day of winter to hold a gun for a deer of any kind till the season of 2014.

Back at camp, I decided I wanted to go to Chihuahua for a night, get a room, and get some good rest. That I did, until I stepped outside and heard a racket in the hall. Then I got my butt caught in my Fruit of the Looms when the door closed behind me and locked automatically. It was about nine at night. Now, this was a fix, so down to the front desk I went in my underwear, in front of everyone. To the right of the reception desk was the packed-full dining room, which just so happened to have glass walls. So there were at least twenty people who got a good story to tell that night. I just took it in stride with a smile. What else could I do?

I rested well and was up at seven o'clock. I showered, ate, and headed to Mass in an awesome church nearby. When the service was over, I hit the streets walking, seeing what I could of the city of Chihuahua and taking in the culture.

I would be boarding the plane at one thirty to fly home if there were no problems with my gun. I had no problems at the Quality Inn I stayed at. My hunt and experience here and the friends I made were well worth the trip—another one to remember. This city seemed to be like most, with people just trying to ride through their short time on Earth that God had given them. For me, each day is a special one. If you can, make some time to see the planet God has given you. Better yet, see the wild side with Mother Nature.

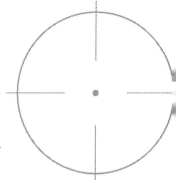

Amazon Dream

Red Tail Catfish

On January 12, after Tiffany dropped me off at AEX, I took an hour-long flight to Dallas, Texas. Then it was two hours to Miami and four-hour layover before the five-and-a-half-hour flight to Manaus, Brazil. I was about to begin my adventure to Rio Travessao River in the Amazon. Seeing the Amazon River was a dream I'd had since I was a kid. I would be primarily fishing, but I hoped to get to hunt with indigenous people as well.

This was my first time in Miami International Airport, and I didn't hear much English spoken there. I'm not sure if they had ever seen Lacrosse rubber boots with pant legs tucked into them either. They looked at me as if I had no legs. I did have a great dinner for an airport at Las Vegas Cuban Cuisine. My body was catching a bit of hell adjusting to the antimalarial pills (about $200 for twenty pills). It seemed some of the people at the airport thought I was the foreigner because of my southern accent and slang words.

The flight to Manaus, Brazil would take five hours. Other fishermen and I were met at the airport and cleared customs without any problems. We arrived at a tropical hotel on the water. It was a huge five-star hotel with twelve-foot-wide hallways and two-hundred-yard-long halls. We rested for a glorious two hours before packing up after an awesome tropical breakfast.

Day 1

At the airport, I skimmed through with my luggage being just under the thirty-pound weight limit. It was my first trip on a float plane, much less being over the Amazon jungle, so I was stoked and couldn't believe that, after all my life, I was finally here! The flight was about an hour long before we landed on the river.

We were greeted by Wellington, who runs the camp, and on getting there, I couldn't see how it could have been any better. Wellington had his whole family helping. It was about as homelike as you could make a place on a small island in the Amazon jungle, surrounded by rocky waterfalls. After meeting his whole family and the native guides, we quickly started rigging our gear to go fishing after a quick lunch, regardless of our lack of sleep. We got sprinkled on a bit but missed the rain and headed to the river. I was a bit flustered on discovering that I was somehow missing a part of my new Ambassador 7000.

On the water, I came to realize that I was actually here, in the Amazon. There were new sights, sounds, smells, and landscapes that I had wanted for so long to experience but could only image what it would be like. There were thick groves of forest along the banks of the river, with parrots flying overhead. All kinds of insects were chattering inside the forest. My fishing partner was George, a Canadian who also has US citizenship. He had fished the river before, just not at this spot; therefore, he was a great asset. Not many people have been at this location of the Rio Travessao. Wellington had us pay the natives to enjoy this spot, and now we were looking forward to the adventure it would bring for the next seven days.

Soon the sun broke out, and I caught my first piranha, later a pacu, and then a jundia. Unfortunately, I got my bait too high and lost one of my best topwater baits. Mr. George caught a few peacock bass.

Day 2

After breakfast, the morning was cool and foggy. We went up the river, starting out at a hairy spot in rough water. After about one and a half hours of running river, I was ready to fish. We started fishing around rocks in front of and behind some falls. Mr. George hung into a good peacock bass and later another. I had only a few hits. I was getting frustrated, and we figured out why. It turned out my Power Pro line was spooking the fish in the clear water, so I changed to my invisi-line and then started catching some. A few minutes later, we turned up a split, running into river that was narrower and denser. There we ran into a few caimans, and a bunch of beautiful blue morpho butterflies caught our eye.

After a few casts more, I caught another jundia. It was a long way back to the camp through rough water, so we headed for open water with a bit more depth and used cut bait and circle hooks. Right off, we were getting hits, and we had a caiman slip up behind us, looking for a handout. It was about five feet long. Then my line took off, and we knew that what I had was not a piranha. After about twenty minutes, I got him up. It was a redtail catfish—one of my main targets—a beautiful fish! Once George got him in the boat, I was a happy, happy man. He was about thirty pounds, which was good enough for me.

Soon the line was running again, and I got a really good piranha—about seven pounds. The sun started going down, and it was about this time we were thinking about heading in. Then Mr. George's line ran and he landed a sorubim—a light brown catfish with jagged black bars on its back. It was about twenty pounds. Today was a good day for peacock, now that I had gotten a few lessons.

Back at camp, we got some bad news. Wellington's wife had been stung by a stingray in the water, and she had been in pain all day. This meant we were going to lose our cook. All of us got all our antibiotics out to try to help her. We'll see.

Day 3

I got up and about, feeling a bit less energetic than yesterday. We grubbed down on breakfast, and I changed partners and went with Egor. He started with a topwater bait, and I did so as well. We threw our arms out till about eleven thirty in the morning. Egor caught two trairas. I hooked one, but I had taken my leader off to try to get more action. Most fish here have teeth, so the line gets cut easily. We decided to find some shade and have lunch so the guide could get some rest from working the boat through the current with a paddle.

Two more hours into it, we decided to go for big cats early. I had nearly decided peacock bass weren't in God's plan for me. After we caught a few piranhas, we decided to try a bit longer and worked our way back. That was when we passed George and Tom. Tom, a Missouri boy, had gotten the end of his thumb cut off by a piranha. They were headed in to try to fix it and maybe sew it back on.

We hit a spot and started slinging. Egor caught a seven-pound peacock bass. *Damn!* Of course, I backlashed and then threw again. Yep, I hung up my jig. I got it back out and hooked another one—one nice enough to break my rod tip and get away. I threw back in, and *bam!* I put him in the boat. It was another dream come true! I was ready to take the picture and I decided to wash it off to keep it from sand getting in the boat. Yep, sure enough, I lost him. But I recovered, putting six more in the boat, with the biggest peacock bass being twelve pounds. *Yahoo!* Egor said he had never seen anyone do that. Later we attempted catfishing as I lay on cloud nine, happy, happy, happy!

Day 4

Sitting there after dinner on the river's edge, with the full moon breaking past the tops of the trees, I decided I would attempt to explain my day. I had given up a day on the river to go into the jungle where some streams met the river. We were checking for spawn, and while at that, we came across where some peccaries had been. We later saw a print that looked like a calf's. As it turned out, we ended up tracking it; we were just trying to see it, though. One native did, but I didn't! They call them tapirs, and they look like huge aardvarks. The jungle was super thick and full of things we always had to be conscious about.

Farther along, we heard the sound of a crested guan. It makes a noise that vibrates. This is one thing that I was kind of shocked by. It was a familiar sound from the jungle in Mexico near Campeche. The native guide—named Lucas in English—held his nose to make a calling bark at the bird. It worked, and the bird came from two hundred yards to fifty yards, even though we never saw it. I think turning off my GoPro scared it because of the beeps.

One thing about these natives is that they pay extra attention to detail while in the woods. If you watch closely enough, you will see they are different from someone who hunts for pleasure, as they hunt because they have to for food.

We struck out on the trail of a smaller animal—a paca. The native, Lucas, sounded as if he was whistling a song, and the thing ran right to him. When it came in a third time, I almost got a picture.

It was interesting to learn about the things you don't want to touch and things you can. We also learned some habits of these animals and what made the sounds we heard. We headed back to camp for lunch, and then we went out again for some fishing. As Wellington had said would happen, his wife stomped us. We proceeded to get wet when a storm blew in, as happens there almost every day.

Day 5

We went out a bit late for my standards. Getting started, we began fishing for bait and then catfishing. Twenty minutes into it, George locked on to what we figured was a piraiba catfish, which can get up to three hundred pounds! Because of the way his drag ran and the way the boat was moving, we were stoked. Right when we assumed we were about to see him, he got off the line! Man, what a letdown!

We tried a bit more, till the current got strong and the wind got even stronger, and then we went after a different pacu than the big one I caught. After a few hours, I caught two, and then George caught one. While trying to catch more of those, we both brought in two more species we had never caught before. They were not very big but were different.

Toward evening, while fishing for peacock bass, we ended up close to some howler monkeys. Unfortunately, I thought I was recording the awesome sounds, but I forgot to press the button on my camera one more time. We ended up catching a few and losing a few. I lost a traira, I think, right at the boat. Man, I was sick! This was one I had hoped of getting; it is also called a wolf fish.

We finished the evening with catfishing. After finding a hole deep enough that piranhas weren't in it to cut our lines and steal our bait, we gave it a shot, but we had no luck. Just a short time before heading in, we got stormed on.

Day 6

We started out for catfish and piraiba in a deep hole close to camp, up the rapids. About thirty minutes into it, my line started flying. I reeled when I could and pulled on the rod, and he was pulling the boat a bit. About the time I felt we were going to see the fish, the line broke. It was 150-pound Power Pro line. Later we drifted and caught some pacus on small tackle. These are small fish about the size of bull bream, but silver, white, and thin. We went into a creek flowing into a river. There we tried a few holes and caught unwanted piranhas, although some were only a pound and a half away from the world record. There are different species in different parts of the river.

I got some pics of caimans and parrots and various types of vegetation, and I found a little spot that looked promising where the creek ran fast over the rocks. I baited up and had just dropped my bait over and was cleaning my hands with a rag when a big traira almost took my rod in.

After several bait-and-tackle poses, we headed on up. We met Larry and Martin, and we all started bringing in trairas. My biggest one was twenty-one pounds. Suddenly, losing a five-pounder seemed to be a really silly thing to be disappointed over. Later I landed a sorubim, and then I got a jundia in another a hole. Now I was starting to feel as if I just might get the target fish I came here for!

As darkness fell, we headed for the main river to try for a few peacock bass and one spot for piraiba catfish, one of my main targets, but we had no luck. On the way back, while resting in the bottom of the boat for a two-hour ride, I decided that if I could go out at night, I would catch one. Sure enough, I struck a deal with Wellington, the camp manager, and even got my fishing partner, George, to go.

Out before dark, we slipped lines into the water. We were throwing as far as we could toward the middle. The boat was backed up into the brush. We got a good laugh at some kind of bird that sounded just like a telephone. When it was dark enough to need a light, my line started flying off. The native said, "Sorubim." Now I was excited. With the native working the boat, George was ready with the gaff, and after fifteen minutes or so, he finally appeared in our headlamps. I couldn't believe it was the one I wanted. I figured him to be fifty to sixty pounds; we had no scales in the boat. I was happier than a cat in a tuna factory. I wouldn't have cared if he was three pounds. This fish had been my last target, and I ended my trip with a grand slam on catfish with one species extra—a barba chata. This one was no monster, though. It was a small cat, two to three pounds.

For a trip that started out rough with some funny luck, I had done what many haven't, and with some of my fish at reputable sizes. We fished till the moon came up and then headed in slowly, stargazing. I truly thanked my lucky stars and the man upstairs!

Day 7

I awoke with a laid-back attitude toward fishing. I was content with what I'd already done on the trip. The sky was clear, and I knew it would be hot, so we planned a run up the main river to the creek—and, if possible, far beyond where we had already been. I wanted to explore some of the bends in the creek and fish. I seriously didn't think I could do any better, but after thirty minutes at the first hole, my line took off. I left the reel unlocked. With big cats, you just let them run a bit and then start reeling to set the hook. I did this, but with the drag set tight, it still kept running. We knew right off this was a big fish. Without seeing the fish, we were thinking it was a big piraiba. Finally the line stopped, and I tried to reel, but it wasn't going to happen. So I pumped the rod a few times and got a few turns, pumped again, and got a few more. Confident I had gotten the fish off the bottom, I held the rod high while Lucas paddled to it—and while it pulled along our sixteen-foot boat containing three people. After about eighteen minutes of pumping the rod, he got close to the bank, and worry set in that the big fish was going to snag my line on the rocks and cut it. About this time, I was glad I invested in 150-pound Power Pro instead of the 80-pound line they suggested.

At one point, the fish almost ran the line into the motor. I hollered at Lucas to pull the motor up. Soon the big fish broke to the surface, and I didn't have to look twice to see he was a giant. We ended up pulling it over to the bank to get it out of the water. It was a huge redtail cat—a beautiful fish! It was wider than me both ways, and it had a hanging belly bigger than a basketball. It was only about sixteen inches shorter than me. I'm five foot seven and weigh 167 pounds, so I'll bet he was 100 pounds and maybe a tad more; there's no doubt he was at least 80 pounds. We had no way to weigh it, but they said it was one of the few redtail catfish that big caught anywhere. Now I was not *on* cloud nine, but *on top* of cloud nine!

Here's the part that sounds like a fishing story. Two hours later, I did it again in another hole, and the fish wasn't much smaller. We also caught some huge piranhas and a good sorubim cat, along with another large traira. It was my last boat ride out of the fishing area in the river, and I was feeling the sense of gratefulness to the man above and the emotional feeling I sometimes get when God grants me a wish and another thing taken off my bucket list. The sun was setting behind the boat, and I felt confident that this was a time I will never regret: the Amazon, the river, the natives, the fishing challenge, the time in the jungle, the new friends, and my still having the good health to do it all. The beauty of wildlife, from parrots to butterflies crossing our path, and all the sounds it made all came together to make it a one-of-a-kind trip.

I sit here now at the tropical hotel waiting on the restaurant to open, and I realize how precious a time it was, knowing that in less than twenty-four hours I will be home. I am happy and sad. This just a part of life that I must go home. Adventures like this is hard to come by for a simple man. Now I'm ready to get back to fight the devil. I trust in God that I will soon see another adventure, and I wish the same for those who wish it too!

Good bye, Brazil!

A Few Hours out of
Thousands for Deer

I guess I want to remember this little story because I needed this hunt to remind me that dedication will pay off as well as time in the stand. The events took place during the 2013/14 season on Wallhanger Hunting Club's 1,860 acres across Highway 28, where I live. The land is between Leesville, Louisiana, and Alexandria, Louisiana. Calcasieu River runs through it. It is a mixture of swamps, piney woods, and hardwood bottoms. Over the years, I have grown to love the woods there, as I hunt so many other places, and along with it I love the animals there also. The landowner is Roy-O-Martin Timber Company.

Now, this was one of the first years in a while I decided not to venture off into another state to hunt whitetail, mostly because I had worked so hard at home on my own property and leases, and I also had a half dozen or more trophy-class bucks located in our neck of the woods. Most folks find one every two years at home. There wasn't just a couple of trail camera pictures; there were many pictures! I had put time in all year, no less than two days a month, prepping places; doing tractor work; using a bulldozer; trimming; brush-hogging; placing many mineral licks; planting, moving, and setting stands; etc. I guess I could say this year I planned to come close to getting things in one place to stay one way or another. All these bucks were scattered between about five places. The obsession started for the season at the Wallhanger Club, where three different timber types cornered up along the river's edge about 150 yards away. Actually, this was where I always felt I needed to watch and hunt but never did. I was spoiled by my box stand down the road.

I had three shooters around, with two being good deer—one better than ever, and more than average in the area. Here is where I decided to start. I think you really need to get in a tree stand to see more than twenty yards, but I decided to bring out a ground blind. My stepdaughter, Devin Rogers, helped me pick it out at Academy, set it up, brush it in, and add some leafy camo over it. Then I used the four-wheeler to run down some tall grass through an old pond that had been dried up since the droughts in 1950 in that area. When the wind was right, I clipped limbs and broke limbs out as far as I could, never touching anything as I worked. I placed a few deer cameras near the trail and where I had seen scrapes in years past. I sprayed them with a little oil-based cover-up scent—my favorite to cover the smell from the oil off my hands. And of course, I always wear rubber boots.

I split a bag of rice bran and a bag of corn in two locations about seventy-five yards out. I have better luck not getting pegged at that distance or farther. I backed out for a few days and then eased in one afternoon to check cameras. One camera showed two of three deer had been there—a nine-pointer and a twelve-pointer. At that same location, there were about six smaller bucks on camera, and I decided there was something the bucks liked about this area. Rarely did the camera show a doe here. The season would open in about a week, so

I decided I would start right here! This kind of hunting is tough in a small blind with a three-inch inch slit in the front; the most I could see was about the seventy-five-yard and thirty-yard areas, in most places. It was pretty much like this for the first six days. I hunted no less than eight hours each day through all kinds of weather, no matter what.

On the seventh day, one afternoon, I ran up to a piece of my property and checked the camera and saw a reason to maybe try there awhile. I moved to my high side stand, as I called it, that evening. And the next morning, I decided to go back to my big box at Wallhanger to check my camera just before daylight. A big ten-pointer had been there for about an hour from around nine to ten in the morning. Talk about feeling as if I had made a big mistake!

Well, I sat it out till two in the afternoon that day, did an evening hunt, and then went back out the next morning. About eleven in the morning I got scented about twenty yards behind me. The lucky part about that was that the darn wind had been different up until about ten minutes before that time. I felt it was him. He had also made a scrape there that night. I stuck it out for a few more days and saw a few does and turkeys. Then, on another side of the lease, I got a picture of a monster there. I sat on a stand that Jessie West and I share until ten thirty in the morning.

When finished, I walked the road out, looking down for fresh tracks while heading to my Kubota 1100 ATV. I looked up and saw a big buck cross the road at a trot. By the time I got my gun up, all I had in the scope was his ass. So that evening, I ran back to the park for a hunt. Nothing was there, so I decided to break out my climber and go into the woods where the buck had come out from the road and hunt. Again, nothing! Four more hours passed.

That evening, back in the climber about twenty minutes till dark, I heard a shot right behind me. It almost made me crap myself and jump out of the stand at the same time. I didn't think anyone was around. This is why hunters need to wear orange! Not long after I heard the shot, there was a bunch of loud talking and hollering. At first I kind of got mad. Then I thought maybe someone fell out of a stand, got shot, etc. I had seen two deer run by behind me about twenty minutes before the shot—no doubt a buck chasing a doe. So out of the stand I came, and I then rode the Kubota up the highest hill in the area to try to see if I could hear something. Sure enough, low voices were in the distance.

About that time, a good friend, Billy Gordy, on the lease right next to us, called on his cell phone. He was happier than a pig in a watermelon patch. He said Blake, his son, had just shot a stud. I knew exactly which deer it was. Down in a sapling thicket, there he lay. There couldn't have been a happier dad-and-son team in the world, and it spilled over to me as well. That deer was meant for Blake.

Bear Hunt—Valdez, Alaska

Day 1

Hello, folks. On May 12, I was on my way to Alaska to hunt. After the plane ride from Alexandria, Louisiana, to Dallas, and then on to Minneapolis, Minnesota, and Anchorage, Alaska, I got picked up by my good friends Bim and Vicky. Soon we got our bear tags and groceries, and then we went back to the airport to pick up Joey Sullivan and Paul Olson from Manhattan, Kansas. Now jet-lagged, we decided to get car-lagged on a six-hour drive down through beautiful country to Valdez. Then we spent two hours unpacking before we headed to our bunks on a fifty-five-foot boat with Captain Bob. By now we had all been up for twenty-four to twenty-eight hours or more. I filtered in a nap or two on the plane and had just gotten back from a turkey hunt in Sonora, Mexico, so I was ready for bed.

Day 2

After barely surviving their snoring, I awoke looking for the coffeepot. It's dark here only about four hours out of every twenty-four hours. We geared up in the rain and drove a bit out of town to check the guns, leaving the bows behind. We rolled back in, unloaded the skiff boat, aired it up, and tied it to the back of the boat. By now I was ready to do something other than travel and try to sleep.

It wasn't long before we saw more than just boats and docks as we eased into Prince William Sound. We were blessed that Mrs. Vickie wanted to come help cook and keep some drinks made. Slipping through the water, we passed some glaciers, sea lions, sea otters, and mountain goats. Snow-covered mountains were all around us. We planned to cover a good bit of ground today, all the time looking for a bear on the coastline. We came alongside a shrimper and bought some huge shrimp called "spot shrimp" for our dinner. They were prime shrimp! These wouldn't be going to China for sale.

The weather was dreary and rainy with patches of fog. Soon we saw a whale that allowed us to get beside him for some sweet pictures. Our boat was fifty-five feet, and he was about half as long. What an awesome sight! It was cool listening to Mr. Bob tell his stories of fishing, duck hunting, oyster farming, and fox farming. Mayday calls, diving trips, and times before the *Exxon Valdez* oil spill. As a side note, Valdez is the snowiest city in Alaska.

A few hours later, Paul spotted the first black bear. It was a nice one, too. We slipped past slowly in the boat and dropped the skiff, and the bear eased back a ways. I had a shot at eighty yards, but she had a cub, so that was a wrap. It was a fine sight though. We ended up anchoring in the area to watch and take a break. During the break, we wet a hook and brought in a few flounder, all along cooking the shrimp, now and then glancing over the hillsides. Scanning the area, we found several eagles, and there were a few seals that got our blood pumping, as we thought they were bears. We looked over one hundred–plus miles of shoreline. We saw a few small boats fishing for shrimp. We made it through the night; after anchoring in a cut nestled back in the mountains, we got cozy and got our eyeballs rolled down for some sleep. It felt like seconds later when I heard Mr. Bob's alarm clock go off, which was the anchor being pulled up.

Day 3

Morning was cold but comfortable and foggy, but there was no rain yet. I knew there would be rain, though, because this rain forest gets more rain than any on the continent. Soon, when I didn't have the binoculars up, we were eating oatmeal for the morning. We were in the area where the Aleutian Indians were present a lot in the 1930s and 1940s. Fox farming and copper mining were present as far back as the 1800s.

About nine in the morning, in a cutout on a gray rock bank, we saw a black spot; after studying it, we agreed that, yep, it was a bear. We eased in around the curb on the boat, the Artic Light, and then dropped the skiff. We slipped around the bank in the skiff then got out onto the bank. Up the ridge, there he was, about a 170-pound black bear. Paul hit the ground on his belly, military style. Paul served in Afghanistan and Iraq and is a wounded warrior. He aimed at a low white spot between the bear's front legs and squeezed a round off, scoring a hit. The bear wheeled and slung rocks, digging out, and Joey backed him up with a shot to the back, dropping the bear in his tracks.

All along, Bob and I were watching with binoculars. Everything went just right. It felt good to have a bear and boat and see a fine man take his first bear ever and see how happy he was. Joey was equally happy, knowing he had helped him achieve the dream and that he had tightened the bonds between two men's friendship through hunting. Paul was Joey's employee, and he was showing his appreciation.

About an hour or so later, luck fell again with another bear out near the water's edge, in the distance. It was hard to see through the binoculars from a distance, so we eased our way very slowly and set the skiff out. Joey and I eased in around the bend with the trolling motor on low, slipped back up the bank, and went through some trees. When we looked up, there he was, close to where we had first seen him. In a sitting position, I aimed slowly and squeezed the trigger, dropping him in his tracks. As we approached the bear, we saw that he was a boar and was much bigger than we thought. He was an old warrior with chipped teeth, large paws (super claws), and a massive head. He ended up measuring sixty-four inches–plus. It was the biggest black bear Bim and his group had ever taken, according to him. We were all happy! We proceeded to skin the bear out, and I decided to do a full-body mount. The other guys went off to hunt while there was a break in the weather. The old boy had been eating barnacles growing on a rock. While skinning the bear, we had a couple of sea otters keep popping up, checking us out.

We came in for a sandwich and then started rigging boxes to try catching some shrimp, and rods to fish with as well. Next we loaded up in a skiff and headed deeper in. We banked and attempted to hike for a while, but ponds, streams, and lakes hidden below two to four feet of snow changed our minds, forcing us to stick to hunting along the banks. We came in and worked on bear hides, gulped down some lasagna, and hit the hay. The day was full of rain, sleet, and hail but was not super cold. We were guessing that when the tide went out, more barnacle-covered rocks would be exposed and the smell would attract a bear. An hour later, it happened. Paul, Joey, and Bim took the skiff out down the coast about half a mile or so and stalked their way to the bear. All along, Mr. Bob and I were stopped at a distance, trying to keep the bear distracted from their stalk. Soon the bear moved, and we knew it had seen them. Joey never got a shot. It's all about the hunt.

Soon a windy storm blew in for a bit, so we headed for cover back into a bay to have supper. We had turkey on the grill for six hours or so and then went out for bear again. All along, we were still telling stories. Mr. Bob told us of his days as an orphan and how he made his life. He ran with Steve Pantone and knew him and his sister well. The evening was filled with heavy rain, making it hard to see through binoculars. There was a lot more snow than usual for this time of year, and it was making it hard to see the bears we would normally see. We finished out the evening and went to bed early.

Day 4

We slept in a bit later, but soon Mr. Bob's anchor alarm went off. Clearing off the window, binoculars in hand, we started searching. Paul walked to the back to take a look and noticed we had lost a skiff; we were dragging it behind the boat. Thirty minutes later we found it, thank God. It was about a $4,800 skiff with an outboard motor that had been used only three times. An hour or so later, we spotted another bear, but it split before we had a chance. We soon saw a nice group of seals on the rocks nearby. Later we saw a few pairs of loons. We drifted into a bay surrounded by big mountains and cliff walls covered with snow. It was a place like one out of a dream. We had no luck there, and we headed out, but not before we made a little hike to check for tracks. Then the rain got heavy, so we ran for a spot to get out of the weather and settled in for supper. We watched a couple of movies and bedded in.

Day 5

We slept a bit late but were in no hurry, because the tide was going to be late and we hoped the rain would slow. Valdez averages 500 inches of rain a year (accumulation) and about 180 inches in the ocean nearby throughout the islands. We saw a lot of ducks this morning. They are funny to watch; sometimes they eat so much fish they can't fly up. They puke while trying to get up if something chases them. Now five of us were looking through binoculars at once, and the sea was forcing us across to the other side.

Soon I saw a bear to the left of the boat, and at about the same time, I was sure Bob had seen it as well. Seconds later, Joey called out, "Bear!" We realized then that we were looking at two different bears. Neither one even came close enough for us to unass ourselves to have a chance.

Finally we found a cut to hide from the elements a bit where it was calm, so we watched another movie, snacked, and dozed a bit. We watched *Mystic River* on a mystic ocean. The rain slacked off a bit, so we got back on the move, but a few hours later we decided it was time for supper, so we served up a few burgers. Everyone but me and Captain Bob stayed up and watched *Rio Lobo*.

Day 6

After a few hours of darkness, we all broke out of bed slowly and headed out. There is a lot of daylight here, and it makes for a long day sometimes. A few hours into it, I was glassing a small grass flat when I noticed a black spot. After watching it a while, I saw movement. I showed Joey, and we made a little stalk. We moved to within about 152 yards of him. The bear started to move, and Joey squeezed off a round. He didn't appear to hit it, but four of us went to make sure. A bit disappointed, we sucked it up and started back hunting.

Later we came across two groups of mountain goats high in the cliffs. We found most of the game was on the points. Animals come there for the winter. It's as far as they can go to get out of the very heavy snow. We were hunting in an area they call Nunya Bay, as in "nunya business". Finally there came a break in the liquid sunshine. Just then we came upon a lot of floating ice that had broken off a glacier; the chunks ranged from the size of a lawn mower to the size of a truck. There is awesome beauty around every corner in every way through these mountains. These glaciers are thousands of years old and have a beautiful blue color to them that's hard to explain. A lot of them are around Columbia Bay and Heather Bay.

The rain stopped, but wind came—and so did the sea, with four- to five-foot waves. It was time to tie down and secure everything for two-plus hours on our way to another hunting area on the way back to Valdez—a trip of some forty-five miles. With all the floating ice and wind, we tucked off in a bay. Joey and I took the skiff and headed to land. We hunted for a few hours but saw no sign, and the snow was very heavy. We ended up making brownies for supper and watched a movie as it started getting dark at midnight.

Day 7

We were up early, and the day was nice, calm, and clear. The plan for today was to cover about 125 miles and cast a line on the way in. The Indians of the village of Tatitlek were looking over us now. Wow! Today we had a group of three humpback whales alongside the boat, close. One was jumping up halfway out of the water. I'm telling you, there's nothing like seeing them in their natural habitat. It's not like seeing them at SeaWorld. We also saw a few killer whales. This experience in itself was a trip. It's the closest thing to the size of a prehistoric as you can see today. We didn't see any bears, but the scenery was awesome. Sea and liquid sunshine helped make for a fine day.

Back in Valdez, we all ganged up, getting the boat unloaded for the seven-hour trip back to Anchorage. The drive was a totally different trip with sunshine, and we were now seeing it from a different perspective. I drove awhile and Bim drove awhile. We got a motel, and we all but depleted their hot water taking showers. Later we went out to eat.

After boarding the plane for a six-hour flight to Dallas, Texas, I asked the pilot to fly where we could see the mountains. He said he would see what he could do. Looking out the window, the sight was amazing. I ended up with all three seats in my row to myself. Well, I hope your dream trips come true as most of mine have. Thanks to God! Y'all have a good one, and remember: my coffeepot is always ready, so stop by my taxidermy studio.

Tarpon Fishing in Nicaragua

Day 1—July 8, 2014

I got my girlfriend, Tiffany Edwards, to drop me off at Alexandria Airport for a trip to Nicaragua. I knew it had started; excitement had built. I now had the chance to top Jeremy Wade's tarpon trip on National Geographic. I took a one-hour flight to Atlanta, where I got to eat lunch with a good friend I hadn't seen in a while, Darrel. Then I took a four-hour flight to Managua with some layovers. I arrived after dark. Customs was easy, though it cost ten dollars. While waiting on my luggage, I went to convert $250 to córdobas with an exchange rate of 25,985. I x-rayed my bags and then saw Carlos with my sign: "Victor." Soon I was in a car and on the road for an hour trip to Granada.

We picked up a passenger, and that kind of worried me at first. Running about sixty miles per hour down the road, we saw half-starved horses, dogs, cows, and goats. Most were tied up. Folks on bikes and motorcycles without any lights missed us by only feet. We arrived at Hotel Los Chilamates. The gate was guarded, and the hotel was fenced with concertina wire. It wasn't long until I hit the hay. The rooms were nice, and I was glad to see a good AC unit.

Day 2

I met with Carlos; it was to be just him and me today. We planned to see the good side and bad sides of this place, along with the normal attractions. We first went to the Mombacho Volcano, where we sneaked into a part where I wasn't allowed. It was an awesome sight! Then we went to see a military base and Lake Cocicbolca. This lake is twenty-six-thousand-plus years old. We saw churches, poor areas, rich areas, and a coffee bean farm, and then we went to a market downtown for a little shopping. There we went to see how indigenous people made pottery. I stopped along the way to pick mangoes and other fruits and ate them. We ate a native lunch from a roadside vendor; it was awesome. Then we just drove about the countryside, seeing more how folk lived here in Granada and some of the surrounding small towns. Once back at the motel, I wound down with supper and drinks. I visited the poolside outside before bed. A lot of things are different outside our own world in the United States for sure—some better rather than worse. I loved visiting the Catholic graveyards because they were quite different than ours in the South.

Day 3

Today was busy. Again Carlos picked me up at nine in the morning, and we headed back to the airport for my flight to San Carlos. On getting there and weighing my bags, I found out that I was gonna have to do something with most of what I thought I needed. I was not very happy. This plane was a prop plane, a Cessna. I could carry about ten people and was not much bigger than a crop duster. Finding no lockers to store my belongings at the airport, I went to the nearest motel and booked a room for the night before I was to fly home. This way I could talk them into holding my stuff for me. I was glad I had the time to do that.

I boarded the plane and got near the cockpit for some GoPro action. It was hot! Once we reached about 7,500 feet, things cooled down. These planes are not like the big boys. Your guts get knocked around in the turbulence, and sometime we could see only two feet out the windows because of the cloud cover. Most of the time, the view was awesome. Flying over volcanos and jungle canopies, I think I saw most of Nicaragua from the air.

Of course, we landed in two more places before San Carlos. The one in San Juan was in the middle of nowhere. The San Carlos airstrip was pure dirt and rocks. The trip was about two hours of flying and landing; it was kind of fun and scary at the same time. The view from the plane let us see towns, forests, rivers, mountains, and oceans that could never be seen any other way but by plane. I was met by Champa (his real name was Moses). We got a taxi through San Carlos. This town was built all on and around a mountain. It looked a lot like a town from one hundred years ago.

We traveled down the river to my French friend Philippe's lodge, where I would be staying for the duration of my trip. The only way in here is by boat. Unique to itself, it is nestled right between the river and the lakes. Tropical vegetation had grown right up to the front door. Wild birds were right outside the window. It was about as warm here as at home in Louisiana. Quickly they made me lunch, and then we headed downriver. The weather was very windy and rough. About twenty minutes in, I had a huge tarpon hit my line, only to lose him fast. Talk about my crappy luck. We trolled the rest of the evening. I had no more luck, but I did get a few hits. We sped out before dark because things tend to change then on the river as far as safety, etc. More tired than a one-legged man trying to cross a mountain, I was about to crash hard.

Day 4

I got up a little late. Soon breakfast was complete, and I was pumped. About an hour or so after the bait hit the water, the rain hit us. But the cloud cover was welcome. We fished until noon and then we went and ate with Moses's sister-in-law's family. These folks lived on the river way out of town. They had no electricity or running water, and they used an outhouse for the toilet. Interestingly enough, they did have a few solar panels. They cooked me what looked like mullet, rice, beans, and veggies. Lemon water was about all they drank. Everything was cooked on a clay grill with firewood. I tried to kick back for a rest but ended up playing with two kids.

After lunch, baits went back into the water from all four reels. Soon I got a huge strike and a tarpon was airborne. *Wow* was all I could think. *Will I bring this baby in?* Well, with a lot of coaching and just over an hour on the first full day, I got my tarpon. It was no easy task. I even got some video of it as well. The journey here in itself was an adventure just in making this happen. Moses said he was 115–125 pounds.

About thirty minutes later, another fish was on the line. This tarpon almost jumped on a boat passing by. I would reel him in but then lose my progress because of his power; he was stripping seventy-five to a hundred yards each time. Moses was excited, and now so was I, because of the size. In a little less than an hour, we landed a tarpon that was probably twenty-plus years old. They said he was easily 145 pounds, maybe even 160. Wow! I was so happy. I rarely have such great luck early in any trip of any kind.

With the moon full, I had been worried. I think the storms helped, and the 60 to 80 pound test PowerPro braided line was a plus also. I was content for now. I told the boys, "Let's go, I'm gonna buy y'all a six pack." When we got back to the lodge, Philippe, the owner, had made it in. After some camaraderie, I was out. Sharing my story of my catch wore me out.

A family of four from Belgium arrived. There were four different nationalities at the dinner table, where we ate steak French style. After I knocked a tarantula off the porch by my room, I felt okay to go to bed.

Day 5

Today started very early, about two in the morning, with me throwing up over the porch in the rain. Looks like I caught a jungle virus. After about twenty hours of no sleep, hurting to the point I could barely get still, and then being weak, I wanted to try. I was lucky the best doctor in the country happened to be in the lodge that night. He comes to San Juan for only two days each month. They all worked hard to try to make it better for me.

Day 6

I was still queasy and weak, but we went out. It was a little late, but I was determined to try. I'm sure glad I did. It was rough, but I managed to land two tarpon. One was about 100 pounds. The other was a monster by Champa's standards, weighing in at 160-plus pounds. He's weighed many while studying and tagging them. That big boy worked me pretty good; I fought him for one hour and thirty-seven minutes. I got some good pics and video.

After all that, and feeling about 50 percent healthy, I opted to go in and try to eat my first real meal in a while. Then I went to lie down a bit and try for their catfish in the evening. Philippe's lodge sits at an intersection where the rivers diverge at the entrance to the lake. I decided to fish this evening to see what kind of species I could catch. I caught quite a few tiger bass averaging about one pound and many mojarra bream—enough for supper for everyone. Many tarpon swam by, breaking the top of the water. The Andres family canoed down the river to visit and see the looney white American man.

I spent the rest of the evening relaxing, watching numerous waterfowl, and preparing to go across the lake to fish the islands in it. One thing I've learned in all the places I've visited is that there are people who love nature and the environment, as I do—those who understand the importance of preserving it—and then there are those that would choose to exploit it to the end.

Man, catching these tarpon was like catching fifty ten-pound largemouth bass.

Day 7

I woke up from a night's sleep with no pain. For the last few nights, the city of Managua had been celebrating the thirty-fifth anniversary of Nicaragua's Sandinista revolution. Every year on July 19, hundreds of people from all over the country commemorate the event of the fall of the militarized Somoza family dictatorship with music and celebrations. The celebrations had now stopped, along with the excitement over the World Cup game between Argentina and Germany. That helped, since the commotion was only about a mile away. Of course, there were still howler monkeys all about in the distance, and all the birds came alive at night.

I was greeted this morning by some hummingbirds by my window, so I'm hoping today is a good day for sea bass. I had scrambled eggs for breakfast, along with toast and some peanut butter I brought from home, thanks to my girlfriend, Tiff. The night guard cracked me up; he was snoring when I got up. He also worked as a custodian, gardener, etc., in the camp.

It will be all freshwater fishing today; it's all they have here. Of course ole One Eye joined me for breakfast. He is a feisty-looking dog weighing about four pounds. He lost his eye and got his mouth deformed in a fight with some other dogs, and he was so old about all his teeth were gone. It was looking to be about a steady eighty degrees with clouds overhead.

At the first island we came to, I must have seen fifty different birds, no doubt. Quickly we caught some bass and other kinds of fish; none were very big though. We were using a lot of lures similar to the ones we fish at home with.

They say there are a lot of boa constrictors on these islands. Some of the islands are inhabited, and boys at early ages are out with the men working. It is just about impossible not to see a bird of some kind every five minutes. Trees hang over islands with strings and webs of roots hanging down, reaching for water. It is lush, with many types of vegetation all around.

Later we decided to troll. As best as I can understand, we are in a central area. It is a dry forest where everything loses its leaves. The summertime is in January. This place and my home are definitely opposite worlds. Before lunchtime, we had landed twenty-eight fish, but still no big ones.

We passed some nice homes that some richer people had hidden up in mountains under the forest floor. The islands here look to range in size from ten acres to one thousand acres, from what I've seen.

Around noon, we found the lodge we were staying at in the islands. We ate chicken, rice, beans, and juice squeezed from fresh fruit—not too shabby. I felt good enough to lie back on the big porch and doze in the breeze a bit. We then went out and tried to find some bigger fish, but we pretty much just saw a lot of pretty country. The lake became more like an ocean fast. We tried for about three hours without any luck—not even a strike. So we opted to stop early and just relax by the water's edge. We didn't care too much for the lightning and rain all around us—and on us from time to time.

I kicked back on the porch, and it dawned on me that over a period of time of hearing repeated conversations in a language you don't understand, it eventually becomes more of an annoying noise. So I decided to move up the mountain to my own little bungalow for the quietness of nature and to reflect a bit. And what did I see? Another guest—a huge tarantula!. This was the biggest one I'd ever seen, sitting on the post handrail by my door. Now, this thing was creepy. I'm guessing he was after one of many, many lizards I had seen scurrying all around. I wanted to take a walk through the island forest, but I would need a machete to be able to enter the places I wanted to go. I wished I could just gather seeds from all these plants with flowers and see if I could grow them at home. These little stories or articles— whatever you want to call them—are mainly for me and the mind that I hope to maintain as an old man, for God's given days are good most of the time. But at this moment I'm thinking about compiling them all into one. Maybe I'll give it a name like "Simple Man's Journeys.

I don't study a lot about where I go. It seems to be more enjoyable to figure it out as I go. I think it makes it more of an adventure. People, cultures, and cities are interesting, but it is what's off the beaten path that compels me to go. The new surprises in my own eyes are those of the sights never seen, the sounds never heard, and the spooky situations that I barely passed by. It is always interesting to see the struggles different folks go through in different places to be happy. I always visit the good and the bad sides of a place when I get the chance. A lot of things don't really seem fair to write about though. When I lived in Russia, building the US Embassy, I was told by the American Department of Defense that they truly didn't think they had ever known an American to know the city so well or have been through it as I had. I never wasted a moment there when I wasn't working. I didn't sleep much—I never do anywhere I go.

I ended this evening with pork dinner and a cold shower. That is all they had here. There wasn't any internet, TV, etc. Dinner was healthy—full of several kinds of veggies. Back in my little screened-in box up the hill, I stepped out on the deck after I scanned the room for critters, taking out a few spiders as always. However, there were some that slept under the wood-frame box spring that I was about to sleep on. I just hoped that they stayed on their side of the bed.

Right off I saw many flat black spiders all along the porch. Most of them were ugly and about the size of a silver dollar. Many frogs waged war on the insects all along the walls. Some were as big as my foot. Most of them looked a lot like our toads. I always hunt creepy things at night wherever I go, and I couldn't say I was not glad for what little protection I did have here. I constantly heard things outside on the walls and the roof. Wild flying insects—big ones—were attracted to my light. Some had eyes that glowed. Man, this island was as full of life at night as it was during the daylight. I was so mad that my camera battery was down and I would have to wait until I got to San Carlos to recharge everything.

Tonight was going to be rough, as there was no wind. It was easy to see why so many people sleep in screen-covered hammocks instead of beds out here. I plan to sightsee outside a bit each time I wake up tonight. I have an awesome light. I use LED headlamps.

As I was about to turn in, I brushed the small gnats and flying critters off my bed and turned in with them. The water hitting the bank sounded nice. The singing insects were mesmerizing, and all so strange too.

Day 8

I managed to roust myself to step outside for a look last night, but I did sleep well otherwise. Of course, I found more huge spiders. My light seems to attract them. They look a lot like our wolf spiders, but some are bigger than my hand and furrier than wolf spiders. I started out breakfast with an omelet and tea, and I then headed to big, open water. I was trying once more for a big rainbow bass. It's kind of like a peacock bass, weighing from five to twenty pounds. We had to leave early to make it across the lake before the lake became as rough as an ocean from wind.

We caught some machaca. They look a lot like our shad, but longer. We were also doing some bass casting. Sure enough, we got caught in the wind on the lake. All we could do was hang on, stand up, and take the pounding, and I was hoping the boat would survive. The entire console was all over the place, and cracks along the side were moving in and out. Closer in, it calmed a bit after a one-and-a-half-hour beating. We ran into about eight thousand ducks, give or take a few. I don't know how many there really were, but it was enough to stop and watch and get some photos of them as they flew off the water.

I went in for lunch and quick nap, as well as to recharge all my cameras. We soon left for our daily permit for the boat each day. I will no longer gripe about the sticker we have to put on our boats. I gave the staff their tips for the day. They were happy folks.

We were heading a few hours down the river to a different spot—a more remote spot than where we have been so far. All along the way, we tried a few places. This water looked like dark tea. Today I realized I really no longer knew what day or time it was. My cell phone was in a locker in Managua near the airport. We had seen a few caimans but not really much wildlife. However, most of the wildlife here is nocturnal. If you were stranded or lost here, you would sleep during the day so you could survive the nights without a hammock, nets, etc. And without a light, you would just be screwed. You would have to sleep and move when you could. I don't think hunger would be an issue though. Water would be a serious issue, though, I would think. The birds shit everywhere in it.

Another thing I'd seen was some beautiful dead wood—stumps and logs. They would make some beautiful furniture. Sometimes, all of a sudden, along a riverbank in a small opening, I would see a hut, and around it a small family. The hard life they live easily showed. The men look rough, with faces of leather. Quite frankly, tangling with them would be like fighting with a lion.

We were somewhere between San Carlos and El Castillo, right on the Costa Rican line. Philippe's twenty-acre piece of land was at an intersection of Rio Frio, Rio San Juan, and Great Lake.

Everything got calm this evening. There was some rain off and on, but we didn't even get a strike. We stopped a little early so we had time to find the lodge. The lodges there are not like the lodges at home. Ours was more like a ten-by-ten-foot tiki hut on stilts. Around 90 percent of folks live in these here. Leaves and straw make up the roof, and it is open underneath with three-quarter-inch cracks in floorboards.

Day 9

The night in the tiki hut was interesting, but the first time I got up to use the bathroom, I saw about nine of those big spiders. So this time I dropped the net over my bed. I took some photos of them. On top of that, there were about a hundred cockroaches. The thing was, when I would turn my headlight on to go to the bathroom, the cockroaches would scatter. And then the spiders would pounce on them! They were super fast for being so darn big.

I had a tough time getting to sleep because of the heat. It was the hottest night yet. Then, as always, it finally cooled down and I was out.

If something went to sleep with me, I didn't know it. During the first few hours, it seems everything that crawls at night is either hunting something to eat or getting eaten. Then, when it cools, it's like they are all lying down after Sunday lunch.

Right at daylight, I had a farm pig creep under my hut and wake me up. About that same time, something must have upset the monkeys. They were raising all kinds of hell back and forth. Then the rest of the world followed, waking birds and so forth. Of course, the occasional chicken crowed too. The people here have to raise most of their food.

It was watermelon and bread for breakfast. We went a bit farther down the river into some small cuts off the main river, which are my favorite kind of spots to explore. I saw more wildlife there. The day was dark and gloomy, with cloudy skies—one of the kind I like to fish. No joke, just before I started this line, I had a tarpon strike! The fish flew plumb out of the water. Then I had another hit. It took me until the fifth one to finally get the lure to stay in one's mouth. It was strange but awesome action. I got some great photos and GoPro footage of the fish launching himself. After about forty minutes, I got him to the boat and the hook pulled out. We got a photo though. He wasn't long but was fat and wide, with a huge head. I would guess he weighed 150 pounds or so.

All of a sudden, fish were on lines everywhere. We got in some snook. I was happy, as snook was a new species for me. Later, I changed to a bass rig I use at home, which helped me catch some from seven to twelve pounds. They can get up to twenty-five pounds or so, I think, but I hadn't seen anything like that yet. I also landed a few fifteen-pound gar. I was kind of hoping not to get a tarpon on these rigs though.

The overcast was soon gone, and the sun came out. It was extremely hot but tolerable. There is crazy weather here—at least in July. Three different species of snook pass through this river year round.

We definitely made some locals along the river happy by giving them some of our fish. They were fishing with a piece of line by hand for bream. These bream are a lot like ours but differ in color. The job of many people along the river is just to find food and fruit to live. That's how jobs used to be in the United States. It's hard to say if jobs are bad these days. It used to be great to work; folks were proud to work and of their jobs in the States. Now it seems to be what people hate the most. This makes things terrible, and I'm glad it wasn't this way for me. The only reason I don't want to work as much in these times we live in now is that there are so many freeloaders looking for a handout. The federal and local governments are making it easier for them. On the contrast, our government in the local and federal levels seem to be hindering citizens from achieving success. It's a bad deal now.

We were about to have a watermelon for lunch. About halfway through the melon, one reel started singing. My first thought was that it was a tarpon, but I ended up landing about a thirty-pound gar. This sucker was shooting out of the water like a tarpon.

With that we decided to head back to San Juan, which was a few hours down the river. Today was my last full day. Shortly into the boat ride, a Caribbean monsoon set in with what looked a lot like a southern Louisiana turd floater. After drying out a bit, we grilled some snook while I listened to some of Philippe's fishing stories. We discussed maybe taking a trip deep into the Caribbean sometime. At about four thirty, we lit out to burn some gas, which cost seven dollars (American) per gallon here.

We headed up a swift little river called the Rio Frio for a short trip. It looked like I would have to give up my new Ambassador 7000 reel; the last tarpon killed it altogether. I had taken only three tarpon. I decided I was going to be a Penn reel man on the next go-round.

The Rio Frio was nice. Just a few hours before sunset, we saw a lot of little white-faced monkeys and howlers. I cast some big baits all along the banks and hooked one good tarpon. He exploded out of the water and spit the bait out at us. It was a cool sight anyway. I was ready for my last night in San Carlos, though, so I went off to bed quickly after.

Day 10

I had a few hours before my flight back to Managua, so I thought we might run out to the lake so I could try to catch a rainbow bass. I caught some sea bass, and Champa got one rainbow; I so wanted it to be mine. Back at the lodge, we found some wasps. I found out that if you are stung by them, your throat will swell shut fast. Getting into the water quickly is the only way to stop the swelling. Then I got some good news. Philippe said I now held the record for tropical gar. The record had been twelve pounds, and mine was well over twenty, if not more. I was glad I got pics so it wouldn't be just a "fish story."

After a little food, camaraderie, and some time in town at a festival, I taxied up to a little dirt runway at the airport. I was wishing it was noon, but it was four in the afternoon. This is the same at airports everywhere, I reckon. I was ready to go now for sure. After one more night in Managua, I hoped to be on my way home.

That night in Managua, I got a taxi just to drive me all around town so I could see the place. There were a *lot* of folks in this place. I stayed the night at the Best Western, which was really nice. It cost one hundred dollars a night (expensive)! The trip was definitely one of those that leave you feeling as if you had a glimpse into a second life—as though you escaped and got away for a while. As I always do if I get the chance, I visited the local church and said my prayers. God is good, God is great, and I am sure that without His help, this trip would have been just a wishful thought.

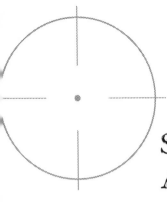

Sonora, Mexico—
Across the Border

Hello! This trip and story are continued from the one I took in 2014 to hunt Coues deer—the one I had to redo so I could complete my slam on all species. You just about have to hunt across the border to achieve this.

Leaving home for the flight was great. It looked as though there would be nice weather all the way. Everything went smoothly until we landed in Monterey and I made it to customs with my gun. If I had flown through Arizona and made Hermosillo my point of entry, I would have been fine, because Jim would have been there to meet me with the original gun permit he had gotten for me. That was the problem. I had only a copy. They made such an issue out of it Tiffany and I missed our last two-hour flight. Now we had a layover for nine hours. I was far from a happy ole country boy. Then the permit was for one hundred rounds, and I had only thirty-two, so it was a mess. We were flying on Delta, and they gave us vouchers for lunch and supper, so we went and had supper and decided that eight more hours of sitting in an airport was just too much. So we got a motel room, cleaned up, rested, and relaxed a while.

Eventually we made it back to the airport, where we had a meal. When we got our boarding passes, they wanted to make me pay for some of our luggage again, even though we had a receipt showing we had already paid. *Good God!* was all I could think while sorting this out. I was about to explode when I had to run my gun over to customs to go through some of the same crap all over with them even after my permit had been stamped and cleared.

In the air, it wasn't long before I saw that this two hours was gonna be rough with no AC working. And there was nowhere to put my carry-on, which held all my money. I was determined it wasn't going with them. They just gave up and allowed me to sort of slide it under the seat. By the time we got to camp, it was about three in the morning. After half-assedly unpacking, I slammed into bed with my girlfriend of two-plus years, Tiffany Edwards. The ranch we were staying at was Ranch Ojo de Aqua.

Day 1

We were up at five thirty. We headed down to the cook shack, slurped up a mess of coffee and a burrito, packed up backpacks with some lunch and fruit, and lit out on a Polaris Ranger. Without a windshield, I quickly learned that I needed more layers. Back to the ranch house we went. This was not a guided hunt, so from a map jotted down on a piece of paper, we did our best to find a spot to hunt. Right off the bat, I saw the amount of fun that could be had with thousands of doves all around and a couple chubby quail.

Just about a quarter mile away from the bottom of the mountain's edge, we jumped our first deer. We later jumped our first javelina, which was what Tiffany was hunting, but there was no time to pass her the gun. By then we were a few hours into walking, and we were feeling the lack of sleep. Never quite seeing a place I wanted to settle for a sit, we stayed on the move, skirting small canyons and glassing with binoculars. We ended up jumping and seeing about five more deer. Quickly the day's heat swept upon us. Temperatures were about fifty to fifty-five degrees at night and reached the eighties fast during the day. It wasn't until about three thirty in the afternoon that it started to cool down.

Back to the bunkhouse we went. We scarfed down some lunch and tried to murder the bed getting into it.

While in the field, I pulled a stupid stunt. I allowed a cactus to stick me in the leg and tried to use my finger to pull it out, and then dozens of tiny needles ended up in my fingers. Attempting to get them out with our fingernails, Tiff and I had some luck. Next I came up with the bright idea to use my teeth, which led to needles in my tongue. This was not the greatest way to learn from a mistake. I ended up having to use tweezers on my tongue.

About two thirty in the afternoon, we headed back out to hunt near a water tank. After making circles, trying to decide where to sit for a shooting spot, for comfort, and to play the wind, we found our spot and settled. The wind was all over the place. We had seen a good trail about 150 yards out. We wanted to be sure we were able to see. About one and a half hours later, sitting together back-to-back, Tiff and I saw two does walk the trail we were watching. Later, about five, three more does came out. They could smell us, and one even blew a couple of times but never really spooked, but they fed about 125 yards out.

Soon I spotted a buck coming our way. It being so early in the hunt, I wanted to be sure it was a shooter. After deciding he was, I felt a bit rushed to get a shot. I threw up my gun, keyed in on him, offhand, and shot. I was shocked to see I had made a clean miss. He was still walking, as if nothing ever happened. After that I decided I had to kneel down and hope I could get another shot in an opening it looked like he might come through. My bipod was already down. Sure enough, God once again was on my side; my second chance was there. I whistled, but he would not stop, so I drew a small breath and squeezed the trigger, dropping him in his tracks.

I was happy and relieved in knowing I had just closed another chapter and achieved a dream. The first thing in my mind was to thank God; the second was "Let's see the antlers." The size of the antlers wasn't all that important. I just wanted to be successful on this trip with a reasonable trophy. I ended up with a more-than-worthy trophy that was equally unique, owing to a good bit of palmation in his antlers. I knew he had broken one tine right there somehow, because I had seen eight points. I was quick to lay my hand on him with Tiffany and say a prayer for his soul and for the opportunity. We could not find the broken tine. He scored ninety-eight points.

We loaded the deer and headed back to camp. Soon another four hunters came in, but they had nothing for the day. We talked about my hunt over supper, and then I caped him and prepped the skull for boiling. The cowboys and guide later prepared the meat for themselves to eat. Nothing was wasted here.

Day 2

We got up about five o'clock. After waiting on the cook like vultures over a dead carcass, we scarfed down some fruit and pancakes. This part was nice, and we had a good cook. We were now on a mission to get Tiffany a javelina, but just at daylight, a coyote ran in front of us, and I popped him as he was on the run while sitting in the Ranger. A little farther down, eating dust now and then because it was so dry, a jackrabbit blew by and stopped, providing Tiff a good chance to shoot my rifle for the first time. After two shots, ole Jackie was coyote food. We spent the rest of the morning slipping through cacti, stalking, and scouting all the time, wishing for a little luck, but it was a no-go. We had a good time hiking though.

We went back to bulk up again with lunch. We tried to catch a few winks because one of the dogs had decided to bark all night.

In the evening, we went after coyotes and had one come in, but I thought it might come in more, so I had Tiff wait. The coyote ended up going to nowhere land. We then decided to go over to an ole dried up riverbed to do a bit of scouting over by some charcoal makers. They had cut down many trees in the area to make charcoal to sell. We saw a lot of tracks among the cacti, so we decided to get in the middle of the spot on top of the Ranger and wait. Watching many doves pass by gave me the itch to want to hunt them; they were much bigger than the ones at home. We saw a few hawks after a quick call from my predator call. All we ended up seeing was a decent sunset.

Day 3

Again I had a good breakfast and a cup of coffee with just a hint of Amarula in it. With brake dust trailing down the road, we headed higher to the hills and got set up before daylight where we could see all around. We started glassing for game. After about two hours, all I had spotted was one bedded deer. We weren't really in good deer areas, as we were trying to stay clear and keep from messing with other hunters. The spot where we were was a thick cut down a mountain made by rain. It was thick with cover, so we started creeping down and through it. We were hoping to have Tiff see a javelina, but not with it sinking a tusk in one of our legs. It wasn't long, though, before we started seeing a good bit of deer sign. And sure enough, we saw a deer off and on, peeking from above us. There was also one decent buck at about eighty yards. We tried to mark the spot in case some other hunters wanted to try for deer there. On the way out, we picked a few ridges and sang the desperate cries of a dying rabbit, but all the coyotes must have been full.

For the evening hunt, we crisscrossed through a different area with dry, thick riverbeds. We stumbled across a good trail at the edge of some thick groves and opted to sit for the evening out there. We did see one doe but were a bit disappointed. We also had to move out of our nice room in the big house to a tent with cots down by the cowboys' house. I was more than ready to get away from that barking dog. I was about to mistake it for a coyote. Apparently a Rockefeller man (of the billionaire Rockefellers) was coming and needed our room. That evening, three bucks were taken—all nice deer. After more work, more good food, and a lot of camaraderie, we slid into the bags for some much needed sleep and a chance to give our sore feet and calf muscles a tiny break.

Day 4

After a pretty cool night, I was up early building a fire, ready for some warmth. We had to double-layer our clothing for a cold three-mile or so ride through the hills to hunt. Ten minutes out heading to our spot, I saw a coyote ahead. I was quick to pass Tiff the rifle. The little thing did her best, but she couldn't steady the thing and keep a good bead on the critters. She let them slide by, missing two. Shortly after I took the gun back, I popped one in the head with a 150-grain Ballistic Tip, helping to sustain the coyote population with more food. We spent the rest of the morning at the crossing and saw only a few does. Then we took a javelina. I took it back to the charcoal camp and was welcomed with open arms for the meat. So we went back to try to sneak up on some in the direction they ran. Carefully we made our way through the cacti. We didn't see any, but we schooled ourselves in some areas to hunt for the evening. After a quick rest and lunch, we headed back out and spend longer than necessary debating where to sit, but we ended up finally settling on a spot.

Soon the sun settled behind a distant mountain, and ten minutes later the temperature dropped until it was cool enough to put on a light coat. Then the wind calmed. Sure enough, during that magic hour we heard faint grunts—yep, just the kind of luck I'm used to getting. There they came, right behind us with no clear shots. I managed to stand and get Tiff up. She spotted the first one at fifteen yards and tried to get a shot on it while it was standing still, but it wasn't happening, so she dropped the hammer with no luck. Minutes later, another one followed at about ten yards. *Bam!* She pulled the trigger again but again had no luck. She was in the learning stages, but my gun was sighted at two hundred yards dead on, so I think she must have overshot the pig. She was disappointed, and I was not believing in the good luck or bad luck of the situation. Either way, we were seeing game and she was getting to squeeze off some rounds. As I told her, the only difference between the hunt and the experience we had was that there wasn't a photo of the animal taken, that gave us the great experience. This story is still a story and sometimes it's the animals you don't get that drives you to try again and remember the most.

Day 5

We got up and were moving fast. The morning was cold this time. We settled into a spot we hoped would be "the spot," but we'd had no luck after a couple hours. I figured the deer were bedded, so we stalked and scouted for the evening hunt at the same time. Later we set up to call coyotes a few times. Back at lunch, two more deer had been taken—nice deer—one being the biggest this particular man had ever taken in twenty years. It measured about 115 inches. This is very good for the Coues species for sure.

We kinda halfway packed, ready to leave after the evening hunt.

After a short rest, we lit out with dust boiling behind the Ranger. We settled up in cacti after moving a few times before I was satisfied on a location, yet I was still not satisfied. We were trying to savor the last few minutes of sun setting behind the mountain. We were in an area I figured a good buck should be in, and I said to Tiffany, "Man, it would be sweet to see him anyway." Well, guess what? Now you say "What," and I'm gonna say that with about thirty minutes of light left he walked out about sixty yards away. Tiff spotted him first. Sure enough, he was a very impressive buck. Another tag would have been sweet. Tiff was happy at having spotted it first, and I was glad to have gratification in having been right.

Ten minutes later, some cattle moved up behind us making all kinds of racket, so I got up and threw some rocks at them, and in doing so, I scared off that darn buck, who was right behind us. All I could say was "Crap!" He would have walked right over us, and I would have loved to get a better look.

We then went back to camp for our last supper. Gordon Rockefeller came in, and he seemed as down-to-earth as we were. There was another good deer in camp; Andy had taken it. We all took some group shots, and we had all had a good hunt.

As usual, the trip home through customs was an adventure. Not registering my gun was the biggest issue in the United States. And this time, unlike the last time, I was on the other side of the border. The USDA inspection with my antlers went well. Trying to put them on the plane as a carry-on didn't. All in all, it was an awesome trip to have, and it had allowed me to finish up taking one of every deer species in the world. I had made new friends, and the trip had given me more reason to give glory to God for the hunt. The journey of taking one of each species seemed long until it was over; along the way, I took white-tailed deer, Rocky Mountain mule deer, desert mule deer, Coues deer, black-tailed deer, and Sitka deer in Alaska. Well, enjoy the wild, my friends, and see God's blessing for it.

My First Moose Hunt

My first moose hunt started with a ride from a good friend, Pamela to Alexandria Airport. The total flying time was about ten and a half hours to Anchorage, Alaska. I spent some visiting time along the way with Johnny Rae and Melony Dowden. They were on their way for vacation too. Tagging along with me was Trenton Johnson, who was trying to take his first black bear.

As soon as we hit the ground, we were running to Cabela's for locking tags, licenses, and more gear. All along we were trying to figure out how to stay under the 350-pound weight limit for Above Alaska Aviation in Talkeetna. This weight includes body weight and all. The plan was to be in the bush for twenty-plus days. We ended up bedding down at the Lakeshore Inn in Anchorage on the first night. I could have done without the snoring from Trent though.

Once up and at 'em, we needed to be at the Alaskan Railroad Train

Station for a three-hour trip to Talkeetna. It was a nice and interesting trip along the way. This trip, for me, was a sign of changing times in my life. As I write now, I need glasses, and my bones hurt. I saw a few moose along the creek inlet at forty feet elevation.

August 29

We reached Talkeetna and wasted no time before meeting Sarah Russell, Drew Haag, and Eric, our pilot, to reorganize our gear. We had to confirm our correct weight, which was limited to 350 pounds. After about an hour and a half flight over mountaintops covered in snow and glaciers, we scouted around, looking for game. We spotted some.

We first thought about landing at Crater Lake, but we ended up landing at a small lake about four miles away. We had a good-sized running stream nearby, as well as a few small trees. We were about a thirty-minute hike from where we able to get the pontoons off the plane and up the bank. I alone made four trips to the selected campsite. There were only a few flat places to be found. Trent was supposed to be in about three hours later.

About the time I was logging in our GPS location and was done with my tent, I heard Trent's plane flying in the distance. He packed in his stuff, and while setting up, we saw some caribou. Later on we made a little stalk, and Trent got within about one hundred yards of a brown bear. We ate and bedded down for sleep—or so I thought. It didn't take long to realize my zero-degree-rated sleeping bag was not enough for the snow and twenty-four-degree temps. It was a miserable, cold, and very scary night—no fun at all.

August 30

As morning broke on day two, August 30, it was no better. Now we had about 15 mph winds. I made it down to the creek anyway for breakfast and a drink of water. The water had to be filtered and was all we had to drink. I ended up running for the tent after about an hour, praying for the weather to clear. Lo and behold, after a few hours of us being flat on our backs, the sun finally broke through and the wind started to calm down a bit, with the temperature rising a few degrees.

Soon, packs loaded, we lit out and saw one lone cow moose. We decided to split up and spent most of the day glassing the ridges, moving now and then to warm up. I eventually ended up seeing another lone cow moose and a few caribou way off. There were still a few blueberries, but very few, and they were starting to go bad, so we were not expecting to see too many bears. We hoped to see one for Trent. (Just one.) We came back to the camp a bit early to get supper down before it turned colder. All day I was dreading the thought that it was going to freeze again. It was darn near torture. The worst part was having to crawl out of the sleeping bag three times to go to the bathroom.

Day 1: September 1

Moose season officially opened today. Last night saw forgiving weather, with the temperature hovering right about freezing, at thirty-three degrees. As soon as I saw ice crystals that had melted a bit on top of my tent, I eased out of the ole sleeping bag and into the open air of the cold tent and got moving, throwing on clothes. I crawled out of my tent to a beautiful sunny day, though it was cold. It was an awesome sight to wake up to the big snow-covered mountain in the background, with nothing but wilderness and big sky all around.

I woke up Trent, and we wormed our way down the creek and cook area about one hundred yards away. Again we were glad to see all the food still hanging in the tree. We broke open a pack of Mountain House granola and blueberries, scarfed it down, and headed out. We worked the river's edge on the bank, sitting, warming up, scoping out the hillsides, and then moving again when the wind cooled us back down. We always moved slowly so as not to get warmed up too fast, because doing that will cause you to get tired and have headaches and dry mouth. We split about two miles out from each other, and I went about a mile more before I thought, *I'm ready to pack a moose at forty-nine years old!* I'd been humbled at what a few years could do to a hunting man.

All I saw was a few eagles, and I picked up a few sheds from caribou along the way. Trent found quite a few as well. He saw one moose and a calf and a thick-coated red fox. We both got headaches from the cold wind that morning, so we decided to take a nap. With only a few hours of daylight left, I decided to just take binoculars and a gun, and head out a mile or so to do some glassing. Not too far off in the distance, I saw a bull's antlers glistening in the remaining sunlight, but the shot was much too far for the daylight left for sure. So I watched him and thought, *Lord, he must be a good one to be so easily seen that far away.*

After getting back to camp, as I was talking with Trent with maybe twenty minutes of daylight left, a cow and calf walked within 150 yards of our tents. When the temps drop, they drop here. So we got in bed soon as the sun went over the mountains.

Day 2: September 2

We woke up to a nice thirty-six-degree morning. I decided on a granola bar for breakfast and headed out early, alone, to see if the bull was still in the area. A plane was passing by to drop off a father-and-son group to hunt caribou toward Lake Louise, and it was also going to drop off some waders for Trent, so he slept in.

After about an hour, I made it to a spot where I could see for four miles in most places. After about twenty minutes, I spotted a big bull way off—even farther away than the one I had seen last night. About my luck. I watched him in the same area for about thirty minutes, contemplating the whole situation. I had to at least get closer. About two miles was what I'd been telling myself was the farthest we should try to pack a bull moose out, but a mile was more like it in this country. Well, I decided to let the good Lord call it. I decided I was gonna go to him if I could, moseying my way through swampy grass, crossing streams, going through thick bushes taller than my head, and trekking downriver for a mile or so.

I got to a spot where I could look again. Sure enough, he was still there, now about a half mile away. I took time to look at my GPS to see how far from camp the pack distance would be. I was already 3.42 miles away. I thought, *No way; too far to pack.* This would never have crossed my mind in the past.

The more I watched him, the more I realized this was a very big bull. It was an easy trophy by any moose standards. Going closer, I crossed a good-sized stream and expected him to be right over the ridge, a couple of hundred yards away. I decided to shoot, thinking I could use the stream to keep the meat cool for a time. Just as I eased over, a darn cow saw me, moved slowly off, and then accelerated to a trot. The bull stood on top of the hill for a long time, looking back now and then. I might have been able to hit him but decided against it, hoping he would start to ease over the hill to feed. Then, being out of sight, I could get closer, rushing the hill. That I did. He moved even farther into some bad stuff 326 yards away. I decided it was too far to try to pack him out. I felt sick, but I got pictures anyway, and then I watched three cows bed down over in a small canyon, and a bull went over into it as well. I never saw them come out. I figured the bull had spotted me and I just couldn't see him the bull ease out. Now, I'm just glad I could have got one and sick at the same time.

I looked at my GPS and saw I was 4.27 miles from camp. And that was a straight shot. By the time I worked my way back, zigzagging through the countryside, I would probably have traveled 5.5 miles. I was about five hundred yards from the top of the hill where they had broken over and disappeared. Now my adrenaline had slowed down, and I realized how far I had to go back. I was feeling a little laid out but decided to go up and make sure the bull had not high-tailed it down the valley. I peeked over the top of the hill and saw the ears of the moose bedded there to my right, along with two more. *Where did the bull go?* I watched for about fifteen minutes and decided to make a cow-in-heat call with my mouth. They all stood up, but there was still no bull. There was one little spot he may have gone through undetected. The cows stirred around and then moved along. I was still convinced there was a bull somewhere close to where I stood. All alone, I was thinking, *Will I shoot this time—in even a worse place than before?* Well, I never saw him again. I felt kinda glad and kinda sad. I don't like to boast sometimes, but I'm pretty sure this was a better-than-average bull even for an avid moose hunter's standards.

I decided to lie down right there and sleep. Then I made the three-and-a-half-mile hike back to camp. During the last two miles, this ole boy was tuckered out. Back at the camp, it didn't take me too long to head for the food down at the creek and get some groceries down. Trent had watched me walk back from a hill across the way, but he hadn't seen any moose. A cow and calf came into the camp later that evening.

Day 3: September 3

The night was the warmest yet. In the morning, I woke Trent, and we scarfed down some Mountain house eggs and bacon for breakfast. Then we lit out about one mile or so to a spot I wanted to glass. We spotted five caribou and twelve moose. One of the moose was a small bull, but Big Boy was nowhere to be found. I gave up finding the big bull, and we headed in to fire up a couple of MREs just in time to beat the rain. We dashed for the tents. We could see six miles or so away that snow was coming. So I wrote as it rained, and then I curled up in my Ascend sleeping bag. By the way, I highly recommend a half-gallon Borden milk jug in your tent if you don't want to run outside in the middle of the night.

Day 4: September 4

Well, last night was forty-five degrees, and it rained all night. I spent a long time in the tent. Daylight came, and I was ready to roll. The rain had slowed a good bit, so we dressed with all our rain gear ready. The minute I walked out, I was sick! There was fog! Visibility was only about one hundred yards. So we walked for a bit of a stretch and headed right back into the tent. Trent didn't come out for some time. After an hour or so, the rain slowed to a drizzle, so I headed out anyway. As the morning passed, so did the fog a bit; but at higher elevations, the fog lasted all day—and drizzle too. Right away, I saw some moose!

I sat a bit and then slowly and steadily moved all day. I sat and glassed spots now and then. I shot a small bull with my camera as well as a porcupine, after it almost shot me first. I saw half a dozen moose, but no bulls! I also had a hawk try to attack me; I think I may have been invading his space or something. I found another awesome lake, and there were some goldeneyes—a type of duck I had always wanted to shoot. After doing a little gun cleaning, I got out of most of my wet clothes, scarfed down a chicken fajita MRE, and went to bed.

Day 5: September 6:

I woke up Trent, cooked some eggs quickly, and went to the hill I call "the Perch" and started glassing for moose. It wasn't too long before I spotted a few cows and calves. It was a little windy, as usual, making the forty-one-degree morning cool for sitting. Trent was laid back on his backpack, trying to stay warm. About that time, I was going to chew him out and tell him to get his binoculars up. About two miles behind us, he spotted a bull. Quickly we started trying to put together a game plan on how to stalk him. But with our usual back-and-forth ideas, we weren't getting too much decided, so we just lit out toward him, trying to stay hidden behind small hills and tall brush, all along checking whether he was still feeding along the mountainside. The closer we got, the more we felt as though this bull might exceed the fifty-inch requirement for being legally taken, or that he might have the alternative requirement of at least four brow tines. The bad part was that there was a cow with him on the ridge. We needed to get close enough to see him, make sure, and maybe get a shot.

Sure enough, we got almost there, and the cow popped up and looked at us for ten minutes until my arms felt as if they were gonna crack from the weight of my gun. All the fast moves and warm clothes had me about to drop from being hot. Thank God we had dropped our packs about a half mile back. Luckily the cow just eased over the hill without acting as though we startled her, and we hoped the bull was still about one hundred yards out. Now on top of the hill, four hundred yards or so out, we eased over it, hoping to see the bull. There was no bull!

We were looking frantically, trying to comprehend where he went, thinking maybe he spooked without us realizing it. We were glassing when Trent saw a speck of white up the mountainside a bit. Sure enough, thank God, the bull had bedded down and was looking our way. Now all our game plans were going again back and forth. So we eased up three hundred yards and thought about trying a shot there, but we then decided to get closer. We got to 150 yards. The plan was for me to be ready, and then Trent would yell, making him stand up so I could get a good look. I hoped he would be legal to shoot. Well, the plan worked, and when he stood and looked back, I saw his horn bump his back, which is one way to identify a fifty-incher, so I shot and hit. I shot again and hit, and he crumpled to the ground but was still moving, so I slung another one into him. We were excited—but not too excited until the tape came out. He measured fifty-two inches. *Praise God!*

Then we looked at him closer as he lay there weighing approximately 1,500 to 1,650 pounds. Just the sight of him made our bodies ache, knowing the work was about to begin. During the hunt, it had begun to sprinkle rain now and then. Trent decided to go back and get the packs, and I started to skin the moose just enough to not mess the pictures up. These things have about 950 pounds of meat you have to take out on bone, and about 600 off bone. Unfortunately, our area required it all to be left on the bone. Now, if you're not ready to work—and I mean *work*, then spend big money and get an outfitter to do this for you. We did it ourselves, and it is tough—very tough! You skin them where they lie without moving them or hanging them.

We got one side laid open and put some aside and hiked the mile and a half or so to camp, where we got pack, game bags, saws, etc. We headed back up and went ahead with finishing the tough task of quartering him, using tarps to flip him around now and then. We got almost all of the meat into game bags to help keep insects and debris off it, and we started packing. I knew right off the bat this was going to be tough on this forty-nine-year-old man. I will never get another bull out at the four-mile mark.

Trent made two trips, and I made three—one right at dark. On each trip, we were hoping a brown bear didn't want the meat worse than us. Each step had to be precisely placed when going up and down the mountain through rocks and bushes, being careful not to fall. Trent did fall once; his knee landed on a rock, making it doubly hellish for him. I'll tell ya, everything that had kind of hurt on us now hurt more. Each load was one hundred–plus pounds, and I had no problem taking a muscle relaxer that evening, even though I don't usually do that. In the sleeping bag that night, I could barely turn over or lie on my shoulders, as they hurt so bad. The weather had warmed up that night, and the creepy-crawlies started coming out and biting, leaving some nasty marks. I thought Trent was gonna die before it was over.

Day 6: September 7

It was time to finish packing. We had already scheduled a pickup with Above Alaska Aviation the next day, and today we had to bring in the back hindquarter. Trent tried to carry one whole; took about ten steps and knew there was no way. So we had to cut them in half, which hurt, because we added two and a half more trips at two and a half miles a piece. Not that the morning was cold.

We ended up making three trips each, loaded down all the time, hoping a pack of wolves or brown bears would rather have fresh meat than us. We didn't tote a gun, as we had enough to tote already. Anyway, we got everything down, including the trash, quicker than we thought. We stacked the meat on piles or rocks so air could circulate around it, and sprayed it with citrus spray to help keep bugs off. The weather was already warmer than we would have liked it to be, and I was worried as to whether my carrier could get out here. They had wrecked one of their planes, so they had only one now. I was a bit worried that I might be fined for the meat, but so far so good.

Day 7: September 8

They are supposed to get us and the meat out of here today. One of us might have to stay if we run out of time. Trent will be going first, so I half packed, and Trent will bring it all down. The night was good. We always know when it's about to get dark, because we can hear the wind howling in the mountains, rivers, and streams, raging down the hills from snow melting up high. It was a smooth forty degrees.

About four in the afternoon, we saw the plane top the mountain with a light on its wing, and we knew our ride was finally here. We had seen a few more fly by while at this spot. The deal was that Trent flew to Lake Louise and then came back, got some more moose meat, and went back to Lake Louise. Trent is gonna go back by truck to Talkeetna and hopefully make it back to get me; then we will fly back to Talkeetna. I sat there hoping, 'cause it was clouding up and I saw some rain in the mountains that looked to be about twenty miles away or so. I'd already packed all my gear—tent and all. At least I had beavers and ducks swimming in the lake near me for company, but they won't keep me warm when I get wet.

It would be about a one-and-a-half-hour flight back to Talkeetna in the super cub. I planned to have my little talk with Jesus this evening under the awesome sky he had made. I truly felt he had answered my prayers all along on this trip so far. I could only hope he would give me the time and energy to share more of the good parts of what is left in these times on planet Earth and one day brag about the good things in his creation.

Well, Eric made it back to get me and the rest of the moose meat. He also had just fueled up the plane, so we tried to take off two times, but there was not much headwind left and we ended up being too heavy. The third time, after trying hard and shutting it down, we kind of ran aground, so we had to unload the meat to get in the air. This meant a trip back for Eric. It also meant we had to abort our plans and go to Lake Louise, as well as try to land in the dark on the lake with no lights. The four of us ended up in a cabin at the lake, with Eric on the floor.

The next morning at breakfast, we met Mr. Gene Moe. This man killed a grizzly with his buck knife while it was attacking his wife in the loft of a cabin. *Outdoor Life* wrote an article about it. It took 589 stitches to put him back together. He is a smart and interesting man and still lives in Anchorage. Then we made a five-hour drive down beautiful Highway 1 through glaciers and mountains full of aspens. It was rough through most of it, and we passed areas where massive wildfires had done a lot of damage this season. It was the stop in Wasilla at Hardee's that ruined my day, making me sick.

Day 8: September 9

We got to the motel, ate, washed our clothes, and hit the hay. We then woke up and started processing two hundred pounds of moose meat. I prepped my antlers to bring them back on the plane, but not before setting enough meat aside to grill. We had steaks, some of which were over 1.5 inches thick.

Day 9: September 10

I woke up ready to do what sometimes gets old and gets into your pocketbook while on a trip—eat! We can't live without doing that! There can be two thousand–plus tourists a day on the streets here in Talkeetna. I'm getting antsy to get back out. It has to happen soon.

Day 10: September 11

Well, Trent finally got off the water and into the air about one thirty. I stayed back for the second flight. This hunt was mainly for him, so he wanted to pick the hunting and camping site. Two hours or so later, I was in the air. While on the way there, Trent had decided on a different spot than we had picked. I planned for us to do the best we could. The country was thick, and we would be about two miles from what I perceived from the air to be a place where we could shoot with best chances, but one never knows. We couldn't hunt the first day, and it wouldn't have mattered, because we had only about two hours left to set up the cooking area, get tents up, and prepare for the next day.

Day 11: September 12

The first night was not too bad once the beavers stopped slapping their tails in the lake. They were down the hill about seventy-five yards, near the cook area. There were a few different birds I had never heard before as well. We got up a bit later than I wished. I told Trent we needed to be out early for bears. We grabbed some quick grub and headed out one way, and right off the bat I saw it was going to be what I had seen in the swampy areas of Prince of Wales Island. The ground was soft, and after we went through the thick spots, it was like climbing a stair tread. I found myself needing water much more often than when we were hunting moose, and I grew more tired at shorter distances. Unhappy with that, I knew even more that I didn't like the spot, but I hunted on. At 2.72 miles on my GPS, I'd had enough and still hadn't gotten to where I needed to I be. I had jumped a few pairs of grouse, but I imagined there would not be much of them left to eat after a .300 hit one.

By the time I got back, four hours later, I found that Trent had arrived back early, aggravated at me for raising Cain about the location and worried about his knee hurting. I was beat, and that was not good, as I needed to look for a better spot, so I napped an hour and we ate, and we then went in another direction, looking for hope through open swamps. We tried to call bears with a predator call. We saw very little sign, but we had a nice view of Mount McKinley when the sun popped out a bit. The wind was ripping cold all day. We made about a four-mile circle and still saw nothing, but our hopes were up. Back at camp, we were quick to hit the bed and aggravated enough at the hike from the lake to the mountains and severity of it that both of us were mad enough to plan to cut the whole trip short and carry our butts home early if we could. We made a call to schedule a pickup, which we hoped would arrive tomorrow, on Sunday.

Day 12: September 13

The night started out cold—cold enough to make me put on two pair of socks. It ended up a bit warmer, but it was still very foggy. Drew said the pickup would happen about noon instead of three in the afternoon, as was first scheduled, so we broke camp. Big mistake! The weather turned far worse, so we had to put it all right back up again. This was another unhappy time for me, so I went fishing on the lake for an hour or so, having no luck. I decided to retreat to the tent to catch up on writing this story.

Lying there a few hours later, I heard a plane in the distance. As far as we knew, we were not going home. Then we heard a swish in the lake and realized they had made it out to get us. Trent broke camp again as if he had done it one hundred times a day, and he flew out. Me? Well, the storm was breaking, and I knew the plane would take about two hours round trip, so I broke down all but my tent. The pilot did make it back, and I did get out; and just as I landed, the rain started.

Back in Talkeetna, we quickly started rearranging our gear to ship it and bring it home on the plane. I plugged in a cell phone to see what options there were to rebook an early flight. I was sweating the cost. Luck had it we could fly out at six o'clock the next evening for $325 if I could get there. On the way back, we stopped at a Subway and arranged a ride from a young man that worked there. We paid him what it would have cost for train transport, both of us wanting to help him rather than take a train.

Day 13: September 14

We paid the young man $200 for a ride to Anchorage, dropped the meat off, and went to the airport. We also went to eat, and of all the restaurants, we ended up in the one our new friend Gene Moe (the man who killed a brown bear with a knife to save his wife) was in. We wanted to visit him at his home. Next time, maybe. I ended up having to cut my moose antlers in half, place boxes around the tips, shrink-wrap them, and duct-tape every inch to get them on the plane. They no longer want any antlers showing (a crock!), all because a man shot a lion lured out of a park in Africa. I don't think the man knew the lion had been lured out. Maybe the outfitters knew. He had enough money not to have to pull an illegal stunt like that. This was another dumb mistake made that affected so many in the hunting world when it shouldn't have.

I can barely live with the way Americans just fall to the feet of so many. Kinda like when a few folks died on three-wheelers, it was "Hey, let's just stop making them." What a crock! Anyway, Marco Rivera ended up coming through for a ride, but I had a lady from the motel as a backup. It's rare that I need help and ask, but I didn't want to lose the plane ticket we had booked over the phone and have the fare go up to $750 the next day.

All in all, even though the trip was cut quite short, once again I'd seen God answer my prayers in more ways than one because of my continued belief and understanding, by my standards, that if one helps oneself along with prayer, prayers can be answered. I'm a firm believer that being in a place far from normal life is as close as one can find to real heaven. The awesome part of nature is that it can always open my mind, soul, and heart enough to straighten the good side of me back out every time. Also, I have to thank my good friend Trent Johnson for coming along having my back. I thought I was gonna have to go alone. He truly had my back, helping me pack out that moose. I also have to thank Scott Bagi for getting me the permit in the moose draw. I missed hunting with my ole buddy, but I felt our original plan might have put too much strain on all of us as a bigger group.

Yeah, I know a man can quit a lot of things and be all right sometimes, but if he quits on his dreams, then he has to quit being happy. Find hard work, clean living, and God together, and go for them, my friends! It also helps to have a strong woman at home, like my Tiffany Edwards, to help handle things while you are out living your dreams and understanding your passion.

Brown bears, grizzlies, and at least one caribou are my next dreams, and an even bigger dream is taking one of each species of caribou in the lands they live in. So bow up till you throw up, my friends. Dig deep for what you want, and don't stop till you drop.

Canada Pronghorn / Mule Deer Hunt 2015

Hello! This hunt was what you might call a spur-of-the-moment kind of hunt through my friend Scott Eskar, from Ohio, who shoved it in my face. I had been hoping to get out to hunt pronghorn, but I had never thought I would do it in Canada; going to another country was right up my alley.

The flight from Alexandria, Louisiana, to Saskatchewan, Canada was about seven hours. We arrived in Saskatchewan about midnight. We would be hunting on a Cree Indian reservation. We stayed at a small motel in North Battleford. We were met by our first new friend, Gus. A couple of hours later, we were already up, dressing before daylight and meeting Dennis for about an hour's drive to the start of the hunting ground. The Cree Indians have several different tribes, and they all share the hunting grounds.

At daybreak I was floored to see the massive flocks of sandhill cranes, ducks, and geese. There were birds in every hole of water over the miles of farmland. I was also quick to notice that there was almost no litter along the roadways. Quickly we glassed ridged canyons along the edges of wooded areas, manmade windbreaks through standing crops, etc. We saw some moose and a few mulies, but no shooters.

The second day was a bit tough for me, owing to my new friend Robbie Warner's snoring. I have to have quiet to sleep. So I moved to Scott's room. He assured me he didn't snore. *Wrong!* He snores, all right. My ear plugs were shoved in so deep I had to tie a string to them just to get them out. That second day was tough, with winds over thirty miles per hour, so we headed to a thicker wooded area along the North Saskatchewan River. There were awesome sights! We saw a good bit of sign from moose and deer but ended the day without seeing even one animal.

Day 3

We were out before daylight. Today was Cree Thanksgiving, which always falls during the second weekend of October. We had left early to try to get out on the edge of the canyon. It was cooler than normal, but the wind was still rolling about ten to fifteen miles per hour with heavy fog, so visibility was low. After a few hours, we eased along the canyon's ridge, all along our toes getting colder. We were seeing a few does pop out now and then. All were mulies. There were also coyotes. I shot a bit of video with my GoPro of them howling. They had heavy coats compared to the ones in Louisiana. About the time I was thinking of shooting one, we spotted two bucks moving our way. They were still about a quarter mile from us. The more I glassed the buck, the bigger I wanted him to be. But he was just a tad bit small. Interestingly, we saw a coyote bedded down near the river's edge, and the buck was headed straight toward him. Sure enough, the buck walked to within about two feet of the coyote when both animals realized what was happening and scared the wits out of each other.

There had been a sixty-inch elk spotted in the canyon, so we looked for him. I wasn't dead set on shooting whatever species I saw on this hunt. You can hunt elk, moose, pronghorn, whitetail, and mule deer here.

We rode to some hills and spotted seven more small bucks and a dozen does or so, as well as a small group of whitetails. That night, we went to the casino to chomp down on big steaks. We saw seventeen coyotes that first day.

Day 4

The next morning, after a quick stop at a twenty-four-hour McDonald's, we headed out. Not much later, all of a sudden, while we were driving at seventy miles per hour, there was a tree across the road about the size of my leg, with what looked like a big stump on one end. We hit the tree and discovered there was a big beaver dragging it across the road to a pond. We figured we jarred his head pretty good, maybe loosening a few of his teeth.

That morning we saw a few small bucks, and about an hour before dark, we spotted a group of about fifteen antelope, one of them a buck. He looked like a shooter, but we wanted to be sure, so we were wearing out the binoculars sitting behind some rock about quarter mile out hillside. About that time, Dennis drove up, and they all got out of the truck, which made the antelope nervous about, three hundred yards away. With them there, I was assured the buck was a shooter. I popped my bipod open, and stretched out, and as I was about to take my first shot before they went over the hill, the right side of the bipod broke just at the time I wanted to shoot. Soon they spooked, and we sped after them across the fields, hoping to see them stop, but it never happened. We were about to give up for the day when we saw one lone buck out in a field, and he was a shooter, all alone. So I got out and crawled, or sort of hopped, for a few hundred yards, trying to stay under the ridge he was just over. I got to about 275 yards and made my first shot, and I was shocked! I missed! More shocked than I was, he stood there. I slammed another 180-grain Nosler Partition in my Browning .300 WSM, shot again, and got a hit. I shot a second round with it for an on-the-run hit. I had been wanting a buck antelope since 1987, when I took a doe antelope on the Colorado/Kansas border. So I was one happy ole boy.

Day 5

After breaking out of bed and flying through the local McDonald's for a burrito and coffee, Robbie, Leroy, Dennis, and I were together hunting. We saw a few moose and one small bull that was in rut, slobbering at the mouth and hanging on to the hind end of an ole cow. Robbie had come on the hunt primarily to try to shoot a moose, so he was also foaming at the mouth, wishing the little feller was a shooter. After a few hours of joking and fooling around, we spotted a good many deer way off—a lot of small mule deer and one decent whitetail buck. We went back to camp, and after a short nap. Few hours later, it was a deer hunter's dream. We saw not one but about seven bucks ranging from 140 to 180 inches. Robbie opted to let me shoot the first nice buck, so after hiking about half mile in I scoped down and pulled the trigger on the one I thought was the biggest one. He fell in his tracks. Everyone said, "You missed." I said, "What? I'm looking at him on the ground in my scope!" About my luck—I had shot the wrong one. I ended up with one about 158 inches. That was bad for me but good for Robbie.

Soon Robbie popped a shot. It was a long shot at about four hundred yards, but he hit. The deer ran over the ridge, and we saw him go down. Then he got up, so Robbie popped him again. Robbie's deer was about 160 inches. We both agreed that seeing deer scattered atop that ridge on the skyline with an orange haze in the background was a sight we would never forget. That night, heading in, we were feeling excited and happy with our kills. We got to see a tad bit of the Northern Lights. That was something totally unexpected.

Day 6

The next morning, I intended on getting an elk if I saw a great big one, or even a two-hundred-inch mule deer, or nothing. Over one ridge, we saw one animal but were not sure what it was. We all went back to investigate, and as we topped the hill, we saw that pronghorn were everywhere. Robbie broke out and slung a bullet for a hit, lying down, to bag a good trophy antelope. We saw two small moose bulls with three cows and a few coyotes. During the evening hunt, we saw three cows, and I spotted two good bucks in an uncut canola field, about like the one I took, so it was tough to pass up. In all, it was a great hunt with great friends, we got two more trophies!

Alaska Caribou Hunt 2016

Day 1

Tiffany ran me up to Alexandria International Airport for my first caribou hunt in Alaska on August 15, 2016, with my good friend Bim, from Kosaloft, Alaska. After a delay for an hour right off the bat, I managed to make my way to Fairbanks International Airport; it was my first time there. I had to gawk at the polar bear that had been mounted in 1966, the year I was born, and the big grizzly, while waiting for my baggage. Bim was there to pick me up. Right off, we left to get me a tag, some trail mix, and a bone saw. Then we went to the motel, where we split a room. The next morning, we mauled the breakfast provided by the motel at Best Western, which cost us $175 a night! Jeez! There I met Gary and Jordan from Oklahoma. They were joining us on the hunt.

Day 2

On our long five-hundred-mile-or-so drive down the Dalton Highway, it didn't take long to see it was going to be a beautiful drive. Bim drove the whole way, explaining about a lot of what we were seeing—especially the Trans-Alaska Pipeline. Parts were not paved, and it was rough now and then; the paved parts were rough too. We definitely passed a lot of stories back and forth between us. Of course, we had to stop at the Arctic Circle sign and get pictures. We fueled up at Coldfoot and had a scare when the AC belt went bad. We were worried that it was the serpentine belt.

Day 3

After staying the night at Arrowhead Outfitters' base camp, near Deadhorse, we were sweating being able to fly out when finally the weather broke a bit and we were told to go load up. When we got to the plane and unloaded the gear all four of us had, it was easy to see we had too much stuff for the seventy-pound limit allowed each person. Bim and Jordan left first on a plane with floats. Gary and I left about twenty minutes behind them.

We landed on what looked to be a twenty-acre lake in the wide-ass open, spotting a few caribou while flying in. As quickly as we could, we began setting up tents to try to beat any messy weather that might roll in and wet all our gear. That is one thing we didn't want to happen! The bad thing was that it took a third flight to get the rest of the other guys' stuff in. But I didn't have to wait; I even got my tent after sorting our stuff. LOL.

Bim lit out to search for water, hoping to find some better than the lake water; and he did, about a mile away. I had already shuffled up my bag and found one of my filters for lake water just in case. It is risky to drink out of lakes.

Later we worked on some sandwiches we had left over from the drive down Dalton Highway from Fairbanks along a lot of the Trans-Alaska Pipeline. It was a very beautiful drive, and most of it was dirt and gravel and was rough most of the way. We saw a few caribou, musk oxen, and golden eagles, as well as some hunters with bows along the road. Hunting with rifles is not allowed within five miles of the pipeline.

It was still daylight when we turned in for the night at about a quarter to seven. It started getting dark about twelve thirty and got light again about five in the morning.

On the first day of hunting, we broke out of bed. The night hadn't been so bad. Poking my head out like a turtle from my Cabela's Alaskan Guide tent, I noticed that it was windy and cold but bearable. Right off I scrambled for some grub, and I heard Bim and the others milling around like rats in a wall in their tents. I lit out walking around the lake we had camped on and found a vantage spot about three-quarters of a mile out. Glassing, I saw a few caribou—miles away, for sure—so I decided to stay posted and keep an eye out. It didn't take me long to pull my little three-by-four-foot tarp up against me to break the wind. Slowly the clouds parted and daylight began peering through them. I could see the Brook Range Mountains in the distance. They were beautiful for sure! Many ducks and geese flew about, some in groups as large as one hundred. Later two ravens nearly alit on me, landing two feet from my head. I sat still to see how close they might come.

About midday, I decided to head to camp for some freeze-dried Mountain House teriyaki chicken. Then, after a nap of about one and a half hours, the wind died down a bit. At my first stop, a beautiful white-and-black owl flew up close and personal to investigate me. A bit later, two loons, as beautiful as any duck ever, swam along the lakeshore. I soon saw a caribou about one mile away. There were four that passed well out of shooting range, and one black bull at 206 yards, which I passed on. I hoped it would continue down the lake's edge out to Mr. Gary. It was a bit small. I got to use to my range finder during that time. My girl Tiffany Edwards gave it to me.

At 8:28 p.m., I headed off to bed.

Day 2

I got out of bed about seven o'clock without ambition, a little bit like the first day, owing to a few old man pains in my ole fifty-year-old body. Nevertheless, I headed out for my two-mile-or-so vantage point I had picked out the day before. It was much farther than I wished to have to go, but I wanted to be where I felt I had a chance—and I was right. Not too long after sitting and wrapping my small tarp up around me to help break the wind, I saw two cows and a calf in the distance nearby. Sure enough, they breezed by me at two hundred yards or so. They ran one hundred yards to stop and eat and then ran again, as if following a migration pattern. Later I saw others doing the same thing farther off, so I felt a bit better, thinking that maybe some groups would swing through. I decided to move farther up to where more had passed through, and I got a few photos of those at about one hundred yards. I watched several flocks of geese fly right over me and had my little talk with Jesus after observing how beautiful the sky was with the snowcapped mountains in the background. I am never surprised at the beauty I find on these trips off the beaten path of life. I wished I had brought a book to identify some of the plants I was seeing.

About 5:22 p.m. there came a good rain with high winds. The other boys saw three bulls—one good one—but could not close the deal. I wished I would not have forgotten my dang comb. My GPS said I was 3,470 miles from home.

At 8:40 p.m., the wind picked up. It was about fifty degrees, and I would guess the wind was twenty-five miles per hour. The lake was about two miles long and one mile wide, and it had whitecaps. We were camped at a lake called Nipple Lake in Area 26.

Day 3

At 8:07 a.m., it was still raining pretty hard, showing no signs of relief. Being all alone in a tent with nothing but time is one sure way to work out things in your mind. It's funny, but hard times on a hunt are usually good times, allowing one to think uninterrupted about many things.

Soon I suited up in my gear and lit out. About three hundred yards was all the visibility I had, so I had to mind my p's and q's to not get disoriented—or should I say lost. Now there was a lot of water everywhere, so it was a bit harder to navigate. Little streams were running deeper, making them more difficult to cross. I hunted for about three hours and saw nothing, so I headed back. I made it in about five thirty in the evening, and all I wanted was water and gut wadding right off. I dipped some water out of the lake and boiled it, hoping to make it safe to drink, preventing my getting sick (and maybe dying). But for now, it was underwear city and the flat of my back, Jack. I needed rest.

Day 4

I'll tell ya, swapping clothes out is not an easy thing in this dang little tent. It was 11:01 a.m. and still rolling, and I was tired of counting bugs crawling around on my tent roof. The situation was not worth a flip! The rain was one thing. All my stuff was wet. Also, I couldn't see very far with all the fog and rain pounding my binoculars. It had me being a lazy hunter. Stuff just doesn't dry out in a hurry out there. Get everything wet, and it just stays wet for a long time. The biggest killer was Howard, owner of Arrowhead Outfitters. He'd been here thirty years and said this was the worst year he had ever seen. So either we missed the migration or it was still yet to come. It will probably happen the day after we leave. He also said none of the camps were seeing much to talk about. My chances for caribou were looking slim. I felt it would take a miracle now—a herd coming through for migration. At least the monsoon had started.

It was still sprinkling when I went out to hunt. I saw two way off in the distance and three in the other direction, but they were nowhere near close enough for me to take one. I don't think either was a bull. But before we did anything else, we had to move Bim's tents. They were in low spots and were about to get flooded. The temperature dropped to forty degrees with about a 5 to 8 mph wind—just enough to rough up the hunt a bit. Beef stroganoff was for supper, along with some Tang. I then hiked a hill to glass over some ridges one last time before bed, just to look. I saw five way, way off, so I felt I might as well turn in.

Day 5

I woke to the rain slowing almost to a stop, but no one had rolled out of any of the tents yet, so I made another hike up to a high spot on the ridge to glass. It was slim. There were just a few caribou way off, so I came down to give a report. By then everyone was up milling around, waiting for food. I joined in, and we talked about many things till the rain broke again, and then we put a game plan together.

Up the hill we went slowly, taking our steps cautiously. This was the type of terrain I like to walk on; it was like a bunch of half-aired-up basketballs covered with hay. George and Jordan went one way, and Bim and I went another. Soon we split up with Bim making a huge loop, hopefully trying to run a caribou toward us. After about two hours, I hadn't seen him, but I knew he was down there because seven caribou ran by us as we had intended—but no bulls!

After a while, I was getting colder. It had been sprinkling, and my butt and back had had all they could stand of sitting on humps. I didn't see any caribou between where Bim and I had split up, so I decided to go straight down about a half mile to the end of the ridge, where Bim was, and find him.

I figured he was just over the ridge toward the end, sitting and glassing. I planned to meet him and figure a new plan. We spoke, and it was a good thing. I managed to talk Bim out of a Snickers bar and got to see a flock of ptarmigan, which are kind of like grouse.

One of the hardest things about hunting in this environment has been the lack of toilets. Mine has been a twenty-ounce Gatorade bottle while in my tent.

At 2:12 p.m., I was sick of rain. I had twelve hours behind me and counting. I kind of needed the rest after yesterday, but this was enough.

I had spent twenty-eight hours last year in a tent while moose hunting, but I was not all about record hours in a tent. So about the time I made it to the end of the ridge, I ran into a river. There was still no sign of Bim. I was thinking he might be trying to find a way around it, so I started walking it too, and I was about to where I should have been able to see much better all around when I saw antlers over the ridge across the river. After sitting a bit, I could see better. There were four bulls; two were smaller ones. To me, at the time, they looked big and were in velvet. I remembered that Bim had said they can look bigger in binoculars. With no experience of this, I just kept going down the ridge I was on, trying to watch them and not spook them. About twenty minutes into that, I saw them at maybe one hundred yards and decided one of them had to be big enough. I would not take a shot, because firstly, I had no idea how I was going to get them across the river, and secondly, I didn't know where Bim was.

It wasn't too long before they started moving pretty fast, as they do. At least they were moving back toward the other guys. About that time, I saw Bim up the hill behind me, waving his hands. I wasn't sure if he was saying "Shoot" or "Don't shoot," but either way, the one I was eyeing was across the river—still not an option.

Now I was kind of heartbroken and excited that I had seen some bulls. I decided to go back to camp. It was a long walk back—about three miles. About halfway there, I spotted Bim moving like the Energizer Bunny, way ahead of me. The bulls were long out of sight, and there were no signs of any other caribou, so I decided to fall in behind him and head in to camp. About halfway there, all of a sudden, I saw four caribou. Lifting my binoculars, sure enough, I saw the four bulls again.

Just about that time, Bim slipped over the hill. The bulls were a good ways ahead of me, still on the side of the river where I couldn't shoot. About thirty minutes later, they ambled to about one thousand yards from me, and it looked as though they had crossed the river. Wrong. I glassed back behind me everywhere, and no one was in sight. I decided to stalk the bulls and got within four hundred yards. I stuck to taller bushes and got nestled in them, sat down, rolled my arm up in my sling, sat my gun on my knee, turned the scope up, and picked the bigger of the two. The smaller bulls had moved on a good bit, closing down to about four hundred yards. My BDC Nikon dialed in on the number-three circle inside, and I grabbed a short breath and squeezed the trigger. It sounded like a good hit, and the bull appeared to stumble back. I fired two more times just in case, but I'm still not sure if those shots hit, because of the way he fell behind some stuff.

The other bull was reluctant to leave. I was wishing someone else was there with me. So down I went toward them, and the other bull circled me, heading toward camp, which was good. The bad thing was that it was still across the creek. Now I felt like crap. After ten minutes spent walking up and down the river and finding no spot to cross, I headed back to camp to get my chest waders. Then I saw Bim sitting way up the ridge. Behind him came another bull, so I waved and whistled, and it ran right to him. He saw it and lay on the ground, but he never shot. Like any good guide, he had been trying to get it up to Jordan, who was over on the other ridge. (I found this out later.) I went to camp and then back to the kill site with Bim. Bim and I were already worn out but proceeded to get the bull, which meant me having to get naked and swim twenty-five feet across the river; it was as cold as hell! Bim threw a soft parachute cord tied to a stick across the river, and then I pulled my clothes over. That action went back and forth as I skinned it, quartered it, and packed it up to the riverbank, all the time getting hammered by mosquitoes. And it was one cold swim back across the river, naked and cold. We loaded the packs and together headed back to camp. After all this, I was dead tired, hurting, and ready for bed.

Day 6

At this point I was pretty much just recuperating, trying to stay dry, warm, and hydrated, plus eating. We all managed to go to Bim's tent long enough to eat, and we let our feet get so cold we had to run for our sleeping bags. It was thirty-six degrees with a light rain and winds about fifteen miles per hour, making it feel as if it were twenty degrees. I managed to cape my big caribou, and by the time thirty minutes was up, my hands were really cold. I could hardly unzip anything. I had to hold them under my arms for about an hour to get them warm again. I decided to go watch spiders chase bugs on top of my tent till dark, and then I slept.

Day 7

I woke up, and not long afterward, I heard Bim say he saw two bulls up the hill from camp. All three of them lit out. I stayed in, scratching bug bites I had gotten after I swam the river and my bug spray was washed away. While I had cleaned my bull, I had been torn up by mosquitoes on my white legs. Bim said it looked as if I had measles. It was thirty-four degrees this morning with 20 to 25 mph winds. My inner thighs were so sore they hurt to the touch as a result of the hike out while carrying the head, as well as all that fast stalking.

A few hours later, I heard shooting—eight shots in total. I heard four hits, so I finished getting ready and prepared to pack meat. Shortly I saw the others all coming over the hill. It was still as cold as hell, so we all went to Bim's tent to eat and listen to stories of the two bulls they had gotten. After breakfast we went up the hill with skin, guts, capes, and deboned meat. By the grace of God, the weather changed just in time for us to get it done. Otherwise, I think there would have been a few frostbitten hands. We played with capes and peppered and sprayed everything with citrus, which helps keep bugs away. We then had just enough time to absorb a bit of sun outside before suppertime. Bim decided to make a little hunt. The night was calm, with a little wind. It was about forty degrees.

Day 8

I woke up from a good night's rest, and it was about forty degrees. I heard everyone get up to go hunt. I was tagged out, so I spent some time catching this story up and kind of packing, hoping to head home by August 26. So today day I shot snow owls, caribou cows and calves, ducks, vegetation, and more with my camera. The crazy weather turned to seventy degrees and clear. I could see a lot of mountains in the Brooks Range. There were a few small, scattered showers in the mix of sky and fragments of rainbows scattered about. Bugs were out in full force. Some I hadn't seen on this trip. More spiders. We watched Bim send an arrow through a cow at about sixty yards on top of the hill right up from camp. Then we all had pancakes and went back to debone her and pack the meat down.

Day 9

Today was the last full day we would spend here. We were quickly up and out, hunting up some scrambled eggs, having had a good night's sleep. It was the quietest night we'd had weather-wise. It sounded like a jungle out there, with all the swans, geese, ducks, and other birds. Everyone headed for the hills, glassing them over one last time. There were four caribou cows and calves in the valley by camp. They were after one big bull or a wolf. I later went up to sit by Mr. Gary for an hour and a half or so, but then I couldn't stand it anymore. We had to have some of that caribou meat, so I headed down, cut some up, and got it washed and ready to cook. It was a nice day for it, for sure. We all ended up as full as pregnant armadillos. Then we just sat around and told hunting stories. I packed for the next day, hoping to leave early, a little worried about getting to my flight on time.

Day 10

We were awakened by some rain. It was the last thing I hoped to hear. We had to break camp to fly out. Luckily enough, it didn't last long, but it wet everything. We were supposed to catch the flight at midmorning but ended up being there until about one in the afternoon. After three flights in, we all got back to Arrowhead Outfitters base camp. We opened up our last Mountain House meal for the trip—or so we hoped. I had chicken and mashed potatoes. We loaded meat, capes, antlers, etc., and proceeded to see Dalton Highway going in the other direction, back to Fairbanks. This was a trip in itself. We could already see a slight change in vegetation since coming down.

About six hours later, we made it to Cold Foot Truck Stop for the buffet and fuel. A few miles before we arrived, the terrain changed all of a sudden again, pretty much going from tundra and mountains clear of vegetation to brush and trees. We went a few more miles and then set the tents up to stay the night in the woods and get some rest.

We did have kind of a small problem on the way. The brakes got hot going over the Antigun Pass. All along, the Koyukuk River was beautiful and was crisscrossing the highway with many lakes alongside. Many jagged gothic-looking mountaintops stood along the road. There were small storms along the mountaintops, some with rainbows. I did see a nice black bear walking along the highway, and then it darted into the woods behind us. We moseyed our way to the Yukon River, where we stopped and had a burger at the Yukon River Café. We then headed off Dalton to Steese Highway and drove on into Fairbanks. We enjoyed the sights. We didn't waste time finding a motel to get cleaned up, and searched out a nice place to eat.

It was a tough hunt but was well worth the memories. By the grace of God, I am lucky enough to have lived it. Thanks to my great friend Bim!

So Long, My Friends

Hello, folks. First I want to say thanks to all of you who find my stories, a few of many, enjoyable. I started out writing them for me, mainly, to remember them and the people I shared camp with in what is a short life.

Many of these hunts were hunts I truly only dreamed of as a boy in the woods and as a young man. We weren't rich but were well cared for. Truly never in my wildest dreams did I imagine that the good Lord would grant me such opportunity to enjoy the wonders of Mother Nature and the animals that live in her realm, which I love so much. I've always said a person who sees new places and things through his or her eyes is blessed. What excited me most was being blessed to have friends who did not stop and smell the roses and wished they had done so earlier in their lives. Also, I lost my dad, Victor L Scarinzi, when he was fifty-two and my mom, Carylon, when she was fifty-six. Pondering on that, it was easy for me to feel the need to do whatever I could to live out some of my dreams. I have never feared death; however, I have feared not to live life and pursue my dreams.

So I write my stories to push me, and I hope y'all know that through hard work, discipline, hope, and a lot of trust in God, truly all things may happen. Many men have done much more than I have done, and they have done things many more times than I. But as for me, I couldn't be more thankful, as a simple boy growing into an average man, to have been lucky enough to live out a few dreams and to have been healthy enough to do them.

I have lived in Anacoco, Louisiana, most of my life. I now live in Hicks, Louisiana, where I run my taxidermy studio and spend most of my time hunting or preparing for hunting season. I've hunted all over Louisiana and several other states. I was a guide in the mountains of Colorado in my younger days, and I've also been blessed enough to hunt in South Africa. I've had the opportunity to listen and learn through my taxidermy business, and I've made my own studies about the animals around here. Like I said, I'm no expert, but I really enjoy sharing my experiences. Mostly, I love to just be in the woods and out of the house, anything but sit on my butt in front a tv and watch others enjoy their lives.

Like me, other hunters don't just hunt to kill everything they see. We hunt for the challenge and to share a deep love for the animals, the environments they live in, and more. The meat they provide is just part of it and is more of the reason we respect it all so much. I, like most hunters, never forget that an animal gave its life so I can enjoy my own life and have food on the table. You can and will never get the same kind of care and love for wildlife and the environment by buying your meat at McDonald's and the supermarket.

I feel that this book is not just for hunters but will appeal to anyone who loves a real-life adventure. I hope you feel the excitement of the hunt, the disappointment of the miss, and the elation of the kill. My friends, I hope you, too, reach deep down and go for some of your own dreams before your last days. Thanks for reading my book, and may God be with you always. He usually allows you plenty of time to fulfill at least some your dreams, if you are lucky. But he helps those who help themselves, so you can't just sit and wait for it to happen.

Through these stories, I hope you get to know me—Victor C. H. Scarinzi, a.k.a. Swampman—a little bit and appreciate all my perseverance, dedication, and true love for hunting. Also, I hope you understand my love for the great outdoors and God's presence that abounds in it like no other place. This is where I gather my great sense of compassion, which he probably would like all of us to have more of these days. And I hope that maybe y'all can find the same on y'alls' next adventure as well. Thanks, and may God be with you till your last day.

Printed in the United States
By Bookmasters